ITALIAN LIVING DESIGN

Giuseppe Raimondi

ITALIAN LIVING DESIGN

Three Decades of Interior Decoration 1960-1990

Interiors photographed by Carla De Benedetti

RIZZOLI
NEW YORK

Acknowledgments

I wish to thank all those who have contributed suggestions, information and illustrations, making this book a possibility. In particular I would like to mention: Gian Antonio Gilli, for his insight into Italy's social transformation during these years; Giorgio Donna, for his contributions to the economic analyses of Italian industry; Giancarlo Perini, for his advice regarding and photographs of automobiles; Franco Ballotta, for his drafts of the sections on television programing and for obtaining the archival materials accompanying them; Giulia Carluccio, for her important contributions to the sections on cinema; Donatella Sartorio and Rosella Denicolò, for their assistance with the sections covering the fashions of the Eighties; Giovanni Dondena, for his advice on the analysis of furniture-distribution networks; Lalla Murgia, Fulvio Ferrari, Paola and Rossella Colombari, Simone Dreyfuss, and Sandro Verga, for the materials and helpful information they contributed for the design sections; Tucci Russo, for sharing his knowledge of art.

Special thanks go to Giulio Lupieri, Cesare Baroni, and Paolo Cajelli at Fabbri, whose enthusiastic and competent assistance contributed greatly to the publication of this book.

And lastly, my deepest gratitude to Carla Tanzi and Mario Andreose for their continuing support throughout the project and to Anna Maria Mascheroni who took care of the English edition.

Photo credits

Aldo Ballo, Mariarosa Ballo, Santi Caleca, Giorgio Colombo, Falchi & Salvador, Paolo Mussat, Paolo Pellion, Rino Petrosino, Laura Salvati, Ugo Casiraghi archives, *Casa Vogue* archives, *Domus* archives, the Triennale archives, Fiat archives, Giugiaro Design archives, Gruppo GFT archives, Ilte archives, Club Francesco Conti, Centro Kappa photos, Studio Azzurro (Milan), Studio Blue (Turin), *TV Sorrisi e Canzoni* photos.

Endpapers

Sottsass Associati (Ettore Sottsass, Marco Zanini), project for the Italian Design Exhibition in Tokyo, February 1984. Print HPL plastic laminates, Artemide floor lamps, Cedit tiles, The Milan Style collection.

Frontispiece

Andrea Branzi, House with Axial Layout, 1986.

First published in the United States of America in 1990 by RIZZOLI INTERNATIONAL PUBLICATIONS, INC.
300 PARK AVENUE SOUTH, NEW YORK, NEW YORK 10010

Originally published in Italian under the title *Abitare Italia*

Library of Congress Cataloging-in-Publication Data

Raimondi, Giuseppe
[Abitare Italia. English]
Italian Living Design by Giuseppe Raimondi; photographs by Carla De Benedetti.

Translation of: Abitare Italia.
ISBN 0-8478-1191-3
1. Interior decoration—Italy—History—20th century.   I. De Benedetti, Carla.   II. Title.
NK2052.A1R3513 1990
747.25—dc20   90-31692
                                               CIP

Design by Cesare Baroni and Paolo Cajelli
Translated by Carol Lee Rathman
Produced by DIMA & B., Milan
Printed and bound in Italy by Gruppo Editoriale Fabbri S.p.A., Milan

CONTENTS

FOREWORD

*O*ver the past thirty years, lifestyles have changed enormously. Our cultural point of reference and models have changed, along with the objects surrounding us (to such an extent that, thinking of the reappearance in our homes of modern antiques of the Sixties, the words of Lampedusa's character Prince Salina in Il Gattopardo *take on a new poignancy:* "Everything has changed only to remain just the same.").

The tools of our everyday existence are made of different materials, and our relationship with them is different. Man's attitude toward the use of plastic in the home over the past thirty years is a good example of this: the All-Bayer House designed by Joe Colombo for Visiona '69 and the emergence of Swatch wristwatches in this decade demonstrate the transition from the enthusiastic use of plastic in the Sixties to its rejection in the Seventies and its revival in "noble" form in the Eighties.

The spatial organization of the home has changed; the living room has progressively invaded other areas—first the kitchen, later the bedroom in a sort of osmosis that has altered both our way of sitting in armchairs (which is increasingly horizontal) and our way of lying in bed (which is increasingly erect). The television has conformed to these alterations more than any other household object—it has become less and less cumbersome and has found its way into every room; its program material offers a multiplicity of messages, designed in response not only for the audience's different cultural models, but also with regard to the multiplicity of places where these messages can be received, to the point that we may speak of a target audience in terms of which room it occupies.

The widespread increase in electronics applications in the workplace as well as in the home has given rise to a new science, "domotronics," which in turn has given rise to telematic houses. The word "domotronics" attempts to embrace the characteristics of well-being, comfort, and ease attributed to the traditional "domus," along with those of efficiency and innovation promised by electronics.

As much as the living room has changed (its role as the room designated to display the homeowner's status has waned since the Sixties), the kitchen has changed even more. This is due to changes in the family institution and to the growing number of singles as well as to the introduction of new eating habits that involve frozen and prepackaged goods, microwave ovens, and various types of food processors. The bathroom has changed, becoming a room just as important as the others, where one attends to personal hygiene. Finally, the bedroom has changed; because of its symbolic connotations, this was the area that offered the most resistance to change, but it has now become a sort of annex to the living room, where one cannot only rest but also work, watch television, or even receive guests.

But living is not confined to just the dwelling unit: it extends to the building, the neighborhood, the environment. In the urban way of life, public and private spheres intermingle and become dependent on one another. This phenomenon leads us to reflect on the roles played by fashion and societal customs (which are primarily manifested on the street and in collective spaces) in furnishing private spaces, and in turn to seek to identify how much has been transferred from political movements and the various expressive forms of the industrial culture to the design and use of individual living spaces (fixed or mobile, given the parallel evolution of the motor home), and to interrelationships between the individual users.

The furnishings shown here, from Albini to Sottsass, Joe Colombo, and Pinto, cover a highly variegated terrain of styles and themes, ranging from high tech to high touch, from furnishings based on multiple levels and spatial intersections to those constructed as a low-key scenario for emotionally charged objects, from the transposition of advanced technological know-how to the revival of lost forms of handcrafted decorations. These furnishings are representative of various methodological approaches to the interior design of a home.

The illustrations were selected for their capacity to demonstrate a trend, a working method, a relationship between the site and its existing surroundings, a use of materials. This not just for the purpose of review, but also to increase awareness of patterns of response that emerge in particular circumstances to meet generalized needs.

Furthermore, these furnishings are the fruit of cultural interaction between the design architect and the user-client. And since they are presented to us in the form of photographic images, they are also the fruit of the photographer's cultural interaction (in this case, the photographer was Carla De Benedetti, whose work over the past thirty years for the most important interior-design reviews has made her an expert on many Italian homes).

As for the first type of interaction, Carlo Scarpa has defined the verb "to furnish" as meaning "to respond to a need," a transaction in which the stress falls on the concept of meeting the need itself rather than on exploring the possible ways of responding to it. It is undeniable nevertheless that the interpretation of these needs depends on both the architect, with his design knowledge, and the client, with his specific requirements and buying power. The design solution lies in the dialectic of this relationship, which is couched in the culture of the period.

Clearly, it also depends on the size and degree of the design intervention, as well as the context into which it is introduced. In some cases, the work carried out by the architect determines lifestyle in the broad sense of the term: working from the building's foundations to the design objects and constructing the interior as the logical and cogent consequence of the building itself. This takes place, for example, in some of the villas, where the elements of furniture are low-key presences in a strong stylistic context; at times these can be mixed with other layers that belong to periods prior to the life of the user. The functions that the selected objects must carry out are openly declared; the objects present themselves as possessed of lower semantic import and broader utility.

In the case of situations in which the design site and its involucrum are laden with historical or structural givens (as in the Amalfi grotto decorated by Gae Aulenti or the late sixteenth-century palazzo decorated by Giancarlo Leoncilli), we shall see different ways of handling the historical heritage—ways that can range from acceptance to absolute rejection, from a philological interpretation of the past to an awareness of the right to express one's own stylistic independence.

In other cases, little or nothing is known of the involucrum in which the dwelling unit has been inserted. In the apartments of a building complex or in lofts, there is no relationship between the building itself and what has been done with its interior. Like the whale in the story of Pinocchio, it harbors an unexpected life within its body, an existence that – like a multiplex cinema – offers a range of different shows. Paradoxically, in these cases, the "private" seems even more "private," detached as it is from a "public" context and laden instead with richly imaginative products. At times it has been possible to create this setting artificially, as Schenal did with his all-styrofoam furnishings, or as the review Abitare did in the years 1967–68 with its hyperrealistic studio realizations of proposals for living, decorated with all the right design "objects."

The decorative projects shown in these pages

will reflect the changes that have taken place over the years in the approach to mass-produced modern furniture and the architect's use of it. At the beginning of the Sixties, with the dawn of Italian design, many interior designers (among them Albini, Caccia Dominioni, and Magistretti) created interiors that served as testing grounds for pieces that the industry would later put into series production, and there was a climate of fertile exchange similar to that between haute couture and prêt-à-porter. By means of those architects, companies such as Poggi, Azucena, Cassina, and Gavina found opportunities in the modern furniture sector. Clearly, in the Sixties the table or the armchair selected to furnish a given setting had much more importance, more cultural weight, than it does today. The transition from the traditional home, with its period-style furniture and its tendency toward symmetrical placement of the pieces, to the modern home, with its design furniture, was experienced as being part of a turning point in the nation's history—the postwar reconstruction of Italy. As Vanni Pasca noted: "Buying modern furniture in the Sixties meant taking part in the nation's transformation into a modern country as it entered a period of industrialization and urbanization, mass motorization. It was not a question of design changing our lives, but it certainly did accompany, and in some way symbolize, this collective change in lifestyles."

Once this pioneering period had come to an end (the sector's most important trade fair, the Salone del Mobile, was inaugurated in Milan in 1961), the demand for and consumption of modern furniture accelerated as it shed certain connotations and assumed others. Product obsolescence was speeded up, and formal experimentation intensified. Variations upon variations of some archetypes came into being, but the productive sector also consolidated, and qualitative differences leveled out

on the high side, a fact that other countries acknowledged as well. The design of form—that is, the coordination, integration, and articulation of all those factors that in one way or another contribute to the process of giving shape to a product, whether it be clothing, armchairs or automobiles, consolidated into a phrase, "made in Italy." This kind of design, from the outside, appeared homogeneous in all of its various lines of development, thanks to its capacity for dialogue with figurative developments outside of the field of design: arts, expressive activities, attitudes often imported but which, in Italy, underwent new interpretations and syntheses.

At the same time, the study of design evolved: many new interior-design reviews were founded (our country offers the best coverage of this field), helped in part by the solid advertising contributions offered by furniture manufacturers (mainly small to medium-sized companies).

The growth in the number of design reviews and the broadening of the market for design products, however, also created a shift in design aims. For the interior decorator, items of furniture lost interest as individual objects; his focus shifted to interventions at the visual and environmental levels, leaving to furniture-store architects the careful design of single objects that had characterized the start of the period we are examining (though the latter were often too intent on selling the "menu de la maison," and people's homes often wound up looking like outposts of the stores themselves). In these years, the number of middle-class clients who consulted architects was shrinking; they now tended to solve problems on their own or to enlist the aid of specialized stores. In the meantime, the reviews covering this market were in harsh competition and increasingly banked on the publication of unique design situations, showing the work done by a few stars of the interior decoration scene in very exclusive homes. In a parallel trend, some designers shifted their focus from mass production to limited-edition products that often followed the same orbits as works of art. These products arose aut of a new attitude toward the artistic patrimony, which was now considered a vast warehouse of available forms and contents.

In this changed context, the designers of the Eighties (once the postmodern wave subsided) have shed their inhibitions about the past as well as about the myth of the new and the positive role played by the avant-garde. They appear to be more concerned with the architectonic construction of the scenic space, though they are also more permissive regarding the various layers of the past that may be included among the objects contained in that space. Indeed, they seem to seek out the overlapping effects of new values and new tensions that these presences, with their individual emotional charges, are capable of introducing.

The furnishings shown in this book were photographed by Carla De Benedetti, who for over thirty years has worked for the most prestigious interior-design reviews, both Italian (Domus, Abitare, Casa Vogue, and Gran Bazaar) and otherwise (House & Gardens, Progressive Architecture, La Maison Française, and The New York Times).

Thus De Benedetti has assembled a historical document of exceptional importance that has as its protagonists the most famous of Italian architects, in dialogue with a clientele belonging to the Italian upper class.

Therefore, the lifestyles and furnishing products are those that represent a "taste in progress" and which, like fashion, offer us the chance to interpret the way we were—or rather, the way a specific social class was, how it lived and expressed its status requirements. Some of these interiors are no longer in existence, having been replaced by later expressions of different tastes.

It is also interesting to note how the approach to photographing interiors has changed over the years. This is not due so much to technological improvement, since De Benedetti has continued to use large format cameras and film throughout her career (Linhof cameras and 5x7 in. [13x18 cm] plates), as it is to the photographer's shifting attitude toward the setting to be photographed and the use of lighting. At one time the aim was to evoke atmospheres through artificial lighting, working at night, or completely blocking out the daylight. In this theatrical setting, light could be completely recreated artificially in response to the effects sought.

Today, instead, the trend is to work as much as possible with natural light, allowing the exterior and interior to interact. This more uniform, even banal, type of lighting reduces the possibilities for interpreting the setting, for creating atmospheres. In a certain sense, it all becomes more impartial, more descriptive.

The framing itself has altered. Once there was almost always something in the foreground: an object, a person, a face in profile. In times when the value of designer objects was not so inflated, modern furniture often contributed a stamp of modernity to the setting (in the same way that certain Memphis products do today), but the use of the foreground was, above all, a way of working within the space that one sought to represent, of creating a rapport with the image conveyed. De Benedetti's more recent work is more detached, more strictly documentary than before. It is still up to the photographer (and this is what shows De Benedetti's extraordinary interpretative skill) to choose what to describe, the photographic composition of the objects and the choice of perspective, to offer an interpretation of the space, inevitably manipulating the reality of what the visitor may see against what she has decided to show the viewer.

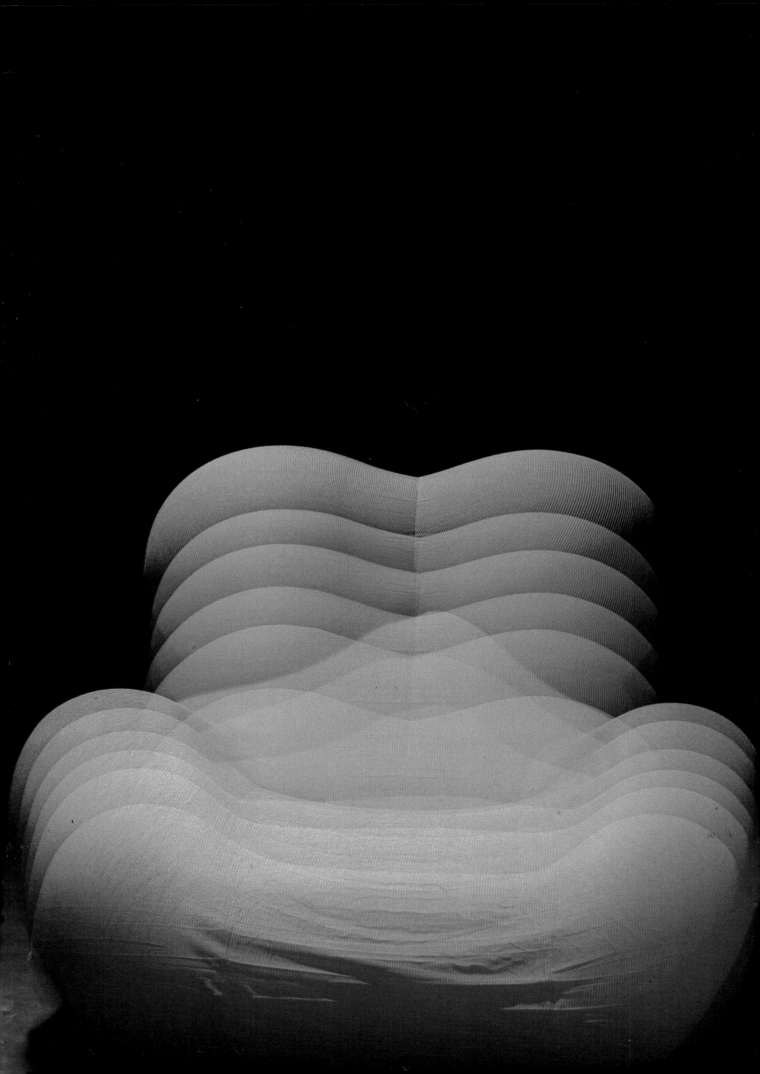

THE **SIXTIES**

The Sixties were a decade rich in ferment and contradiction for Italian society as well as for interior design: they opened with an economic boom that greatly boosted the average Italian's purchasing power and closed with student protests in 1968 and trade-union movements involving various spheres of the industrial and economic sectors.

These were the formative years of an entire generation. They were a kind of watershed between their fathers, who had thrown themselves into the arms of modernity with the enthusiasm of those who have known poverty and are determined at all costs to avoid falling back into its grip, and their sons, who today enjoy modernity with a natural ease that borders on indifference.

These were the years in which the feminist movement was born, sparking a reevaluation of the concept of the home as lair, from which outsiders were barred and in which the living spaces were rigidly structured to safeguard the roles imposed on various household members. People began to seek a lifestyle that was not confined to the walls of the home, but extended outward into the building, the neighborhood. In this urban lifestyle, the public and private spheres intermingled and gave each other nourishment.

What fanned the desire of the new breed of consumers to its highest pitch at the close of the 1950s was the "new." The novelties then available on the market made the buyer feel a part of the American way of life, which had pushed its way into Italian life in the form of industrial foods, the automobile and electrical household appliances. This break with Italian traditions connected with "domestic hearth" did not, however,

"Up" chair in foam polyurethane designed by Gaetano Pesce for B&B in 1969 and vacuum-packed for sale in flat envelopes.

disrupt customary modes of interior design; most Italians continued to furnish their homes as they always had.

In the mid Sixties, the demand for goods became more complex: the consumer, riding the wave of the economic boom, had more purchasing power and exercised greater choice. "Novelty consumerism," which had been aimed at integrating the individual into urban-industrial society, gave way to "status consumerism," in which the individual's social status was highlighted through the choices he made, independent if their novelty.

Air travel and television helped to accelerate the rhythm of change and of internationalization: in 1960 the total number of travelers who passed through Italian airports was one-and-a-half million; by 1970 the total had surged to eight million. The number of television owners went from two million to ten million during this decade. At the end of the Sixties the petit bourgeoisie's dreams of possessing "good clothing" and "good living-room furniture" were partly satisfied, but the class was rudely awakened by the events that took place in politics and by the actions of the trade unions, as well as by the student protest movement, which in its struggle against authority proposed new lifestyles and rejected the aesthetic canons of bourgeois respectability.

A penisula that had traditionally known only poverty was washed by a wave of feminism, radicalism, a growing emphasis on day-to-day existence, the rebellion against well-being and technology, and a glut of goods. This created strange contradictions as different conceptions of life – in the home, the factory, and the schools – arose and clashed against one another.

Jeans, snorkel parkas, long hair, encounter groups (accompanied by a new lexicon of terminology), work groups, and new forms of socializing all had their counterparts in living and furnishing solutions tested by the young in the various "communes," with results that were not always tension-free.

The aggregation of different people, sharing their lives without adopting the formal bonds of family relationships or playing the traditional sexual roles, implied different uses of the spaces that had been conceived for a traditional way of life. These implications were reflected more in the furnishings than in the fixed architectural structures. Room partitions were created with movable elements; panel-caddies akin to haversacks were hung on the walls, along with posters that served more as ideological statements than as decoration; rejected materials such as unused drainage tubes or

The search for the "new" that was expressed in the consumption of various types of goods —electrical appliances, television sets, automobiles, etc.—characterized the Sixties market. The behaviors and tastes that emerged during this decade were shaped by the new ways that youth had of socializing and by feminist ideology.

scaffolding elements were used as shelving; informal seating was cut loose from parlor designs based on symmetry and social deference; artificial materials such as oilskin took the place of natural leather upholstery; plastic replaced walnut in furniture.

The Beatles' Yellow Submarine *record cover, designed by Heinz Eldemann in soft, curving lines, represents a grotesque version of Art Nouveau.*

Below: a dress from Germana Marucelli's "Alluminio" collection with sculptures "to be worn" by Getulio Alviani (1968).

FASHION

In the transition from haute couture to prêt-à-porter, fashion boosted the growth of the clothing industry, whose production for the first time in the early Sixties outstripped that of tailors and dressmakers; from 1960 to 1970, the industry increased the production of women's suits from 390 thousand to 2 million, and of overcoats from 1.7 million to over 3 million.

At the end of the war, 25,000 people were employed in the clothing sector, and by 1980 that figure had jumped to 330,000.

Since 1970, Italy has held the highest market share of all clothing exports from industrialized countries—that is, 25 percent, compared with Germany's 13 percent, France's 10 percent, the United States' 7 percent and Japan's 3 percent. The Italian clothing industry's total turnover in 1985 was 12.3 billion lire.

The great industrial development that took place in this production sector made it possible to increase investments in avant-garde technologies. Under the auspices of such legendary figures as Gucci, Valentino, Schuberth, the Sorelle Fontana, Germana Marucelli, and later Missoni, Armani, Versace, Ferrè, and Mariuccia Mandelli—to name just a few of those who have made Italian fashion great—many individuals poured their energies into offering to fantasy a foundation of logic, so that industrial rationality and the designers' creativity could exist in perfect harmony.

The fashion world imparted lessons—lessons which were absorbed by other fields, such as interior design—not only on an emotional level, but also on a technological level, and the expanding know-how and materials research resulted in innovative options, either through the use of new materials or through the use of traditional ones in new combinations. The clothing sector and that of interior design share a number of qualities, and both have made decisive contributions to the success of the Italian look, the reasons for which can be sought in—apart from the aesthetic or artistic tradition—Italian industry's special advantage in being able to rely on small, nimble businesses that are open to innovation and limited-production series.

As fashion became a commodity consumed by

Paco Rabanne's metallic attire, a pageboy hairdo, Mary Quant's miniskirts, the fashion model Twiggy's spindly physique, topless bathing suits: all fashions of the Sixties.

many individuals, it took on a leading role in the Italian economy, as well as the identification of new stylistic typologies and the leveling of culture, as is manipulated or suggested social behavior.

The Sixties witnessed the expansion of this osmosis between fashion and interior decor: the look of the rising Anglo-American youth culture penetrated all forms of expressive activity everywhere with overwhelming creative energy, modifying not only people's behavior but also the places designated for social interaction. Rock music, op art and pop art, the Beatles, Mary Quant and the miniskirt, Paco Rabanne and his space suits, Courrèges' and his short dresses with geometrical lines and his large multicolored eyeglasses, films such as *La Dolce Vita* and *Easy Rider*, the Living Theater and guerrila theater—all of these represent the Sixties no less than oilskin armchairs, interior design with stepped living rooms, or spaces with cushions on the floor and walls lined with dark-colored moquette.

Of course, for many reasons, not all of them economic, styles of fashion change much faster than styles of interior decoration, but it is noteworthy that in the wake of the Sixties the obsolescence of furniture pieces accelerated, and consumption of replacements increased, just as young people were developing a new attitude toward clothing as one of the many possible means of self-expression, and the generation gap, which fashion had served to highlight, gaped even wider.

CINEMA

Although cinema, theater, television, weekly magazines and literature (each according to its role in society and its own canons of communication) all propose possible dwelling models, Adolf Loos' maxim that "each individual must be his own decorator" is nowhere more truthful than when applied to the field of artistic representation, even the most lifelike, such as cinema.

An artist decorates his surroundings according to his egotistical needs. Everything must work to one end: expression. If documentation exists, it is random—or, compared to the work of art itself, simple-minded. In *A Clockwork Orange* (1971), rather than invent an interior decor, director Stanley Kubrick found a symbolic equivalent for the violent void he wished to represent. In the same way, the empty apartment in *Last Tango in Paris* (1972), rather than being a home, is a place where unrelated persons can maintain their distance from one another.

Piero Poletto and Gianni Polidori (both of whom were Elio Petri's collaborators) should be recalled for their set designs of these years.

In *La Decima Vittima* (1965), Piero Poletto made the interior decor the work's true protagonist, on an equal standing with the other elements of the film's plot. Apart from various references to op art and pop art and the best examples of Italian design in those years, his spaces suggest various decorative innovations and proposals, from the garret apartment to the country mansion and the different types of seating arrangements.

In the film *La Proprietà Non È Più Un Furto* (1973), Gianni Polidori focused on a fetishistic relationship with objects that are installed in a home in which the furnishings are intended to show status.

Giuseppe Patroni Griffi's *Addio Fratello Crudele* (1971) is also noteworthy for its sets by sculptor Mario Ceroli. The furniture he designed of untreated pine for this film was typical of his artistic output and was later produced in series by the company Poltronova.

The Sixties were marked by three other films, and these are worth mentioning for their bearing on the specific topic we are discussing. The first was Francesco Rosi's *Le Mani Sulla Città*, which in 1963 was awarded the Venice Leone d'Oro, a courageous exposé of real-estate speculation in Naples, in which for the first time the decay of a city and the political power ploys behind it were portrayed on the screen in a gripping document of collective and dramatic interest. Marco Bellocchio's *I Pugni in Tasca* (1965) expressed some of the themes that emerged in 1968—rebellion, the emotional trials of education and of family life. And *Easy Rider* (1969) became a symbol for a new generation in search of escape, where the open road and chance encounters take the place of life around the domestic hearth. Collective gatherings in which even strangers were welcomed and hosted on the strength of shared ideology, were typical of the Sixties; in the Seventies, terrorism put an end to this form of hospitality, and the home retreated back to being a bastion of privacy.

For various reasons, the Beatles' animated cartoon *Yellow Submarine* (1968) became a period classic. In it, fantastic colors and graphics are used to create an allegory of the ongoing battle between two philosophies of life—that of the grown-ups, who are the enemies of the world of color (the "Blue Meanies"), and that of the young "hippies", who are preparing themselves for the journey toward a new lifestyle.

Top: Elio Petri's La Decima Vittima *(1965), with set design by Piero Poletto. Note the "Taccia" lamp by Achille and Pier Giacomo Castiglioni, the sheet-metal "Lambda" chair by Marco Zanuso, the "Bastiano" armchairs by Tobia Scarpa*

Above: Detail showing Gianni Polidori's status

home *for* La Proprietà Non È Più un Furto *(1973).*

Below: Giuseppe Patroni Griffi's Addio Fratello Crudele *(1971), with set design in untreated wood by Mario Ceroli. A few of the models developed for this film were later produced in series by Poltronova.*

TELEVISION

The first official television broadcasts were in 1954. In 1959 there were 88,000 television subscribers; the number increased to over 2 million at the start of the Sixties. With this new communications medium, not only did techniques of disseminating information change but lifestyles changed also.

New customs emerged: at the close of the Fifties, people would rush to the home of whomever had a television set or to the local bar to catch popular broadcasts such as *Lascia o Raddoppia?* and *Il Musichiere*. Living rooms were transformed into theater galleries with ranks of chairs. Neighbors gathered, invited not only to see a television show but also to take note of their host's material well-being. In the bars, the television was set up high on a stand, and the customers crowded in, trying to get to the front row. So faithful were these shows, audiences, that even the cinemas risked being deserted if they did not project a few episodes each night, scheduling their film projections around the prime-time television broadcasts.

Most of the shows were broadcast in the evenings, and from 1961 on there were two (state-run) networks vying to entertain the entire population.

On February 3, 1957, RAI (Radiotelevisione Italiana) officially introduced advertisements in its programming, concentrating them in a single time block at 9 p.m. following the evening newscast. The mythical *Carosello* opened with a stage curtain that rose, the classical signal for entry into the world of the imagination, storytelling, representation: it consisted of a series of four (later five) 100-second stories, separated by as many rising curtains, in which the product being advertised was revealed only at the very end. With *Carosello*, advertising became spectacle, but also a spur to consumption. Ever larger advertising investments were poured into television: 17 billion lire in 1963, 47 billion in 1970, and 2,500 billion in 1987.

In its twenty-year run, *Carosello* was to become a fundamental point of reference for all the television advertising that followed: it invented and established genres and characters.

The inauguration of the second television channel, the gradual extension of broadcast hours and the strong reduction in the cost of the sets themselves introduced yet another set of new customs into Italian life.

At this point every Italian family was able to afford its own TV, and later this would extend to individuals within the family unit. Thus, the placement of the TV acquired flexibility, and the tube moved out of the living

Top: July 20–21, 1969. Continual broadcast as astronauts Neil Armstrong and Buzz Aldrin landed on the moon.

Above: Television advertising got its start with Carosello

(1957), an advertisement-show that created famous characters such as Armando Testa's duo Caballero Carmencita (below), of 1965, for Paulista coffee.

Top: Tribuna Politica *(1961). This broadcast brought the faces of Italian politicians into their electors' homes. Its success made television the most important tool of political campaigns.*

Above: The setting for the

talk show Habitat, *created by Gino Marotta in 1970. Focusing on housing problems and the environment,* Habitat *introduced to a broad audience the architects and artists who deeply influence the shape of our everyday spaces.*

room and into the kitchen, the bedroom, and the children's rooms. In the course of this phenomenon of self-multiplication (which took on statistical relevance starting in 1980), not only did types of television sets evolve (large- or small-screen, portable or stationary) but the organization of other components of decor around them changed; although once the TV had reigned supreme (even when it was hidden inside a cabinet), the attitude was now one of indifference. Often left on, forgotten on its cart, the television and its images and sounds were now relegated to the background.

Seen entirely in black and white in the Sixties and Seventies, television programs were clearly dominated by themes aimed at culturally enriching the nation. Dramas in period costume—utterly unrelated to contemporary problems and issues—abounded (*I Giacobini, Giuseppe Verdi, I Miserabili, L'Odissea,* and so forth), while entertainment was provided by mystery stories and soap operas. Sport, even at the minor-league levels, held an important position, and sports events were frequently simulcast all across Europe.

The educational-cultural bias was particularly pronounced in such transmissions as *La TV degli Agricoltori* and *Non È Mai Troppo Tardi.* Films, on the other hand, were rarely included in the programming, in sharp contrast to the 1980s, which saw the advent of private stations.

One very popular transmission was *Canzonissima,* a very Italian-style musical variety show. Launched on October 22, 1958, it ran well into the 1980s.

On November 4, 1961, the second national network was born; television subscribers numbered 2,761,738. Various talk shows focusing on family relationships and daily domestic issues invaded Italian homes.

In 1969 television moved to the forefront of mass communications and aroused deep emotions worldwide with the nighttime broadcast, live from Cape Canaveral, of images from another world, as Neil Armstrong and Buzz Aldrin landed on the moon.

On March 1970, *Habitat* went on the air; it was a weekly talk show hosted by Giulio Macchi for the second network and focussing on housing problems, pollution, and the environment. The show deserves credit for having introduced to the Italian audience the architects and artists who have deeply influenced the shape of our day-to-day spaces, ranging from op artist Vasarely to Riccardo Morandi, who designed the longest bridge in the world (in Maracaibo), to designers such as Joe Colombo, Frattini, and Castiglioni, together with the objects they designed for the home.

chi "Vespa" mangia le mele

From top: Designed by Dante Giacosa and awarded the Compasso d'Oro in 1959, the Fiat 500 was an affordable car for the young, and, for many, the first car they owned after graduating from the Lambretta and Vespa motorscooters.

Above: Lamborghini's Miura, designed by Marcello Gandini in 1966, was the most fantastic automotive creation of the Sixties.

INDUSTRY

The automobile, electrical appliances, plastics, and furniture industries made their mark on the 1960s and modified homes as their product lines expanded.

The automobile. The great diffusion of the automobile (the link in a chain of cause and effect that was to give rise to successive waves of internal migration, the vertiginous growth of the sector, accompanied by spurts of urbanization and modernization, and social tensions that would explode in later years) was made possible by the creation of the utilitarian Fiat model 600 in 1955, and even more so by the 500, which among the younger consumers set off a burst of hectic, chaotic, informal sociality.

When Saturdays were removed from the workweek, the Italians set out on their first weekends in these cars, often heading for their new second homes. These first torrid exoduses led to tremendous traffic jams. That of *Ferragosto* in 1963 (the August holiday) made the headlines: in nine days over five million automobiles —both Italian and foreign—were in circulation, and a record of 700 billion lire were spent during the first mass holiday.

The automobile industry launched a new form of "light transport." The celebrated Vespa and Lambretta scooters were now flanked by the new motorcycles. And in 1964 Carnielli started production of the Graziella bicycle with wheels 8 $^1/_5$ in. (21 cm) in diameter compared to the usual 23 $^1/_2$–27 $^1/_3$ in. (60–70 cm), and foldable, so it could easily be tucked into a car trunk and was nimble in city traffic. Piaggio's Ciao, wheels for the young, dates to 1967. As owning one's own means of automotive transportation became more widespread, people's housing requirements changed: the garage took its place among the features most in demand in the new single-family housing units, along with the recreation room for entertaining friends in the evenings.

Electrical appliances. So rapidly did the electrical appliances industry grow during these years that Italy became Europe's top manufacturer of such products, second in the world only to the United States. Thus, it played an important role in the development and diffusion of design and in the changes in models for living that gave rise to new domestic lifestyles.

Elio Petri's film *La Classe Operaia Va in Paradiso* holds up for analysis the positive and negative effects of this explosion of consumerism in Italian society, and of

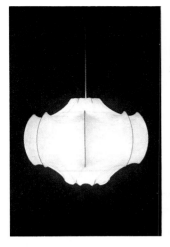
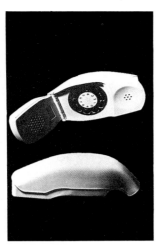

Top, left: Castiglioni's "Taraxacum" hanging lamp for Flos (1960). It takes its shape from a translucent plastic material (cocoon) sprayed on nylon threads stretched over a thin metal framework.

Top, right: Marco Zanuso's "Grillo" telephone for Siemens,

Compasso d'Oro winner in 1967. It was made up of two hinged, molded ABS elements that folded one over the other when not in use; therefore the base and the receiver were no longer separate.

Above: Joe Colombo's molded "Boby" caddy for Bieffeplast (1979).

the frantic search for new status symbols to adorn the homes of the 1960s.

Many of the designers of these objects also worked as architects (Roberto Menghi, Gino Valle, Achille and Pier Giacomo Castiglioni, Marco Zanuso, Mario Bellini, and Joe Colombo), and a like methodology and homogeneity of style is evident in their interior decorations.

Plastics. The triumph of plastics in most manufacturing sectors during the course of the 1960s was a distinguishing feature not only of the decade but also of the history and applications philosophy of the material itself.

From the beginning, the fate of plastics had been conditioned by two contrasting attitudes: disdain for a nongenuine material, whenever the given application was not able to exploit plastics' qualities of newness and adaptability (for example, the plastic doll as a substitute for the porcelain doll); and a consistent use and image of authenticity, when industry (the aeronautic, automobile, and military sectors, for example) exalted its technological potential, or when the design world sought new expressive media.

This ambiguity and the disparity between plastic's applications value and substitution value (it was understood as a low-cost substitute for more valuable materials) shadowed, from the very start, its diffusion in the world. Although it was always regarded as a useful material, plastic has not always been thought of as a "beautiful" material and has at times been faulted for being a nonecological material. In the Sixties this attitude altered, and plastics were seen as offering stimulating design possibilities, thanks to their novelty and low cost.

The broad interest aroused by plastics was confirmed by an unusual exhibition, entitled "Plastic as Plastic," organized at that time by the Museum of Contemporary Crafts in New York. As the title suggests, the exhibition went beyond marketing considerations to focus on the expressive charge that plastics bring to the various products they form—from clothing to armchairs, from objects for the home to eyeglasses —and demonstrated plastic's emergence as a symbol of modernity and technological innovation.

Among the products on display—all of which were made entirely of plastic—what was striking was indeed the coherence between the objects' formal aspects and functional design and the social and aesthetic elements that characterized the period in which they were created. Engineers or artists, tailors or designers—all of them felt that with plastics they could express the

The use of plastic gave rise to furnishings with completely new lines. From top left: children's chair in polyethylene designed by Zanuso for Kartell (1963); Joe Colombo's nylon chair for Kartell (1968); Magistretti's "Selene" chair in reinforced polyester for Artemide (1969); the "Sacco" easy chair—a leather or imitation-leather sack that contained styrofoam pellets—by Gatti, Paolini, Teodoro for Zanotta (1969); various pieces in layered plastic laminate, La Rinascente.

certainties as well as the concerns of the time. This ranged from the lighthearted glitter of Paco Rabanne's clothing creations to Burri's destructive visions. Plastic, emerging from a period of neglect during which it was perceived as inferior to other materials—whose surface appearance it was forced to imitate, almost as if the designers were afraid to let it assert its own identity—was exhibited in all of its youthful beauty and autonomy for the first time at this show.

The new plastic was disruptive, sensual, smooth—whether in the form of Zanuso's "Grillo" telephone, designed in 1966, or in the methacrylate rings that London girls sported at pop concerts. Important objects in plastic produced during these years by Italian designers (almost all are still on the market) were: the "Viscontea" and "Taraxacum" lamps in "cocoon" (a translucent plastic fiber) designed by Achille and Pier Giacomo Castiglioni and manufactured by Flos, 1960; the Perspex lamp designed by Joe Colombo and manufactured by O-Luce, 1962; the child's chair in low-density polyethylene designed by Marco Zanuso and Richard Sapper and manufactured by Kartell, 1963; the "Elda" armchair with fiberglass structure and removable cushions designed by Joe Colombo and manufactured by Comfort, 1965; the "Amanta" armchair with a fiberglass structure designed by Mario Bellini and manufactured by B&B, 1966; the nylon chair designed by Joe Colombo and manufactured by Kartell, 1968; the "Selene" chair in reinforced polyester designed by Vico Magistretti and manufactured by Artemide, 1969.

Items in polyurethane foam, either cut from a single block or molded, represent an entire genre in themselves. They made the concept of the load-bearing structure and padded upholstery obsolete, offering, instead, softness and structure all in one.

Groundbreaking applications of this material were seen in the "Malitte" composition, a seating arrangement of various configurations taken from a single block of polyurethane, designed by Sebastian Matta and manufactured by Gavina, 1965; the "Alvar" armchair designed by Giuseppe Raimondi and manufactured by Gufram, 1966; the "Sofo" armchair designed by Superstudio and manufactured by Poltronovo, 1967; the "Mozza" armchair designed by Giuseppe Raimondi and manufactured by Gufram, 1968; and the "Up" armchairs designed by Gaetano Pesce and manufactured by B&B, 1969.

But the object that embodied all these formal transgressions and also represented a new easy and uninhibited lifestyle in domestic spaces, as blue jeans did for clothing, was the "Sacco" easy chair.

Designed by Gatti, Paolini, Teodoro, and manufactured by Zanotta in 1969 (and still carried by the company), it was a leather or imitation-leather sack that contained styrofoam pellets. Quite a comfortable seat, it conformed to the body of whoever settled into it. Thus, the discovery of its function depended on its use; the chair's deformation permitted its utilization, a process which broke all the usual stylistic canons of the chair.

The product is too well known to dwell upon it here; many articles have already been written about it. Apart from noting its enormous success and its numerous imitators, we shall limit ourselves to the observation that it corresponded then with a new way of sitting—almost reclining, no longer on armchairs and couches but, instead, on cushions that furnished resting places.

Another material that acquired a new image and a number of applications during these years was plastic laminate. Until then it had been used in a material commonly known under the trade name Formica, which was marketed as an imitation wood trim by the American Cyanamid company.

In the mid-Fifties Abet, a recently founded company in the Piedmont region, finally succeeded in undermining Formica's monopoly in Italy by offering the product in a variety of colors and special finishes, with fresh new designs.

"Abet Print Finitura 6" was the rather mysterious reference code for this product, which was everywhere in these years: there was not a single trendy trade-fair stand, colored cabinet, or research project on new proposals for living that would omit what had by then become a password among interior designers. This material represented the ideal solution to every designer's vision. The product—or rather, its treatment—was new, as was the philosophy behind it (never before has a philosophy been so—superficial). The battle cry was "Plastic as plastic; down with imitations and artificial wood!" and, in the name of color, and coupled with the ideas of Joe Colombo, Hare Sottsass, and Superstudio, it evoked a sincere freedom of expression and an indifference to market performance.

The man behind all this, whose sales strategies marched forward arm-in-arm with advances in Italian design, was Guido Jannon. It was he who from the very start had masterminded Abet's company image, evincing a keen awareness and the conviction that "a company cannot restrict itself to indiscriminate production; rather it must participate in its social and cultural context in order to help develop new solutions and orientations."

From top: "Sofo" armchair in polyurethane foam, designed by Superstudio for Poltronova (1967); "Blow" armchair in clear or colored PVC, designed by De Pas, D'Urbino, Lomazzi, Scolari for Zanotta (1967); "Elda" armchair with fiberglass shell, designed by Joe Colombo for Comfort (1965).

Top: "Mozza" armchair cut from a single block of foamed polyurethane, designed by Giuseppe Raimondi for Gufram (1968).

Above: two models in which the polyurethane is foamed in molds: Gaetano Pesce's "Up"

series for B&B (1969) and Giuseppe Raimondi's "Sfera" for Nikol, made up of four sections of a hemisphere, which become individual armchairs (1970). Once molded, "Up" series was compressed to remove all the air and sold vacuum-packed in a flat envelope.

Furniture. The sector's most important trade show, the Salone del Mobile, was inaugurated in Milan in 1961, with 328 exhibitors (modern furniture manufacturers were the smallest group represented), 11,300 Italian visitors, and 800 foreigners. In 1971 the exhibitors numbered 1,552, Italian visitors 42,678, and foreign visitors 6,725. In 1987, the exhibitors were 1,907 (with modern furniture taking up most of the exhibition space), Italian visitors 81,440, and foreign visitors 55,844. Furniture exports in 1961 totaled 9 billion lire and in 1987 exceeded 4,000 billion.

These few statistics are enough to demonstrate the rapid growth of the Italian furniture industry over the past twenty years. At the outset, only a small part of production was dedicated to modern furniture, while today that subsector represents fifty percent of the industry.

Gregotti's observations in his book *Il Disegno del Prodotto Industriale* are of interest in this regard: "It was also decisive to know how to utilize the skills of improvization and creativity, characteristic national vices and virtues. This task was often entrusted to the intelligence of the old craftsmen, whose technological know-how may not have been the most up-to-date, but it was polyvalent and served to carry out syntheses that in other fields had to be drawn at the stage of design rationalization."

Participation in Milan's Salone del Mobile, as well as the Paris and Cologne trade fairs, spurred Italians into an exaggerated race for novelty and the continual renewal of models. New experiences, ever-changing styles, and technological progress were the results; at the same time, there was a twofold risk—of rendering obsolete some products that had not yet even been released on the market, and of creating an abundance of imitations of just a few representative archetypes.

The Salone del Mobile was also an occasion to mount elaborate displays and scenery that would highlight and enhance company images, at times to the point of overshadowing the images of the individual products. Thus, the furniture sector in Italy—unlike its counterparts abroad—came to be associated with lively showmanship, fireworks, even hedonistic displays, that with the years caught up the whole city for the duration of the Salone del Mobile.

Parties, cocktails, and balls created an aura of allure around the furniture manufacturers, one that they increasingly counted on when launching their products in a market that day by day became more mass-oriented and also distinguished by products of uniformly high quality.

Lastly, from the Sixties on, the furniture industry

used every form of communications media—video films, catalogues, posters—to let people know about its products. In this sophisticated form of competition in the race to create new environments, types of behavior, and lifestyle trends, the accent was increasingly on the importance of the buyer's creating a coordinated image through his or her choices.

FURNITURE STORES

Together with the growth of the modern-furniture manufacturing sector and the jump in product sales that took place in the Sixties, furniture stores multiplied at a rapid rate throughout Italy, reaching over 30,000 outlets by the 1980s.

A look at the furniture distribution situation at the start of the Sixties helps us to trace the first signs of the changeover from period-style furniture to modern furniture to around the time of the first Salone del Mobile in Milan (1961). Up to that time, distribution had been in the hands of the large furniture stores, which were usually located on the outskirts of town. These offered period-style furniture (which back then represented 90 percent of production) displayed on several floors, organized into clearly defined zones within the home: the entrance hall, the dining room or dinette, the living room, the bedroom, etc. The "rooms" created were sold in sets and were broken down into various price ranges (thus catering to a broad clientele) and "styles" (Piedmontese rococo, Chippendale, Venetian, modern, etc.).

In the eyes of the consumer, the furniture-store owner was not an intermediary between manufacturer and market. Most manufacturers were anonymous, and the product's name was therefore identified with its distributor. The furniture-store owner was in reality a merchant who commissioned entire batches of complete "rooms" from small- or medium-sized firms.

Thus production, whether at the artisan or industrial level, was highly dependent on the distributor, who controlled the rate of consumption and had a strong contractual grip on the manufacturer. He held his customers in a similar grip through his power to grant credit or not.

It was during precisely these years that the most astute furniture dealers, seeking a client group of higher economic means, began to dedicate more display space to "modern" furniture, sparking a process whereby certain furniture retailers made a name for themselves as specialists in "design" products. In later

In the Sixties the leading firms started to open up the first factory showrooms, calling on famous architects to design the installations.

From top: Achille and Pier Giacomo Castiglioni, Gavina showroom in San Lazzaro (Bologna, 1959);

Gae Aulenti, Centro Fly in Milan (1965); Vico Magistretti, Cassina showroom in Milan (1972).
In the foreground, two semicircular loft structures that break up the very high spaces; the floors are in high-gloss treated wood.

years this differentiation led to the development of a dual market catering to two very distinct client groups: those who wanted period styles, and those who wanted contemporary design.

The Sixties also saw the creation of the very first factory showrooms by the leading firms of the sector. These functioned as publicity for the manufacturers and as a testing ground for their production philosophies and company images. Famous architects were called in to design some of the finest expositions of these years: Carlo Scarpa for Bologna's Gavina in 1960; Achille and Pier Giacomo Castiglioni in Milan in 1961 and in Turin in 1963; Alberto Rosselli for Milan's Arflex in 1965; Gae Aulenti for Milan's Centro Fly in 1965; Mario Bellini in 1968 and Vico Magistretti in 1978 for Milan's Cassina; and the Castiglionis from 1968 to 1972 for Flos in Milan, Florence, Rome, and Turin.

In these elegant expositions—the Centro Fly excepted—what was on display was quality, not quantity, and at times the displays were cloaked in a museum-like, elitist aura. The furniture itself had cultural weight and was created by the few manufacturers of modern furniture who catered to a specific clientele that was not susceptible to overdoses of design.

The Centro Fly was in a category apart. It employed department-store formula very much ahead of its times: free entrance, escalators, Muzak, clearly marked names and reasonable prices for quality products, and scattered among the pieces of furniture, art objects or other elements that reflected the ongoing fashions.

In the second half of the Sixties the advent of furniture to be assembled transformed the production process, making it possible to produce big series of intermediate parts that could be given different finishes depending on the market demand.

Thus a transition was effected between production on commission and planned production cycles. The finished piece of furniture gave way to the "system," made up a given number of parts or intermediates with which it was possible to assemble different typological compositions that could be adapted to multiple end-uses.

Through its product range and its relationship with the manufacturing companies, the furniture store that carried design pieces was no longer simply a sales outlet for a number of products, but a means of communicating a philosophy and proposals for a way of life.

Services—from the financial management of the purchase to project layouts and the complete reali-

The Brambilla store in Corsico, designed by Angelo Mangiarotti in 1968. During his long career Mangiarotti worked on designs of any scale, doing everything from drinking glasses to large industrial buildings. Whatever the scale of a design, he consistently demonstrated great sensitivity to underlying forms and structural logic. In this furniture showroom, one of the largest in Italy, Mangiarotti lined the façade with aluminum panels and, inside, created a dropped ceiling in fiberglass to hide the technical installations, (wiring, tubing, and so on).

zation of design packages—were increasingly crucial to success. This led to the appearance of a new figure in many sales points: the interior decorator-salesman, who was able to dress showrooms for the presentation of new products as well as to guide the customer through his decorating decisions.

Milan's De Padova store has one of the longest traditions of offering home design proposals, with regard not only to products but also to lifestyles. Since 1954, when it first imported and sold important Scandinavian pieces, its store in Corso Venezia has continued to interpret the decorative tastes of Milan's sophisticated upper middle-class, with integrity and professionalism.

FURNITURE

At the close of the Fifties Italy offered a range of furnishing products so rich in ideas that some of them are still successful on the market today—or, following a period of obsolescence, have been reintroduced to the market and are now enjoying a flourishing second wind.

Indeed, the bureau in walnut or rosewood designed by Gianfranco Frattini for Bernini dates to 1956; it was followed in 1957 by a rolltop writing desk and living room pieces in teak. These marked a felicitous encounter between Frattini's talent as a precision designer and Bernini's almost Nordic capacity for woodworking with loving care. This encounter bore fruit not only in the area of furniture for series production but also in Frattini's interior designs, which often relied on the company's top-quality craftsmanship for their execution.

In the same period, for Poggi, Franco Albini designed his famous bookcase with solid wood uprights in walnut and rosewood, and the living room console "MB 15."

Albini's attention to the shape of the supports, his analysis of the load-bearing structures and their expressive potential, and his strikingly rigorous style are characteristics of his talents as a furniture designer and architect. They are apparent in the bookcase and tables he created for Poggi, in his interior decoration such as his 1958 project for Olivetti's Paris store, and in his architecture such as the 1961 Rinascente building in Rome.

A Japanese designer, Hirozi Fukuoh, created one of the first examples of Italian modular furniture for Gavina. Called "Archimede," it expanded in height

Top: a best seller, Tobia Scarpa's "Bastiano" (1960), with a solid wood frame that could be completely disassembled and leather-upholstered cushions.

Above: teak writing desk designed by Gianfranco Frattini for Bernini in 1957. All of Frattini's pieces stand out for their careful design, which catered to the demand of an elite clientele for elegance.

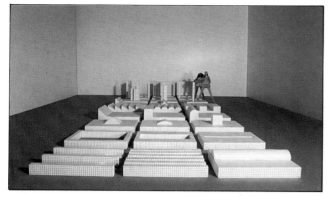

Superstudio, a Florence-based design group, was responsible for a study entitled "Histograms in Architecture," which they proposed to define a set of architectural forms and objects using a two-dimensional grid as their matrix. This conceptual exercise gave rise to a series of primary shapes to be implemented in designing various furniture elements finished in Abet Print plastic

laminate silkscreened with a grid pattern. The "neutral" surface of this laminate became a symbol of radical design.

Below: the influence of Pop art on furnishings of the Sixties: Claes Oldenburg's "Leopard Chair" (1963); Archizoom's "Safari" sofa (Poltronova, 1968). The elements have a fiberglass structure, with upholstery done in a leopard-skin-print acrylic fabric.

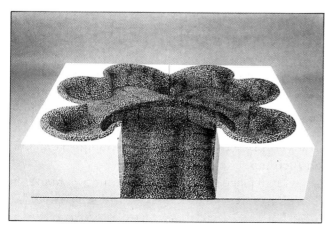

and length by means of a screw device. The Simon company resumed its production in 1983.

Azucena carried elegant furniture designed by Gardella, Caccia Dominioni, and Magistretti, all of whom had returned to the bourgeois tradition of nine-teeth-century neoclassicism, while Fulvio Raboni's creations for Delitala harked back to the "Liberty" style, Italy's version of Art Nouveau.

The period's best-selling couch was Tobia Scarpa's "Bastiano," designed in 1960 for Gavina and still manufactured today by Knoll, the American company that took Gavina over. The model borrowed from Le Corbusier's idea of removable cushions, but in this case it was designed for industrial production: the structure was in solid wood and could be completely disassembled; it was held together by exposed bolts and functioned as a receptacle for cushions resting on flexible steel strips. Thanks to the opulence of the components, the overall effect was one of simplicity and luxury.

Paolo Caliari's "895" couch, designed in 1963 for Cassina, was even more inviting. Widely imitated by upholsterers, it was most commonly sold in brown or green velvet or in leather; it had an upholstered wood structure and foam-rubber cushions with buttons that emphasized their puffiness and softness.

Meanwhile, neo-Liberty-style pebbles had been cast into the still waters of the International Style: the formal challenges of the "San Luca" bergère (whose original design, with its Boccioni-esque dynamic lines and modular parts, required much more advanced production technology than was used for the final version), and Achille and Pier Giacomo Castiglioni's "Lierna" chair for Gavina (1960); the furniture designed by Gregotti, Meneghetti, and Stoppino for SIM; Gae Aulenti's "Sgarsul" rocking chair for Poltronova, in bent beechwood (in the Thonet tradition) colored with aniline dye, and with removable cushion sacks akin to those used in chaise longues (1962).

In 1965 Cassina put four of Le Corbusier's 1928 models back into production, thus inaugurating the so-called Great Masters initiative that in the years to come would re-launch pieces designed by Gerrit Riet-veld, Charles Mackintosh, and Frank Lloyd Wright.

While Cassina was reviving the "fathers" of modern decor amid great debate (as Knoll and Gavina had already done with pieces by Mies and Breuer), Poltronova, a small Tuscan firm managed by Sergio Cam-milli, was turning out pieces by Ettore Sottsass. This company's manager was an unusual figure in the interior-design world inasmuch as he seemed to aspire more to the role of cultural ringleader than to that of a

Top: the "Superonda" sofa, designed by Archizoom and manufactured by Poltronova (1967). This is a destructured sofa in block-cut polyurethane, with oilskin upholstery. The two parts could be positioned to form either the seat and back of a sofa or a platform bed.

Above: Designed by Ettore Sottsass for Poltronova and unveiled at Milan's Eurodomus show in 1970, these pieces made up part of the "Gray Furniture" series, done in gray-painted fiberglass. The bed's headboard contained two fluorescent lights.

successful entrepreneur. Ettore Sottsass, on the other hand, had worked with the company since its foundation, acting in the role of inspirer and consultant for the corporate image. The Sottsass-Poltronova collaboration injected the arena of Italian design with exciting new looks that updated styles seemingly incompatible with those that are more familiar to us. Sottsass showed a highly original poetic skill in integrating elements of Oriental cultures as well as American synthetic textures into his Italian designs.

Sottsass introduced the radical Florentine groups Superstudio and Archizoom to Poltronova. These groups worked actively throughout that period of social and design crisis that struck Italy, inspiring many young architects to "reassess the intellectual input of their personal creativity, while denying the technological input in open criticism of consumerist society" (Gregotti).

In 1968 Superstudio (founded by Adolfo Natalini, Cristiano Toraldo di Francia, Roberto and Alessandro Magris, and Sandro Poli and Piero Frassinelli) designed pieces that were "poor" in technology but rich in figurative charge, using a method based more on formal invention than on production logic. Among these were the modular "Sofo" armchairs in sculpted polyurethane and the "Onda," "Passiflora" and "Gherpe" lamps in colored methacrylate.

Archizoom (formed by Dario Bartolini, Andrea Branzi, Gilberto Corretti, Paolo Deganello, and Massimo Morozzi) was even more influential in the break with traditional "good design," freely employing irony in the creation of provocatively kitschy gazebos and environments such as the installation for the XIV Triennale, although these works also suggested interesting typological innovations to the furniture industry.

Archizoom's "Superonda" sofabed was made of two pieces cut in a sinusoidal line from a single rectangular block of polyurethane foam. Placed one over the other, they formed the back and seat of a sofa, or, side by side, a platform bed. Archizoom also created the "Safari" sofa, a fiberglass structure with a seat and back of polyurethane, upholstered in fake leopard-skin fabric. It was made up of two matching sections that could be joined in different configurations to create an armchair or a two-seat sofa. The message of the advertising campaign distributed to interior-design magazines was threatening, because it was indicative of the hard-line approach taken by radical design in general and Archizoom in particular:

"A regal piece in the squalor of your own home. A piece more handsome than yourselves. A beautiful piece that you really don't deserve. Make a clean

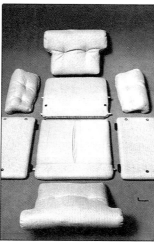

In 1966 Afra and Tobia Scarpa designed for B&B the "Coronado" series (an armchair and two- and three-seat sofas), creating with highly industrial techniques a very attractive object that met the demands for comfort and versatility. The "Coronado" was the first piece of padded furniture to employ the cold-molded foaming process, with deeply sunk metal structural elements. Its cushions contained Dacron padding.

sweep of your living rooms! Make a clean sweep of your lives as well!"

The model was truly interesting: it was a sort of round table (in response to the current ideas about sharing) in which the irreverent prankishness of the fake leopard-skin upholstery (this rather obviously paid homage to the pop fashion of the times, and in particular to Claes Oldenburg's 1963 "Leopard Chair") did not overpower the piece's elegance of line and its capacity to occupy a psychological as well as a physical space.

Both the model's charm and its commercial limitations lay in its monumental appearance and rigid formality (which found a rival one year later with Zanotta's "Sacco" chair).

Afra and Tobia Scarpa's 1966 "Coronado," for B&B, rocketed to success. It embraced formal elements drawn from traditional design (which fit in nicely with antique furniture); optimal comfort, made visible by its soft, quilted cushions; and avant-garde industrial construction that ensured high-quality standards in industrial quantities. It was the first padded piece of furniture to use the cold-molded foaming process, which made it possible to sink all the rigid metal structural elements deep inside the soft polyurethane. It could be disassembled into individual parts and introduced a technique of furniture-making that is used today in about 80 percent of the sector's production worldwide. This model is still one of the company's best-selling items, with a production of about 20,000 pieces per year. The countless imitations of the "Coronado," especially the leather-upholstered version, bear witness to its success both in Italy and abroad (though the imitations often matched the original only in appearance, falling short in their technology and material quality).

In the section on the evolution of plastics in the Sixties we mentioned two chairs, one by Joe Colombo for Kartell in 1968 and one by Vico Magistretti for Artemide the following year. Both were among the world's first chairs in molded plastic; Joe Colombo's model "4869" was in extruded nylon, stackable, with open semicircular legs that were originally interchangeable, in three heights, (low, for waiting rooms; medium, for dining tables; and high, for bars).

Magistretti's "Selene" model was in press-molded, fiberglass-reinforced polyester. A small and large armchair and a table were developed, taking advantage of plastic's applications potential, which had already been tested and confirmed by the seat. The legs in cross-section were an open S-shape, which gave them rigidity and made it possible to produce them with a single mold.

It is worth noting that these two chairs are among the few that are still in production and have withstood the test of time, unlike many other later designs. As Giulio Castelli, president of Kartell, rightly pointed out on the occasion of the international exhibition entitled "La Sedia in Materiale Plastico" (The Plastic Chair), organized in 1975 by Centrokappa, "Among the one hundred chairs on display in this exhibition, only a few have matched the success of this design initiative."

Top: the wood-framed, straw-bottomed "Carimate" chair designed by Magistretti in 1961 as part of his project for a clubhouse near Milan. Later this model was put into production by Cassina and become a best seller.

Above: the "Plia" chair designed by Piretti in 1969 for Castelli; one of the most popular chairs in the world. It is a stackable folding chair, with a chromed or lacquered tubular steel framework; the seat and backrest are done in plastic or straw.

"There are very many pieces that look as though they were made by a good carpenter, and as such are negative examples, though they are often interesting from technological point of view: others exalt their raw material, even to excess, but are poor in technology. Since we are just now emerging from the pioneering phase, a great research effort on the part of the manufacturers is called for, especially in the area of raw materials.

"These manufacturers often have the vice of ad hoc production methods, putting into circulation materials with which they themselves are not fully familiar and which as a consequence are used badly, leading to a rejection of plastics. What is positive and stimulating in any case is that not a month goes by without the announcement of a new breakthrough in this sector, encouraging intensified experimentation aimed at the future."

The products of this phase of Italian design were very successful commercially, and for this reason have been the object of a continuous wave of studies that for the moment shows no signs of abatement. Project design was complicated by the layers of cultural connotations within our own memories, and the archetypes were few and widely copied, with minimal variations. This repetition, rich in echoes and cross-references, is extremely helpful in interpreting the dominant styles during this particular period of design history. We will cite here the two examples that open and close the 1960s: Vico Magistretti's "Carimate" chair of 1961 (manufactured by Cassina from 1963 on) and Giancarlo Piretta's "Plia" chair of 1969, for Castelli.

Both enjoyed an extraordinary success. Common to both is the fact that they represent not a morphological novelty but rather a perfect synthesis of a number of foregoing experiences – and this is almost a paradox in a decade of "innovation" and "novelty."

The "Carimate" was a straw-bottomed chair in lathed wood, an existing typology that was here, in Magistretti's genteel way, reproposed. The solidity of the chair's parts and its high armrests made up a vigorous line, and its red-lacquered frame gave it a fresh new appearance.

Piretti's "Plia" was a folding, stackable chair with a steel frame and a transparent plastic seat and backrest. It was the ultimate version of the old folding-chair theme, in a fully industrialized version with an optimum price-quality ratio; over five million have been sold the world over. The coherence of its lines and the perfect folding mechanism whereby the "Plia" can be flattened to only $3/4$ in. (4.5 cm), have made this article ubiquitous not only in homes but in business and social environments in general. The "Plia" represented the state of the art in furniture manufacturing.

Though the two chairs have the aforementioned trait in common, great formal, typological, and material differences distinguish them. It is worthwhile highlighting these differences because they are indicative of two very different approaches to design and to working within the furniture industry before and after the 1960s.

The "Carimate" chair, like many other products at the dawn of Italian design, arose from a particular interior-decorating problem that Magistretti faced as the architect-designer of a building complex with a clubhouse, nestled in a green estate in Carimate, near Milan. Hence came the name of the model, which was used in the restaurant's decor and was later produced in series by Cassina.

The "Plia," on the other hand, was done on request by the Castelli company (which, in a strategy of dividing the risks and investments, had decided to branch out from the office-furnishings market into the home-furnishings market) by a staff designer; Piretti's role was to uphold the company's manufacturing philosophy and to work in close collaboration with the industrial side of production, while meeting the specifications set forth in an exact briefing.

Continuing in the vein of industrial production, in the 1960s an important series of studies and research projects were carried out in the area of modular furniture for both home (kitchen cabinets, living room consoles, and wardrobe units) and office. These involved many production processes as well as the organization of domestic spaces.

Gian Casé's "T 12" kitchen for Boffi was one fruit of these studies. Presented in 1960 at the XII Triennale, it was the first kitchen done in plastic laminate and exposed wood, at a time when the market was beginning to tire of units in metal, and it was the first in which electrical appliances were given housings in a rational way in the kitchen cabinets.

Many family activities—cooking, eating, and spending time together—began to converge in this area of the home. The kitchen at the start of the Sixties was kept small, and less attention was paid to formal details, especially in the higher ranks of society, because it was a workplace for the servants. Over the years, however, with the shrinking labor supply in the servant sector, it became a larger, pleasanter place occupied by the homeowners as it became either a duty or a hobby to do one's own cooking.

From an efficient but rather aseptic cooking block, the American kitchen (and at the time the word "American" was synonymous with modernity and stylistic in-

Two examples of the evolution of the storage unit in the Sixties.

Top: Ettore Sottsass' modular "Kubirolo" for Poltronova (1967). Its elements could be stacked or placed side by side and were brightened by multicolored plastic knobs.

Above: Kazuhide Takahama's "Olinto" system for B&B (1979). Based on load-bearing uprights (no longer on elements simply placed side by side), it offered spaces into which various components of the system could be inserted.

novation) became more and more Mediterranean and colorful, and towards the end even recovered certain values associated with the nineteenth-century storage pantry.

The "E 15" kitchen, designed by Massoni in 1965 (again for Boffi), was so named for its basic 5 5/6 in. (15 cm) module, a size that on one hand ensured the least raw-material waste and on the other was the smallest feasible for storing objects. This kitchen offered a vast range of laminate or treated-wood doors in different

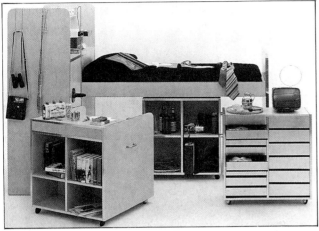

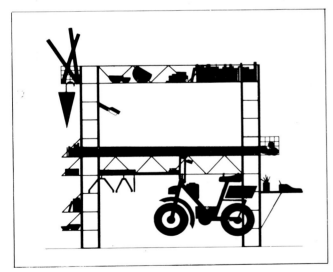

During the Sixties and Seventies various architects and designers worked on the problem of devising living space that combined indispensable household functions within single space-saving blocks. They no longer considered interior decoration as an accumulation of furniture and objects but, instead, proposed solutions that

involved prefabricated blocks that could be mixed and matched in different ways.

From top: Titina Ammanati and Giampiero Vitelli's "Mobile Totale" for Giuseppe Rossi of Albizzate (1966); Joe Colombo's "Box 1" for La Linea (1968); Bruno Munari's "Abitacolo" for Robots (1971).

colors, a continuous surface, electrical appliances tucked neatly away, and was designed for rapid assembly.

Among other sectional wall cabinets and partitions conceived for the home, which today represent the most advanced achievements of the home furnishing industry, we may single out Zanuso's "E 6" wardrobes for Elam (1966); Sottsass' "Kubirolo" container unit for Poltronova (1967); Mangiarotti's "Cub 8" room divider for Poltronova (1968), one of the first Italian convertible wall units with elements that rotated 360 degrees, and still in production today; and Aulenti's and Bartoli's modular units (1968 and 1969, respectively) for T 70.

In 1970, the Japanese designer Takahama conceived a system, the "Olinto" series, for B&B that has been widely developed over the years, and is still in production today. It is based on load-bearing upright panels in fiberboard lacquered in very high-gloss polyester.

New Product lines: all-purpose furniture. In the late 1960s to early 1970s, a number of multifunctional furnishing units were designed and developed. Indeed, these units were more than furniture, being adaptable environments that could serve a number of purposes. They were like big puzzles, in which each piece was individually complete and self-sufficient.

This concept extended to small-scale objects, such as Pierre Cardin's cone-shaped set of cooking utensils, which, starting with a large salad bowl as its base, stacked up various elements of diminishing size, culminating in a salt-shaker.

The limitations of some of these ideas lay less in the success or failure of a given object designed in response to a given need, than in the frequent arbitrariness or rigidity that dictated the activities to be carried out, even in small spaces.

Some good illustrations of this are: T. Ammanati and G.P. Vitelli's "Mobile Totale," designed in 1966 for Giuseppe Rossi of Albizzate. The piece, which measured 106 x 55 $^1/_3$ in. (272 x 142 cm) in its smallest version, was done in layered plastic laminate and incorporated a sofabed, a roll-out bed on wheels, a clothes closet, a vast work-surface, a dining table, a stove burner, a refrigerator, drawers at floor level that could be trasformed into low tables, a bar, and a stereo.

Giorgio De Ferrari and Marco Semino's award-winning "Tramezzino" in MIA's (Mostra Internazionale dell'Arredamento, Monza) "all-purpose furniture" competition, and by Abet Print in 1966. It is a flat,

Above: the "Splügen Bräu" lamp manufactured by Flos in 1961, designed by the Castiglionis for the beer hall of the same name. A hanging lamp, it provides a concentrated beam of light. For better heat dispersal, the exterior of the lamp is corrugated aluminum, with two linings separated by an air chamber.

Below: the "Taccia" lamp, an adjustable glass bell projecting diffused light, designed by the Castiglionis and manufactured by Flos in 1962.

slender piece in which a series of narrow, deep drawers, to be opened from either side, is supported by two laminated panels. An all-purpose article that fits as well in the living room as in the entrance hall, the bathroom, or the bedroom, it could function as a convertible screen-partition, a wall cabinet, or, placed on its side, a cocktail table.

Joe Colombo's "Box 1" for La Linea (1968) is a single living block made up of bed, wardrobe, drawers, bookcase, night table, writing desk, and chair. It is planned to occupy 97 x 50 $^3/_4$ in. (250 x 130 cm).

"Struttura Abitabile Globale," designed by L. Forges Davanzati, B. Munari, and P. Ranzani and unveiled at the XIV Triennale in 1968, is made up of modular blocks that can be assembled in various ways for the kitchen, living room, or bedroom.

Producta's "Gruppo 24 Ore" for Almasio Arredamenti (1970) was designed to meet children's needs. It is made up of three elements: a fold-away bed, a telescoping wardrobe on two sides, and a writing table.

Bruno Munari's "Abitacolo" for Robots won the Compasso d'Oro award in 1979. Designed as a children's room that provided an essential living space for study (there are a table and shelves that can be mounted wherever one likes), to sleep (two twin-bed frames that can be fixed at the desired height on four supports that also serve as the steps to reach the various levels), and to entertain friends. It is constructed in welded plasticized steel and measures 78 x 31$^1/_5$ in. (200 x 80 cm), height 78 in. (200 cm); dismantled, 15 $^2/_3$ x 78 x 19$^1/_2$ in. (40 x 200 x 50 cm). This product is still in production, and sales have improved considerably since its initial release on the market.

Lighting fixtures. Italian lamps hold an important place in the world of international design. Together with a few Scandinavian ideas, such as those of Alvar Aalto, Poul Henningsen, Poul Christiansen, and Norway's Luxo, they offer the most intelligent responses to the artificial lighting problem that the interior-decoration industry has come up with yet. In 1960 two new companies, Flos and Artemide, joined the few firms already existing in which the designer and entrepreneur were often the same person (Arteluce, with lamps designed by Sarfatti; O-Luce with Ostuni's designs; and Azucena with Caccia Dominioni's and Gardella's designs). In the course of the decade Flos and Artemide stood out against a field of small artisanal workshops, not only for the innovative impact and the carefully researched design of their lighting fixtures, but also for the highly industrialized production processes that turned out lamps for an international market.

Flos, founded in Merano under the well-balanced guidance of Dino Gavina and Sergio Biliotti, managing director of Eiskenkill, in 1959 was already experimenting with a new plastic fiber substance, "cocoon," for its lighting fixtures. Flos manufactured designs by the Castiglioni brothers and by Scarpa, whose cultural backgrounds and experience were so strikingly different as to suggest that the firm's stimulating counterpoint of products arose from precisely this meeting of minds. The Castiglionis' experience in designing display installations also contributed to their lamp designs and their highly original use of light—in addition to the shape of the lamp itself—to transform interiors.

Many of the lamps manufactured by Flos arose as solutions to exposition problems, based on experimental research in the field of illumination technology, or as expressive enhancements to architectural projects; they later found their way into many Italian homes.

For example, the "Splügen Bräu" hanging lamp was marked in 1961, but was designed the previous year as part of the lighting installation at the beer hall of the same name; located in Milan, this was an elegant multileveled atmosphere, a special wagon-restaurant wherein eating in good company became a spectacle, without, however, encroaching on the diner's private space. The "Teli" lamp was put into production in 1973 but was designed for the 1957 Triennale. The "Frisbi" lamp of 1978 projected direct light downwards and diffused light upwards; it perfected and adapted for industrial production an effect like the luminous garland of lights suspended in the air that had already been tested at the X Triennale and in the Montecatini Pavilion at the Fiera di Milano of 1962. It was an effect that was revived on a larger scale on the occasion of the "Mobilevante" exhibition of 1980, where for a display of interior-decorative objects in a 9 $^5/_6$-yards-high (9 m) industrial loft, a luminous dropped ceiling was devised using great panels 4 $^1/_3$ x 4 $^1/_3$ yd. (4 x 4 m) of white fabric, volumes of illumination akin to trawling nets, which hung far below the existing ceiling in order to maintain the proper proportions of the objects on display with respect to the enormous size of the loft.

This is not the place to discuss all of the Castiglioni brothers' lamps because, in addition to being well-known and still in production (thanks to Flos' strategy of ensuring product nonobsolescence from a formal point of view, and of reducing to a minimum the products' inevitable technological obsolescence), they

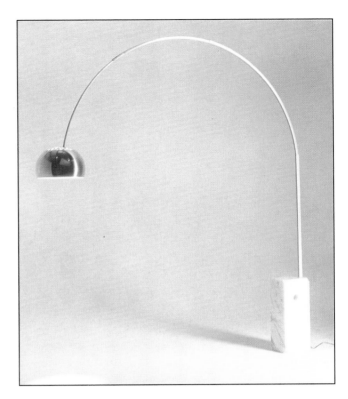

Top: the "Arco" floor lamp with stainless-steel arm and white marble base, designed by the Castiglionis for Flos in 1962; an innovative means of illuminating the dining area.

Above: the "Eclisse" lamp with rotating hood, designed by Magistretti in 1966 for Artemide.
Left: the "Pipistrello" table lamp with aluminum-based, telescoping upright and white methacrylate shade, designed by Aulenti and manufactured by Martinelli Luce in 1966.

have been thoroughly reviewed in countless publications. We cannot help but mention, however, their very famous and much-copied "Arco" floor lamp of 1962. At the time of its market introduction it represented an important breakthrough vis-à-vis the dining room, freeing the dining table from its static position below the ceiling light fixture. The lamp's movement in space had great expressive force, upheld as it was by an impeccable logic.

Artemide was also founded in 1960, by Giorgio Mazza, an architect-designer of many of the company's starting products, and by engineer Ernesto Gismondi, a professor in rocket technology at Milan's polytechnic university. Following its craftsmanlike beginnings, the company became known for its industrial approach and large-scale production. It developed the "Demetrio" tables (1966) and "Selene" chairs (1969), both in plastic and designed by Vico Magistretti

The same architect designed the "Eclisse" lamp (1966), which along with Richard Sapper's "Tizio" halogen lamp (1972) formed Artemide's greatest successes, putting the company on the international map.

The "Eclisse" was a small table lamp in lacquered metal, in which the direction and intensity of the light could be regulated by rotating its spherical hood around the lightbulb (hence the apt name "Eclipse"). Awarded the Compasso d'Oro in 1967, it introduced a design look that over all these years has not lost an iota of its freshness, and one which reflected designer and architect Magistretti's consistent attention to proportion and taste for simple shapes.

The close of the Sixties was thus marked by the coexistence of parallel trends in design (somewhat similar to what was to take place in the second half of the Eighties). "Radical" design turned to Pop and conceptual art to break free of rationalism and functionalism; it offered an "evasion design" based on low technology and low-cost investments for molds and equipment, with limited-series production. Here the product's look was an integral part of the design considerations, which went beyond the practical aspects into the realm of a sort of design criticism.

Sometimes this design process was not even aimed at an object but rather (setting aside plans for implementation) was aimed at developing the expressive potential of the architectural idiom in order to work on the signifying aspect of the design itself.

This could result in an elaborate graphic design or else verged on the artistic developments of the happening, or body art, with the design of gestures, activities or behavior patterns (as in the case of Gianni Pettena or

Superstudio, "The Twelve Ideal Cities" (1970). One of the principal exponents of radical architecture, this Florentine group was founded in 1966 by Adolfo Natalini, Alessandro and Roberto Magris and Piero Frassinelli. At the close of the Sixties, it proposed a series of teaching projects, freed of the constraints of technology and realization, that used collages and films to visualize utopian dwelling situations, magnifications of contemporary metropolitan life. It was, then, a constructive utopia—one that did not propose a different world, but, rather, represented the present at a higher level of awareness.

the UFO group).

These "radical" groups operated outside of the traditional design environments: in Florence and Turin, as well as in Austria with Abraham, Picler, and Hollein. Exhibitions such as "Italy: The New Domestic Landscape," organized by the Museum of Modern Art, New York, in 1972, and "Contemporanea," held in Rome in 1973, took stock of this movement's activities, but also, in hindsight, marked its end as a historical phenomenon – or at least the loss of its initial vitality, a halt in its growth.

On the other hand, there was a "classical" design school, the (preferably Milanese) proponents of "good design": Zanuso, the Castiglionis, Magistretti, Bellini, Aulenti, Agnoli, Mangiarotti, and so forth. This school was oriented toward a broader market in which production investments were an integral part of the object and determined its form; they were a guarantee of quality and distinction, compared to what anonymous competitors offered. Its approach was attuned to marketing requirements, the possibilities of industrial production, and commercialization of the product.

The attitude to plastics, which were in such vogue in the 1960s, and toward the know-how used in their applications highlight the differences between the two approaches. The "radical" designers used mainly block-cut polyurethane (as in Poltronova's "Super-onda" or Gufram's "Alvar" armchair) and hand-molded fiberglass (as in Poltronova's "Safari" and "Mobili Grigi." The "classical" group used molded polyurethane foam (as in B&B's "Coronado," or extruded plastic (as in Kartell's chair and tables), or press-molded reinforced polyester (as in Artemide's "Selene" chairs and "Stadio" table).

EXHIBITIONS

New designs for Italian furniture. In March 1960, an exhibition was opened at the Osservatore delle arti industriali in Milan. Organized by Guido Cannella and Vittorio Gregotti, its participants included Gabetti and Isola, Gae Aulenti, and other young local architects who had coalesced around Rogers' review *Casabella* and had in common—while still conserving significant differences—an abhorence for "stateless and sterile internationality" (Portoghesi). This show was steeped in heated debate, but made an important contribution to the recovery of forgotten prerationalist styles in architecture and interior decoration; the critics hastened to label it "neo-Liberty."

The pieces on display clearly declared their historical inspiration, a highly critical poke at the dominant design ideology. "On one hand, it [the ideology] was seen as being directly dependent on capitalist production methods and mass exploitation: on the other hand, the emergence of the historical dimension as design material triggered the eclipse of the object-as-tool concept in favor of a more contextual narrative connotation" (V. Gregotti).

"What the efforts of this generation seemed to have in common was a rebellion against the 'fathers' who were guilty of having conveyed myths that were difficult to dismantle and whose continuity people persisted in celebrating" (Manfredo Tafuri).

"In some of our furniture's details, there is also a tendency toward elegant or pleasing contrasts, as in the roll-top bureau. It is not a matter of sugar-coating the pill: we think instead that in this way, furniture that has remained outside of contemporary culture can

Three representative products of the Sixties' neo-Liberty style.

From top: console by Gabetti and Isola (1959);

the "Cavour" armchair by Gregotti, Meneghetti, and Stoppino; a table with rosewood top and black legs by Asti and Favre.

"La Casa Abitata," Florence (1955). Above and opposite page, five interiors presented at this exhibition. The Castiglionis decorated a small dining area where they inserted mass-produced elements of their own design (sideboard and chairs for Bernini, table for Gavina, lamps for Flos), together with other anonymous objects (a ladder, a piece of a pile dwelling, steel shelves, a grip), creating a conceptual mis-en-scène. Vico Magistretti presented a living/dining-room area and kitchen for a small apartment in a building that he had planned. The furnishings are pieces of his own design for Artemide (the lamps and small tables) and for Cassina (the armchairs, sofas, table, and chairs).

A. Mangiarotti proposed a synthesis between fixed and freestanding furnishing elements: a wall unit whose elements could rotate 360 degrees. A large chandelier, manufactured by Candle, illuminated the conversation area. Ettore Sottsass designed a bedroom with furniture and ceramics that he had designed for Poltronova and Il Sestante. Marco Zanuso created a living room and a baby's room in a space of about 54 $^2/_5$ square yards (50 sq. m.). To separate the rooms, he used a shelving system, designed for Techniform. In the living room were his "Woodline" and "Fourline" armchair, designed for Arflex, and his "Lambda" chairs for Gavina.

come closer to a 'new line' (an inappropriate word in any case); in particular, we think that, tied as it is to domestic life, a piece of furniture—more than architecture—should reflect a lively and warm taste for people's homes" (Gabetti and Isola, from the catalogue *Nuovi Disegni per il Mobile Italiano*).

This exhibition was pivotal (and had parallels in what was to take place in the Eighties with the neo-modern products of Alchimia and Memphis) to the debate that had come to a head in 1959, the previous year, between Banham, the editor-in-chief of *The Architectural Review*, and Rogers, editor-in-chief of *Casabella*. The illustrious English critic had written a scathing editorial about the Milanese and Turinese architects, lumping together the young architects who later participated in the exhibition and the "fathers," including Rogers, Gardella, Albini, Figini and Pollini; accusing them of having betrayed modern architecture; and criticizing the neo-Liberty style as an "infantile regression."

Ernesto Rogers replied with an article in *Casabella* N° 228, entitled "L'Evoluzione dell'Architettura, Risposta al Custode dei Frigidaires" (The Evolution of Architecture, in Answer to the Guardian of Frigidaires), in which he defended an interpretation of the "Modern movement as a continuous revolution, that is to say as a continuous development of the principle of adapting to life's changing contents," in order get away from rampant conformism (rationalist, functionalist, "organicist"), which had by then become the rule.

La Casa Abitata – biennial of contemporary interiors. For the first edition of the "Casa Abitata" show, which ran from March 6 to April 25, 1965 in Florence, the organizing committee proposed the examination of a fundamental problem—that of domestic lifestyles—starting with a few basic givens (market supply, existing house layouts, and so on). They asked the designers for guidance, suggestions, and interpretations of lifestyle in order to transform an existing, nonimaginary space through its interior decor. The participants were asked to handle with care the layers of sentimental values attached to the furnishings and personal objects—attached to an entire ensemble of emotional and cultural baggage—in a specific place.

Achille and Pier Giacomo Castiglioni were among the participants in this exhibition organized by Giovanni Michelucci and Pier Luigi Spadolini. They decorated a small dining area with mass-produced elements of their own design, and with other anonymous objects: a steel ladder to be hung on the wall; a

It was a true manifesto of the ready-made, done in such a way as to stimulate the dwellers to actively exploit the objects themselves, which, removed from their usual contexts, became loaded with new meaning. The overall effect was to create a situation of suspended theatricality, with the scenery meticulously designed to arouse a sense of expectation in this trade-show environment: a "conceptual" manœuvre that anticipated some of Kounellis's work.

The wall clock, positioned midway between an archæological artifact and the ladder, both made the visitor aware of the passing of time on a small scale—time of a daily, twenty-four-hour kind—and reminded him of the very long time that man had taken to scale the rungs of civilization, to make the transition from his pile dwellings to the industrial product: the steel ladder hung on the wall—a mass-produced object, but also a symbol for hard work and elevation.

Gregotti, Meneghetti, and Stoppino proposed the spatial integration of the various functional areas of the home. Altough this project made use of modern systems then available on the market, their unusual arrangement offered a radical criticism of the entire flow structure of standard housing. In particular it pointed to how the "living-room" function, rather than remaining in a single designated space (the traditional living-room area), tended to spread throughout the entire home. In order to bring apartment design up to date with this trend in lifestyles, the service areas were merged with the wardrobe area, decorated with accessory elements (fireplace, bookcase, etc.), and finished in materials that accentuated their "living-room" function.

Vico Magistretti focused on the living- dining-room area of a prefabricated unit of a building he himself had planned, decorating it with mass-produced pieces of furniture of his own design. The dining area was conceived as the intersection between the kitchen and living room, so that it could be annexed to one or the other rooms by means of extendable partitions, or isolated to make it a small room to be used as a study if desired.

Angelo Mangiarotti, starting from an analysis of existing elements of furnishing in an ordinary home, broken down into elements fixed to the wall and free-standing elements (chairs, armchairs, sofas, etc.), proposed a synthesis of these two types of furniture by means of a wall unit that was later to be refined in his definive design of a room divider manufactured by Poltronova in 1968, marketed under the brand name "CUB 8."

Ettore Sottsass designed a bedroom featuring

grip like those used by grocery clerks to reach the items on the highest shelves; a wall clock with Roman numerals; an old double door made abstract with white lacquer; shelves with potted plants placed at an unusual height and thus changing the relationships among the other things in the room.

totemic elements around the bed, with grids and colors inspired by the Japanese tradition. These helped to create a highly colorful lyrical space, a hymn to love, which Sottsass underlined in his accompanying project description by citing a passage from the *Kama Sutra*.

Addressing architecture students at Palermo University, Sottsass remarked about his work in those years that "I was beginning to get very interested in the sensual import of structural density, no longer as supporting and supported elements, but as a much more complex network of the structural relationships that can exist. Then, also, there was the sensual problem of colors and materials. The piece of furniture becomes a person; it takes on its own life independent of the rest of the surroundings. It does not construct the environment, but settles itself into it, in a certain sense, like a person who in some way concedes to and demands a certain wary reconciliation [with the other elements]. Rather than neutralize the piece, I injected it with meaning...the iconographic elements that were at my disposal in '65 were above all drawn from the peasant culture. For example, the large feet, the broad curves, ceramics; today, instead, we draw our iconographic elements from the urban world, the Pop culture of the urban outskirts."

Marco Zanuso created a living space suitable as living room and as baby's room, bands of light running around its perimeter, subdivided by shelving of his own design that was positioned to form curved theatrical wings acting as screens.

The Eurodomus exhibitions. Another series of exhibitions crucial to interior decoration's development were the Eurodomus shows, sponsored by *Domus* magazine and organized by Giò Ponti, Giorgio Casati, and Emanuele Ponzio. Their aim was to organize "pilot exhibitions" of the modern home, and the four editions (held in Genoa in 1966, in Turin in 1968, in Milan in 1970, and again in Turin in 1972) were geared to bring the consumer in touch with the design professionals—unlike, for example, the Salone del Mobile, which targeted, instead, professionals in the field, and shopowners.

In Genoa, an installation showing an experimental apartment designed by "Gruppo 1" (Rodolfo Bonetto, Cesare Casati, Joe Colombo, Giulio Confalonieri, Enzo Hybsch, Luigi Massoni, and Emanuele Ponzio) was presented. The importance of this initiative (called "Domus Ricerca") lay in the fact that for the first time in Italy, and perhaps in the world, industries with different orientations and production activities joined forces under a single organization whose object was pure

Top: Eurodomus (1966), experimental apartment designed by Gruppo 1, distinguished by its open floor plan with folding partition and by its stainless-steel floors. The living room was furnished with "shuttle-shaped" sofas and armchairs that offered seating at different heights.

Above: the entrance to the 1960 XII Triennale on "The Home and the School" was designed by Sottsass as a hotel foyer, with rest areas and works of art on display.

research, going beyond immediate industrial applications.

"Domus Ricerca"'s apartment measured 211 $^{3}/_{4}$ sq. yds. (162 sq. m.) and was distinguished, first of all, by its layout: it had an open floor plan, made possible by a foyer/access corridor that ran around the apartment's perimeter. At various points this corridor could be incorporated into the space of the different rooms by opening or closing folding partitions. All the other dividing walls were movable as well; the floors were in stainless steel in the foyers and kitchen, and had indoor/outdoor carpeting in the other rooms. The kitchen had a central workblock offering a series of innova-

The XII Triennale tackled the theme "The Home and the School" from three different points of view: the rural environment, the reality of the urban periphery, and the city center.

From top: the city-periphery dwelling decorated by Spadolini and Maioli, with painter Robert Sambonet; city-center installation by Raboni, a dwelling unit featuring two levels separating the zones used during the day and those used at night.

tions that would later be the shared heritage of many other kitchens. In the living room there were strange "shuttle-shaped" sofas in which the profiles of three seats of various height (low seating for the sofa, medium-height for dining, and high for sitting at the bar) were combined.

The Triennales. The 1960 Triennale was dedicated to "Home and Schools"; in 1964 it was dedicated to "Leisure," and in 1968 to "The Big Number."

The 1960 XII Triennale examined the theme of the home and schools from three points of view: the rural

environment, the reality of the urban periphery, and the city center. "This distinction," wrote Ernesto Rogers in his review in *Casabella*, "became a question of social class and not of environmental conditions, especially when dealing with the homes: the middle-class homes took the form of a more or less sophisticated, purely stylistic exercise, while the rural homes smacked of the literary and paternalistic."

The rural home, conceived for a nuclear family of four, agricultural workers in the Novara region, was designed by the firm Gregotti, Meneghetti, Stoppino. It included built-in decor, in line with the notion that the average fieldworker was not able to create his own complete and civilized environment, and that, besides, furnishing was usually kept to a minimum given the continual moves from one farm to another imposed by the job.

The two city peripheries, one decorated by Pier Luigi Spadolini and Marco Maioli with the contribution of painter Robert Sambonet, and the other by Fredi Drugman, were based on public-housing apartments.

The former plan offered highly flexible use of the rooms and great freedom in furniture arrangements thanks to a uniform "pegboard" system for attaching things to the wall; the pieces of furniture were reduced to their most basic functions as containers or resting surfaces. The floor was tiled throughout the house (the work of Piero Dorazio), and the wallpaper was designed by the painter Turcato.

The second home, designed for higher-income clients, included forced-ventilation systems to make freer use of the space. The dining area was contiguous with the kitchen, which offered a view of a fine array of electrical appliances. A series of four teak cabinets, designed by Drugman himself, had drop leafs that could serve as an additional table surface or as a writing table. A 5 $\frac{1}{2}$-yard-long (5 m) carpet designed by Tobia Scarpa ran the length of the living room.

The three city-center dwellings were designed, respectively, by Gae Aulenti, Luigi Caccia Dominioni, and Fulvio Raboni.

The first was a variation on the layout of an existing apartment in one of BBPR's condominiums in Milan, and occupied three floors of the building; it was a luxury apartment decorated with extreme elegance. The living room-dining-room and study areas were on display at the exhibition. Each was on a different level, with the living room, at the center, the lowest by 23 $\frac{2}{5}$ in (60 cm). At the center of the living room stood four supporting piers with niches carved into them for use as bookshelves. Aulenti's design of the marble floors emphasized the divisions and relationship between the

The dwelling decorated by Caccia Dominioni for the XII Triennale, reproduction of an apartment he planned and finished in Milan.
Left: the round windows lighting the hallway to the night zone. One is transparent, the other mirrored.
Below: the central suite of rooms along the "backbone" passageway. The wardrobe doors are lined with silk; the floors are of African walnut.

various settings. Some of the pieces of furniture — a sofa, the cushions, and the fabrics — were designed by Aulenti; one table was by Borsani for Tecno; the armchairs were by Zanuso for Gavina.

The second city-center installation, designed by Caccia Dominioni, reproduced a central access corridor of an apartment in Milan, planned and carried out by the same architect. It was exemplary for its rigorous spatial organization, one of the themes that most concerned rationalist architects, especially in the years following the War, when they were involved in minimalist trends.

"To achieve a functional solution does not mean simply to preordain and guarantee its material functioning, but also to give that function an identity in terms of space and flow and setting. In this particular case, it means going beyond the notion which considers a certain succession of spaces as merely an interstitial factor, secondary in the economy of a house, and as such to be treated in a schematic and approximative way. The old-fashioned anonymous passage, broken down into entrance, pantry, night zone, must be replaced by a system of closely interlocking passages that make up the backbone of the dwelling, and define and separate each function by means of a precise spatial layout.

"The entrance gives access to the living room, the living-dining area and the service areas are linked by the pantry; the night zone is the barycenter of a more private area. The single type of flooring throughout is intended to eliminate the rigid and mechanical subdivision of the areas." (from the XII Triennale catalogue).

The materials used were: mosaic floors in patterns designed by Corrado dell'Acqua; wall covering in light and dark gray straw; the hallway wardrobe in red lacquered walnut.

Raboni instead proposed a dwelling unit in a residence hotel that featured two levels separating the night and day zones. The walls were covered with cotton fabric similar to that used for mattresses; the furniture, apart from a bookcase by Magistretti, was designed by Raboni and put into series production.

The XII Triennale also presented examples of neo-Liberty design by the new generation of architects from Milan, Novara, and the Piedmont, and it was obvious that this trend was not limited to the younger designers or to just a few circles, but could be recognized in the work of the "masters" and in that of the generation in between. Guido Castelli wrote in *Casabella-Continuità*: "This Triennale focused on works that treated the theme in a personalized and mature way, seeking the best expression of a domestic reality or a statement of individual truth, ignoring those of a trite or experimental nature."

Two figures that had a great influence on design in the years to come emerged from this exhibition: Carlo Scarpa and Ettore Sottsass. The former, together with Bruno Zevi, organized a commemorative exhibition on Frank Lloyd Wright: the installation was noteworthy for the lighting effects created by intangible volumes of light and transparent cloth, which was hung from the ceiling in order to reduce the disproportionate height of the exhibition space without canceling its effect. Sottsass designed the Triennale's entrance hall, creating a sort of hotel foyer where people could sit down and linger to look at the paintings and objects displayed in it. The paintings were by Burri, Castellani, Fontana, Manzoni, Rotella, and Turcato; the sculptures by Franchina and Pomodoro; the furniture by Sottsass for Poltronova. The door opening onto the garden was particularly interesting for its graphic impact against the backdrop of the wall.

The materials used were: plaster panels for the ceiling; Montelupo tiles and wood for the wall; and glassy white mosaic tiles with interspersed geometric motifs for the floor.

The XIII Triennale of 1964 focused on mass-consumed items for vacation and leisure by anonymous designers (an approach that was abandoned in the following years, given the inflation of the "signature" as an added value to the product). This Triennale also marked a turning point in attitudes toward art/production, a relationship that had been handled ambiguously in the past; here faith in the reassuring ideological vision of the design of single objects was losing ground, and the field of inquiry was broadened to include an analysis of the questions posed by the total environment.

The following year *Edilizia Moderna* (No. 85) took up these themes. "Nothing guarantees us that the sum total of a number of well-designed items will result in a positive setting: crowding, poor arrangements, overlapping or disconnectedness can cancel whatever the object expresses." (V. Gregotti, *Möbel aus Italien*, Stuttgart 1983).

Inaugurated on May 30, 1968, the XIV Triennale addressed the theme of the great transformation that was under way in all sectors of urban activity and in approaches to designing physical environments. Immediately following its opening, it was occupied by a group of protesters who voiced their objection to "the culture of the bourgeois state and to the excessive power of the professional clans" with the aim of "gaining immediate and direct control of all cultural institu-

XIII Triennale (1964). Top: a view of Marco Comolli's prefabricated vacation home. The furnishings consist of mass-produced pieces designed by M. Comolli and G. Poli; the two-seat sofa is by Albini and Helg. Above: the "Nature Home" by E. Vittoria. Furnishing the living room are lamps by the Castiglionis, an armchair by O. Borsani for Tecno, sofas and end tables by E. Sottsass for Poltronova. XIV Triennale (1968). Below: the tunnel pneu linking the Palazzo dell'Arte with the Park, designed by De Pas, D'Urbino, Lomazzi.

tions and public places of culture, to be run in a democratic fashion." The Triennale took up this "youth protest," inverting it into one of its installations, or better, into a dramatic performance in which under the direction of Marco Bellochio social tensions were made into spectacle and which lapsed into the grotesque when a fake barricade was reconstructed on location.

The interior-decoration exhibition tackled the problem of "demonstrating how, given a series of high-quality furnishing elements, it is possible to use composition to make a single environment take on many different shades of character. But, moreover, it seeks to demonstrate that interior decoration can be conceived of as an operation that involves and modifies the structure of the space in question: particular emphasis will be given to the projects that approach interior decor as a structural element of the living space: convertible wall units, all-purpose furniture, etc..."

On display in this section were:

A flexible living system by Joe Colombo, manufactured by La Rinascente and based on the following criteria: flexibility in time and space; design for collective use; the application of new technology and new materials, such as plastic laminates, plastic bumper elements, magnetic closures, and joints for various types of unit; the feasibility of large-scale production; distribution through large department stores.

The UPIM installation by Carla Venosta with Lucci, Orlandini and Pietrantoni.

The all-purpose built-in environment by Costantino Corsini and Giorgio Wiskmann.

Radical architecture's proposals: the audiovisual self-service restaurant by Ugo La Pietra and Paolo Rizzato; the Center for Eclectic Conspiracy by the Archizoom group.

De Pas, D'Urbino, and Lomazzi had designed a *tunnel pneu* linking the Palazzo dell'Arte with the Padiglione nel Parco, a continuation of their research on inflatable structures, which began in 1967 with their famous "Blow" armchair in PVC for Zanotta.

XIV Triennale (1968). Top: the "Center for Eclectic Conspiracy," designed by the Archizoom group. Breaking with a self-satisfied and complacent tradition, they revived the kitschy elements of Oriental and Alpine folklore.

Above: the Triennale's performance area, designed by Ceretti, Derossi, and Rosso, of Piper Club fame. The space is defined by movable metal structures lined with black polyester. Colorful, painted polyurethane hassocks rest on carpeted platforms distributed about the space.

THE COMPASSO D'ORO AWARDS

The Compasso d'Oro award was an initiative undertaken in 1954 by La Rinascente department store to recognize designers and manufacturers in the field of products for widespread consumption who achieved a synthesis of form and function. It bears witness to La Rinascente's interest in design and

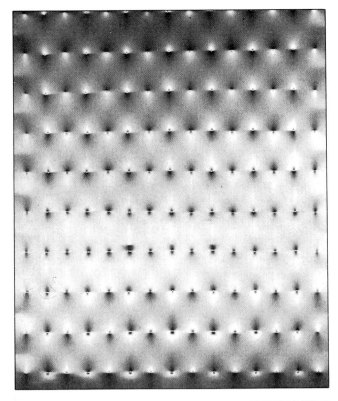

Top: Enrico Castellani, White Surfaces (1967). Founder, with Manzoni and Bonalumi, of the "Azymuth" movement and review, Castellani used a monochrome painting and small incisions or other relief-work on the canvas to experiment with intensities of incidental light.

Above: Victor Vasarely with one of his works of 1968. Vasarely is one of the masters of optical and kinetic art, which primarily uses geometrical designs and chromatic juxtapositions to produce an image that varies depending on the viewer's position. His oeuvre includes a number of serial works.

its marketing, an interest which, as far as furniture was concerned, dated back to the 1930s when a furniture collection designed by Giò Ponti was launched on the market, continuing through 1946 when a model apartment designed by Carlo Pagani was constructed, and on to 1951, when Franco Albini designed furniture for display at the IX Triennale.

During the 1960s La Rinascente counted among its collaborators the likes of Mario Cristiani, Corsini/Wiskemann, Joe Colombo, Ornella Noorda, Mario Bellini, Guido Crepax, Enzo Mari, and Gae Aulenti, who designed a series of high-quality furnishings, many of them in Abet Print plastic laminate. For three years Tomás Maldonado was responsible for the store's coordinated image, from graphic design to architecture, packaging and advertising; this represented one of the few examples in Italian industry (together with Olivetti and later FIAT) of coordination among the different elements of a corporate image.

From 1959 to 1965, the Compasso d'Oro was managed by La Rinascente in collaboration with ADI (Association for Industrial Design, founded in Milan in 1956). In 1967, the latter took complete control of the award's management and organization. In the course of its existence, the Compasso d'Oro has acquired worldwide prestige, becoming the most sought-after honor in the field of industrial design.

ART EXHIBITIONS

The 1960s were years in which the Anglo-American influence had its furthest-reaching effects on many fields of expression, from fashion to music, literature, and painting. Moreover, the climate in Italy was marked by a great hunger for novelties, which were quickly ingested and at times assimilated and then reproposed in original ways.

Various artistic tendencies existed side by side in the period: kinetic art, optical art, neo-realism, Pop art, conceptual art, minimal art, arte povera. These artistic currents had a remarkable influence on architecture, interior decoration, and design; and in the wake of the Sixties, so fertile an exchange of experiences in the fields of art, interior design, and fashion seems unlikely to be repeated.

Op art's experimentation in visual phenomena, its exploration of the effects of light, movement, and colors, was taken up in the fashion world by the likes of Krizia and Germana Marucelli (especially in the latter's "Alluminio" collection, done in collaboration with Ge-

In 1968, the Galleria Mana Art Market in Rome exhibited serial works by artists working in the interior-design sector. Among these were: Franco Angeli's "Dollaro" table (above) and a door by Lucio Fontana (left), both of molded plastic. Below: Piero Giliardi, "Nature Carpets" (1966). Handling the polyurethane foam with astonishing dexterity, Giliardi creates artificial nature pieces, such as meadows and seascapes.

tulio Alviani); in fabric design and wall coverings for the Falconetto company; in furniture design by Sergio Asti and Nanda Vigo; and in graphic design and tile design by Franco Grignani.

At this time design personalities such as Enzo Mari, Bruno Munari, and Ugo La Pietra, or Ennio Chiggio, Eduardo Landi, and Manfredo Massironi of Gruppo N were experimenting in kinetics and gestalt.

Two aspects of this artistic current were to strike home in the field of furniture design: the first was the concept that the work attains status as such only after the user brings it to fruition. Using the work somehow alters it. (A good example of this is J.R. Soto's room with vertical wires hung from the ceiling that vibrated ever so slightly as visitors passed through, disrupting the spaces in a simultaneity of product use and its modification that worked on all levels of sensory stimulation.) The second was the idea that the work need not be an "original piece," but, like a product of industrial design, should be reproducible "in series" where only the originality of the design is preserved, and the piece's "artistic-ness" is identified in this. This "artistic-ness" could be reproduced by industrial means without detracting from its value, even if the artist was not present during the reproduction process.

From 1965 on, the art market was overrun by these replicas from every art genre. Their quality varied, but they fit in well with mass-produced furnishing products and often shared the same sales outlets.

In 1968 the Mana Art Market gallery opened in Rome. It sold "Art furniture": the work of sculptor Gino Marotta, known for his landscapes with vacuum-molded methacrylate trees, as well as for the lamps and fabrics he designed for Poltronova; Franco Angeli's *Dollar* tables; Gianni Colombo's and Martial Raysse's lamps; and the molded plastic doors with hinges and knobs by Lucio Fontana, Enrico Castellani and Gino Marotta. All of these were transpositions of the individual artists' figurative styles to a practical and social context.

César's *Espansioni* date to 1965. This artist was a leading exponent of Nouveau Realism and he filled galleries the world over with his polyurethane foam expansions in very vivid colors, exalting the expressive potential of this medium. César's technique was to mix the components needed for the chemical reaction, letting them expand freely in space and then solidify. In the same years, with great poetic skill and craftsmanship, Piero Gilardi was creating *Le Nature* (Natures), landscapes, riverbeds, stretches of seacoast with seagulls, all in painted polyurethane.

His artistic experiments had an echo in the innovative design of armchairs manufactured by Gavina, Gufram, Poltronova and B&B in the second half of the 60s. Piero Gilardi was a key figure in the Gufram company, not only as creator of famous works such as *I Sassi* (The Rocks), but also as creator of the polyurethane prototypes for a few pieces that in some ways recalled his artificial landscapes (such as *Cactus*, signed by Guido Drocco and Franco Mello, or *Pratone*-Big Meadow, signed by Ceretti/Derossi/Rosso); the idea of painting the polyurethane with latex rubber was his and it solved the problem of the sofa's covering and surface finish.

B&B continued these experiments in polyurethane expansions with Gaetano Pesce's *Up* series (1969). In this case, the innovation consisted in the packaging: extracting all the air from the finished product and vacuum-packing it in a PVC wrapper offered space-saving advantages for shipping and storing the article; when opened, the armchairs took their original form.

Piero Manzoni died prematurely in 1963. He and Frenchman Yves Klein were prime movers behind the expansion and transformation of the frontiers of artistic experimentation that was taking place in the contemporary avant-garde. In his short lifespan (for its brevity comparable to that of Pino Pascali, another key figure), he managed to anticipate many of *arte povera*'s and conceptual art's innovations.

His first *Achromes*, in folded fabric stiffened into absolute whiteness by kaolin, date back to 1958. They were followed in 1959 by his *Lines* drawn on long strips of canvas or paper. In 1960, at an exhibition at the Galleria Azimuth, he invited visitors to eat hard-boiled eggs endorsed with his thumbprint. In 1961, Manzoni executed his *Base Magica* (Magic Stand) which converted the objects or persons set up on it into works of art, and his *Merda d'Artista*, canned and sold by weight at the day's gold quotation. In 1962 he installed in Herning, Denmark, a large metal parallelepiped bearing the upside-down inscription "Socle du monde – homage to Galileo," thus accomplishing the extraordinary feat of aesthetic appropriation of the globe. Scandal and heated debate were the standard reactions to all of Manzoni's neo-dadaist acts, matched only by the provocations of Klein's works. Later radical architecture and design owed much to these artists.

Seminal works by Klein include his *Monochromes*, which showed a single dominant color as the sum of a city's colors; and his *Anthroponometries*, in which he abandoned the traditional tools of the painting craft, using instead his models to color his canvases. That is, he coated them with an absolute blue (later called Klein blue) and had them roll over the canvases laid out on the floor. In this way, Klein worked on two

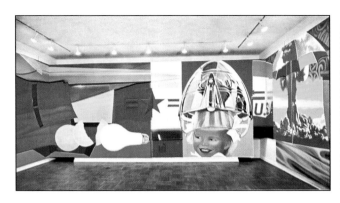

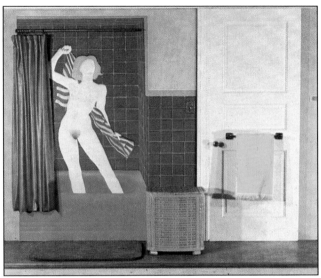

Top: James Rosenquist, F 11 (1965). Made up of fifty-one panels, this painting is more than 32 ⁴/₅ yards (30 m.) long—longer than the American jet for which it is named.
Above: Tom Wesselmann, Bathroom (1963). A few real objects, such as the shower curtain and the towel rack, are inserted in this work.

Left: Claes Oldenburg, Soft Sink (1965), a large, limp vinyl object inspired by an object from the past.

45

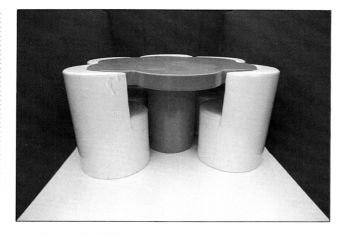

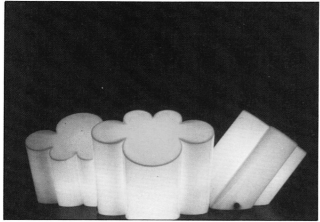

Pop art's influence in furniture design. From top: "Margherita" by Giuseppe Raimondi and Ugo Nespolo, made of six chairs interlocking with a table, finished in oilskin (1966); "Passiflora" lamp by Superstudio, in tinted perspex (1968).

Opposite page, from top: Gilberto Zorio, Il letto (1966); Pino Pascali, Dinosauro, a zoomorphic sculpture in canvas on wood framework; Giovanni Anselmo, Torsione (1968).

fronts later taken up by conceptual art and *arte povera*: he stripped his technical tools (brushes, spatulas, pens, color mixing, etc.) to a bare minimum, using as his sole expressive means the model's body dipped in paint to imprint the canvas with physicality and movement. And he canceled all specificity, all personal skill (of the "only I can do this" type), excluding the role of metaphorical transposition in art, thus freeing the artist of his bonds to his culture.

American Pop artists Rauschenberg, Oldenburg, Jim Dine and others burst onto the scene of Venice's XXXII Biennale in 1964 with a vitality and figurative aggressiveness matched only by Duchamp in his dadaist period.

Pop art showed a new way of perceiving the everyday urban reality (accepting it without the challenge of the dadaists) and reconciling it with the messages offered by the mass media (including their imperfections, such as the smears in Andy Warhol's silkscreens or the comic-book dot screens in Lichtenstein's works), and the mass-consumption of products such as Coca-Cola or of symbols such as flags.

Left by the sidelines, kitsch lost its negative connotations, while the use of fine materials or refined color combinations utterly lacked in experimental charge.

This had great consequences in the fields of architecture and design, reflected in the work of the English Archigram group, the Japanese Metabolism group and Robert Venturi's theories on Las Vegas architecture.

In Italy between 1964 and 1967, a number of avant-garde groups formed, which tapped into the Pop culture on the behavioral as well as figurative levels: in Florence, Archizoom, Superstudio and Ufo, and in Turin, Abaco, Derossi-Ceretti-Rosso and Studio 65.

From the Pop context we have: the Piper nightclubs; some of Ettore Sottsass's pieces, such as his wardrobes for Poltronova (1966) and the *Valentina* portable typewriter for Olivetti (1969); Giuseppe Raimondi and Ugo Nespolo's *Margherita* (Daisy) table (1966); Marcello Pietrantoni and Roberto Lucci's *Nuvola* (Cloud) lamp for Stilnovo (1966); Superstudio's *Passiflora* and *Gherpe* lamps for Design Centre (1968); De Pas-D'Urbino-Lomazzi's pneumatic structures and inflatable armchairs for Zanotta (1967) and the same group's baseball-glove-shaped *Joe* armchair for Poltronova (1971).

In the fashion area, Fiorucci stood out. Surrounding himself with very young designers, stylists and graphic artists, he and his équipe turned out a steady stream of stimulating images, products and ideas.

Trend-setter for an entire generation of the young,

Fiorucci opened his store in Milan's Corso Vittorio Emanuele in 1967, celebrating the event with a big street party. Designer Amalia Del Ponte decorated it all in white and glossy cornflower blue. He managed to keep the fashion world off-balance with his extraordinary sense of surprise, maintaining at length his position in the avant-garde of the fashion scene.

Meanwhile, in Turin, a group of artists formed around the Galleria Speroni – Pistoletto, Zorio, Anselmo, Boetti, Merz and Prini – exhibiting there in the summer of 1966 at the "Arte Abitabile" show. In Rome, at the Galleria dell'Attico, Pascali and Kounellis were working on the same wavelength; the common denominator was a shift in focus from the object to the subject, from things to humanity, from apprehension about technological richness to a preference for materials that had never been used before in art (earth, asbestos, lead, graphite, birds, wax, tar, chemical substances, etc.).

Germano Celant named this artistic current "arte povera," and its approach had points in common with conceptual art, represented in America by Joseph Kosuth, in Germany by Joseph Beuys and in Italy by Giulio Paolini. "Thus a new alphabet for the medium came to be," wrote Tommaso Trini in an introduction to these artists. "If a language lives as cells do, the lifespan of the work of art that embodies it is determined by the artist; indeed, many works last the duration of an exhibition, the time needed for an alchemy to take place. The medium evaporates and becomes an equation, a ratio: two ideas expressed by two successive things. There are no new materials here, as there were no new images in Pop art: many works arise as psycho-physical space (Marisa Merz), an extension of manuality and feasibility (Anselmo, Mario Merz, Prini, Calzolari), chemical-physical reaction (Zorio)."

In the 1980s *arte povera* was a major influence, especially in the new attitudes toward surface finishes in materials used in interior decoration.

Another figure whose art left a deep mark on the 1960s was Lucio Fontana. Since his death in 1968 his stature has grown steadily, and he is now considered one of the leading artists in the twentieth century. To mention Fontana here is not a contrived transposition of the poetics of his works to the field under examination: his works—ranging from the neon-streaked *Ambienti Spaziali* (Spatial Rooms) to the slashed and punctured canvases of *Concetti Spaziali* (Spatial Concepts), the masses of violated stoneware of *Nature* (Natures), and the differently shaped frames making up part of his *Teatrini* (Little Theaters)—served as a guiding light in all the experiments with sculptural lighting and various media of our times, heralding, as his works did, breakthroughs in spatial perception and the intuition of infinite, galactic spaces beyond the wall.

THE PIPER CLUBS

Between 1965 and 1967 in Rome, Viareggio, Turin, and Rimini, a new kind of club environment emerged that was revolutionary compared to the old-style night clubs. The new clubs were places for meeting people, for exhibitions, happenings; they were stopping-off (or, indeed, getting-on) places for young or aspiring artists. They offered a new kind of space, one that was repeatedly broken off and changed by lighting effects, an illusory space created by projectors, reflectors, strobe lights, amplified music—a space that did not exist if it was not turned on and changing. These environments were important for the existential changes that they interpreted, for the role that they played in introducing new lifestyles to a whole generation of people from all social and cultural walks of life. These new lifestyles were based on the mobility of space, the dynamic dislocation of furnishings, a break with rigid plans and *a priori* definitions of (mono) functionality, a preference for artificial textures and the possibilities for their use in domestic interior decor, and a growing awareness of applications for art's expressive potential.

The clubs were spaces for the new music and the "yeah-yeah" lifestyle, suited to the tunes of the Beatles and the Rolling Stones, to performances of the Living Theater, to the New America Cinema, Indian music, Patty Pravo's songs, Piero Gilardi's "nature" carpets, and Marisa Merz's sculptures.

The Piper clubs in Rome and Viareggio were decorated by the architects Francesco and Giancarlo Capolei and Manlio Cavalli. The one in Rome was a big garage with lit-up platforms and suspended balconies. The Viareggio club had padded walls lined with glossy red plastic, "bullseye" chairs with references to optical art and pop decorations, a bowling alley, and a boutique.

The Turin Piper, decorated by the architects Giorgio Ceretti, Pietro Derossi, and Riccardo Rosso and managed by Derossi, had extraordinary appeal and an unusual disk jockey—Gianni Piacentino, whose decorated machines made him famous as an avantgarde sculptor in the Seventies. The club was equipped for various uses, with movable platforms that could be grouped to form a stage, and stadium-shaped varied-

From top: two views of the Piper Club in Turin; the Altro Mondo Club in Rimini. These polyvalent nightspots made use of *highly flexible installation structures, spearheading a trend in dynamic dislocation of furnishing elements.*

height seating arrangements in colored fiberglass.

A kinetic device invented by Bruno Munari projected decorations that pulsed, to the music's beat, against the aluminum-lined walls. Upon entering the club, patrons took a staircase down to the action. Each step was connected to a photoelectric cell and a musical noise machine invented by Sergio Liberovici: during each ascent and descent the staircase burst forth in spontaneous concerts. In December 1966, the Piper exhibited Michelangelo Pistoletto's "Tree of Mirrors" and Piero Gilardi's "Nature" carpets, and people danced amid the works of these two artists at Turin. The Altro Mondo Club, in Rimini, was by the same architects.

INTERIOR DECOR REVIEWS

Italy has more architecture and interior-decoration reviews than any other nation, which conveys some idea of the importance of the furnishing sector in the country's economy. Its influential position is recognized even abroad, since many of these reviews are sold in many other countries. It also illustrates the interest that so many Italians take in their homes, an interest that could almost be considered a national sport. However, these reviews did not always play a critical role in the design sector's development, and often limited themselves to reporting novelties for the sake of novelty.

The 1960s witnessed the birth of new reviews that took their place beside the by-then illustrious *Domus*, run by Giò Ponti up to the time of his death in 1979. Publication of *La Rivista dell'Arredamento* was launched in 1954; in 1967 it was renamed *Interni/La Rivista dell'Arredamento*.

In 1961 *Abitare* came out, founded by Piera Peroni. In 1967 the review *Ottagono* was founded, on the initiative of a group of eight industry leaders of the time: Arflex, Artemide, Bernini, Boffi, Flos, ICF, and Tecno.

Another three reviews came to the newstands in 1968: *La Mia Casa, Rassegna,* and *Casa Vogue*. The latter, initially a supplement to the fashion magazine *Vogue*, held by the international Condé Nast group, saw such success that it became an independent review. From the start, the editors of *Casa Vogue* showed extraordinary intuition in anticipating every trend in the sectors of furniture, decor, figurative arts, illustrating them with rich, high-quality photographic images.

Edilizia Moderna (no. 85, 1964) contributed greatly to the quality of debate in the field of design and was awarded the Compasso d'Oro in 1967. Edited by

Two studio sets proposed by the review Abitare *in 1967–68, designed by Oscar Cagna and Italo Lupi (top), and Costantino Corsini and Giorgio Wiskemann (above).*

Vittorio Gregotti, this issue included contributions by Bellini, Castiglioni, Mangiarotti, Mango, Rosselli, Sottsass, Valle, and Zanuso on their own professional experiences, as well as articles by Gillo Dorfles, Filiberto Menna, Augusto Morello, Andries Van Onck, Enzo Frateili, and Tomás Maldonado that discussed in depth the multifaceted cultural consequences brought out into the open by this field.

Joe Colombo, "Visiona 69." The design of this promotional display for Bayer hinges on a concept that Colombo had already used many times, that of the well-equipped, all-purpose unit with a number of functions concentrated in a single freestanding area.

From top: the "central living space," for making oneself comfortable, reading, listening to music, watching TV; the "kitchen box," a closed off, air-conditioned kitchen area with a dining table that slides out of its housing already set.

The interior designs of famous architects such as Carlo Santi, Giampiero Vitelli and Titina Ammanati, Silvio Coppola, Adalberto Dal Lago, and others, covered in Abitare's issues 47–48 of 1966, 59–60 of 1967, and 62 of 1968 merit particular attention. The installations, executed and photographed so as to create the appearance of a lived-in home, represented various ideas for decorating one home, taken as a typical example of standing housing then available on the real-estate market. The review's editors explained: "We wanted to make an experiment: we wanted to construct atmospheres in the studio to show how the anonymous rooms that are normally assigned by the building industry can with a little care be transformed into unique spaces... The aim of this experiment was to offer a good idea of the possibilities for home modifications, geared to all tastes and pocketbooks. The solutions reflect different starting premises, such as whether the home is rented or owned, in the first case keeping the structural modifications to a bare minimum and in the second case allowing much more radical interventions."

The proposed decor represented the cultural models of the time as adopted by the architects themselves. In the absence of client-architect dialogue, it is steeped in the present and rich in suggestions for fashion materials and colors and on the philosophy of the review and its target public, and is free of historical constraints. In almost every case, furniture produced in series and available on the market was chosen—"each item selected for its expressive value and its immediate response to precise basic needs."

The rooms were laid out on various levels that emphasized the functional differences between the individual living areas. The stepped floors provided spontaneous seating for the most informal conversations. The service areas, like the bedrooms, were enhanced by a "living-room" look. The central overhead lighting fixtures were replaced by multiple light sources that were better suited to the flow of the spaces and lit up the rooms with chiaroscuro effects.

The walls were colored with washable paint, sometimes high-gloss enamel in multicolored bands, or were covered with fabric or ciré (a PVC-treated cotton fabric frequently used in upholstery applications).
The floors often had wall-to-wall carpeting that sometimes climbed up the walls as well. In some cases plastic laminate was also suggested as flooring material. The dominant colors were yellow, orange, red, brown, forest green, and white.

The furniture was in pine, Rio rosewood, or white-lacquered, plastic-laminate- or fabric-covered wood.

JOE COLOMBO'S VISIONA '69

In 1969 Colombo was at the peak of his career, and the multinational Bayer company invited him to design a "Proposal for the Habitat of Tomorrow," a traveling display to promote new synthetic fibers for home use. It was presented at Cologne's Interzum salon under the name Visiona '69 and later, in September of the same year, at Milan's Museo della Scienza e della Tecnica on the occasion of the Salone del Mobile. The proposal was restricted to the "contents" of the home, leaving aside consideration of the "container"—that is, the architectural framework, which according to Colombo should in any case be designed keeping in mind the function of the internal layout. It was done entirely in plastic, and the furnishings were based on Colombo's characteristic furniture blocks, multipurpose units with a number of built-in functions, designed with flexibility in mind. They were conceived as three separate coordinates to occupy about 109 $^1/_3$ square yards (100 sq. m.) of open space.

The first block, the "central living space," was for a living room open on all sides. It consisted of eight modular seats placed around a central unit with built-in radio, tape recorder, turntable, bar, electric cigarette-lighters, and TV remote controls. Above them, suspended from the ceiling, were an aerial bookcase supporting a multidirectional television, lighting fixtures, and an air-conditioning unit.

The second block, the "night-cell," served the night zone and bathroom, including a bed surrounded by a circular closet with folding doors, and the bath with spherical tub-shower, two yards in diameter, all done in plastics with accessories and fixtures built into the walls.

The third block, the "kitchen box," was a well-equipped, closed-off and air-conditioned area that had been laid out so that a person working at its center could reach all the fixtures without changing position.

Today Visiona '69 appears to be an empty construction, concocted for the purposes of publicity and utterly lacking in any cultural value.

The Visiona proposals of later years were by no means any better. Lifestyles are based on complex layers of behavior patterns and experience that preclude conventional futurological solutions, often bolstered by trumped-up interdisciplinary psychological and physiological studies and barring any possible contribution by the end-users. This was Visiona's greatest shortcoming.

In this case Colombo planned a dwelling-space for the future, full of naive faith in the power of technology to set everything right, with no irony or doubt.

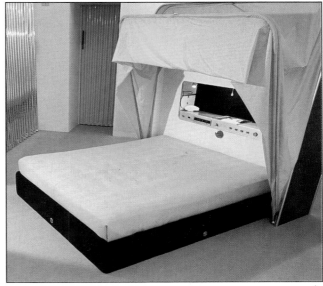

Joe Colombo (1970). This is the home that Colombo designed for himself. There are two multifunctional "living machines" set in a single space: one, the "day machine," contains table, bar, and seats with different possibilities of seating arrangements; the other is a bed equipped with remote controls for lighting, telephone, and air conditioning. An awning that could be raised and lowered made the bed similar to a capsule.

FRANCO ALBINI AND FRANCA HELG

Working in collaboration with Franca Helg from 1951 on, Franco Albini (1905–77) assiduously avoided the din of fashion, constructing over more than forty years not only buildings and objects but also a steady and even approach to his profession. His work reflects a high moral standard and the character of a craftsman who demands much of himself as he relentlessly pursues perfection.

Shown in these pages are two homes designed by the Albini-Helg studio. One is a small, unpretentious country house suited to summer vacations and week-end living. The other is a large apartment on the eighteenth floor of a Milanese tower—the home of a collector of ancient and modern art, the placement of which determined much of the apartment's layout, the type of furniture used, and the finishing details.

Like all of Albini's houses, the country house presents a simple exterior, made up of four white walls and a tiled roof at even pitches. Inside the layout is elegantly conceived, starting with a living-dining area set on the diagonal and occupying the three sides of the house with the best views. Off this are the two bedroom groups and services. The living room itself may be closed off by means of two large sliding doors. The living room ceiling reaches to the full height of the house, and a skylight at its peak provides a source of light to the loft structure which can be used as a small study, accessed by the spiral staircase in gray-enameled iron with slate steps.

The space unfolds around the staircase (a recurring element in Albini's work, from the INA building in Parma to the Milan subway system), inviting continual discovery of new possibilities in flow patterns, views, and lighting. The furnishings are a tasteful blend of unpretentious family pieces common to all second homes and pieces from series that Albini designed for Poggi (the bureau, the cart, the table, and the chairs) and for Arteluce (the lamps).

The second dwelling is almost a house-museum (with works by Sironi, Bellini, Casorati, Campigli, and Miró, and one of Marino Marini's *Horseman* sculptures) which highlights Albini's expertise and his long-term experience in renovating and redesigning museums both in Italy and abroad.

Here a long hall opens into a large living room where screens are set up at intervals to suggest points to stop and look at the individual paintings. A checker-patterned floor in marble tiles in various tones of black and white enhances the perspective and acts as a continuous field for a few isolated groups of furniture.

Albini and Helg designed the black leather armchairs and sofas for Poggi; the lamps for Arteluce; and the low round table and the rectangular table with black iron supports and red broadcloth surface. The arrangements confirm a compositional approach already developed for the Palazzo Rossi museum in Genoa.

The cylindrical fireplace with its black wrought-iron hearth and mantelpiece eases the transition between the hall and dining area without obstructing a visitor's perception of the spacious living room as he strolls through the hall/gallery.

The door frames are in anodized aluminum with doors lined in black leather (in the living room and access corridors; the others are lined with plastic laminate). The wall coverings are in light gray wool fabric with an iron molding fixed at the top for use in hanging the paintings.

The kitchen floors and wall are a continuous checkerboard pattern in yellow and white ceramic tiles; the cabinets and furniture in plastic laminate and stainless steel were designed by the architects.

Preceding page: Living room of an apartment designed by Aldo Jacober, with light- and sound-control booth.

Left: View of the living room from the entrance hall of the country house designed by Albini and Helg.

Entrance and loft seen from the living room. The wall lamp and console were designed by Albini for Arteluce and Poggi, respectively. Opposite page: the living room can be closed off means of sliding doors, and above them, in the loft, is a small study. The floor is in green-glazed ceramic tiles; the staircase is of iron, painted gray.

The living room of the house-museum with Marino Marini's "Horseman." A painting by Mario Sironi is hung on a partition panel to the right.

The kitchen furnishings, designed by Albini-Helg, are finished in plastic laminate and stainless steel. Opposite page: the section of the gallery nearest the living room. The floors are done in marble tiles in tones that range from black to white; the walls are lined with gray wool fabric. The display cases of painted iron and glass were designed by Albini, as were the ceiling lamps, manufactured by Arteluce.

SERGIO ASTI

Since the 1950s Sergio Asti has been in active contributor to the Italian design scene, creating a vast range of products—vases, armchairs, television sets, cutlery, and tiles—all distinguished by a remarkable graphic skill and elegance of line. Among the many articles of the 1960s that bear his signature, those of particular value include his blown-glass vase for Salviati, awarded the 1962 Compasso d'Oro for the way in which the vase's opening resolves after hovering in midair over the volume of the base; and his "Zelda" series of armchairs and tables (1966) for Poltronova. Here the legs are in grooved bent plywood, in the manner of the Viennese Secessionists.

The sophisticated intimacy and almost exaggerated technical subtlety in his interior decoration thus arises from a longstanding habit of attention to detail, the result of his vast experience as designer.

"As in the Japanese home," commented Asti in an interview published by *Espresso* in 1970, "it is important that in a perfectly operative space, not amorphous, there be no fetish pieces of furniture, no totem pieces or monuments, but objects that bear the precise imprint of whoever made them; go ahead and make attractive lamps, handsome sofas, pretty chairs, but then let people make their choices fairly, on the basis of their taste, their means and their lifestyle."

The interior shown in these pages is a studio apartment separated into day and night zones by a slight change in levels following the curve of an oval column. Its style is vaguely neo-Liberty (Asti participated in their Milan exhibition in March 1960), and highlights a rich tradition in upper middle-class interiors and design as decoration. The floor plan reveals well-defined spaces that are seconded by the vertical elements; the effect is completed by the pink silk that envelops the walls and ceiling. The entrance has a dropped ceiling covered in silvery tinfoil that hides the air-conditioning ducts; it is echoed by the silver lamé tablecloth. The high planter columns form a stage curtain to the living area; they are made of metallic-gray enameled wood. The black leather armchair is Asti's "Bellagio" model, designed in 1961 for Adrasteia. The lamps are by Gino Sarfatti for Arteluce.

The entrance hall features a volume of varying height that both acts as a stage curtain to the living area and conceals closet space; on the living-room side, it serves as a small bookshelf. The bedroom area, which is raised in relation to the living room, can be closed off by means of three large folding doors.

The living room area of the studio apartment: the furnishings consist of a black leather armchair, designed by Asti for Adrasteia, and a series of sofas upholstered in linen velvet. The walls and ceiling are lined with pink silk.

64

GRIFFINI AND MONTAGNI

Often written up in *Abitare* throughout the Sixties, Griffini and Montagni's interior designs go hand in hand with their architectural projects of single-family houses in mountainous or natural environments. They are homes in which, like good country cooking, traditional materials have been used in the right doses.

The house presented here was covered in depth in *Abitare* (No. 25, April 1964). The piece opened with an editorial by Eugenio Gentili entitled "Country Consumers," in which he discusses the difficulties of land-use planning and the shortcomings and delays in the few plans that had at that point been drawn up.

The destruction of many tourist areas had become a widespread problem in Italy. The agricultural population was thinning as rural inhabitants tended to move to the cities, and city-dwellers sought second homes in the countryside. These opposing movements had deep consequences, lowering the tenor both of urban life (due to uncontrolled growth) and of country life (due to wholesale destruction of nature by unthinking, unplanned development), as well as upsetting the original socioeconomic structures.

Working to inform its readers about environmental conservation and examining the problem in a broad context from many different points of view, *Abitare*'s editors decided to publish a systematic series of articles on examples of abandoned rustic housing that had been given new life as vacation homes.

This house shows Griffini and Montagni's transformation of an abandoned limekiln on the banks of Lake Maggiore into a home, following painstaking restoration work that left most of the existing structural features intact.

A living room was created at the base of the chimney, where previously there had been a large workroom with a service loft at mid-height, later turned into a guest room; two raised bedrooms were set on either side of the chimney, linked by a ramp where there once had stood stoking rooms. Both the old walls and the new were done in stone and solid brick, roughly plastered and whitewashed. The floor in the living room, originally earthen, was redone in solid brick laid in a herringbone pattern, dry-sanded, and waxed. The guest room and loft floors and steps were done in oak planks.

Tobia Scarpa's "Bastiano," designed for Gavina with rosewood framework and cushions in black leather, was chosen to furnish both the living room and the loft.

Griffini and Montagni's transformation of an abandoned limekiln into a home, with an ample staircase joining the large living room and the loft structure that passes above the kiln's hearth.

Top: the loft structure, with oak-planked floors.
Above: the limekiln after completion of restoration work.
Opposite page: the living room, with Tobia Scarpa's "Bastiano" sofas and armchairs (Gavina).

LUIGI CACCIA DOMINIONI

Luigi Caccia Dominioni was a leading figure in the postwar architecture scene, together with Ponti, Nizzoli, Magistretti, Albini, and Gardella. Both his buildings in Milan and his design objects—from a 1935 radio-receiver to the furniture he created in 1956 for Azucena—merit attention as "a sort of reconstruction of the bourgeois interior, descriptive and nostalgic of a world made up of precise rules of behavior, unchanging certainties, and clear symbols for communication, reinstating a notion of luxury that was new to the twentieth-century tradition" (V. Gregotti).

"Underlying every interior decor is the house's floor plan," stated Caccia Dominioni in an interview published by *Casa Vogue* in November 1968. "The architect should always build a house that in itself presents all the characteristics needed to furnish it. The house should already be decorated by its form. This means maximum simplicity and bareness for the most possible open area in which its architecture of shapes and spaces can be enjoyed."

We present here two interiors: a new seaside vacation residence and a small country castle.

The new construction follows the contour of the terrain. Inside, the atmosphere is mellow, demonstrating Caccia Dominioni's familiarity with traditional construction materials. The dominant colors are the stark white of the walls, the terracotta of the floor tiles, and the gray of the raised platforms in slate and the lacquered doors. There is a very attractive bedroom niche with a low arched ceiling and bed designed by the architect. At the head of the bed a frescoed lunette illuminated by a small window offers a view of the sea. The table with lacquered gray top and iron framework was designed by Caccia Dominioni for Azucena; the wire mesh chairs, also designed by the architect, echo the design of the nineteenth-century chairs set up outside.

The castle makes generous use of simple, almost humble materials, in the tradition of the northern Lombard region—Lombard terracotta tiles, Valtellina granite, whitewashed plaster. The tenuous color of these materials is an ideal backdrop to the fourteenth-century frescos. The window and door casements and railings are in wrought iron. The sweeping staircase leading to the oval dining room is illuminated by a cluster of lights suspended from chains. Both these and the large oval dining-room table were designed by Caccia Dominioni.

The dining room and living room in the seaside house. The doors and shutters are lacquered a dark gray, the floors are terra-cotta. The table's lacquered gray oval rests on an iron support; by Caccia Dominioni for Azucena.

Following pages: the bed, designed by Caccia Dominioni, is tucked into a niche with a raised slate platform.

Caccia Dominioni's restoration of a castle in the Brianza countryside.
Top: the oval dining room. The cluster of lights suspended from chains and the large oval table were designed by Dominioni.
Above: the living room seen from the entrance hall. Opposite page: the sweeping curve of the staircase. High up, on the curved wall, a late nineteenth-century fresco with geometric motifs.

JOE COLOMBO

Although he died in 1971 at the age of only 41, Colombo was a key figure in Italian design of the 1960s. His career was marked by great success (even though it faded rapidly), and from 1960 on was concerned exclusively with design (interior design, furniture design, product design, and visual design). Colombo studied at the Brera Accademia di Belle Arti and at Milan's Politechnico, but interrupted his academic involvement to launch his highly varied design activities, producing everything from lamps for Stilnovo to photographic equipment for Fatif, to furniture for Bernini, and pipes for Savinelli. As Milan's XV Triennale catalogue put it, "The form as the expressive basis, multifunctionality as the aim and technology as the means sum up Joe Colombo's approach to design."

Colombo's premature death leaves many open questions about how his career as designer would have progressed in light of the rapid obsolescence of many of his products, and the advent of sociocultural models that were increasingly at odds with his ideas.
Many of his objects unleashed heated debate, making of him a designer-personality, but in our opinion Colombo's interior decoration for stores and homes is far more interesting, apart from his Visiona '69, which was too much a science-fiction comic-strip fantasy at the service of Bayer company's plastic products. His furnishings show great inventive skill applied to the problem of how to achieve an intelligent utilization of space and innovative handling of materials.

"Man has always created a casing to shelter himself, later outfitting it with all the necessities. In this process the container has almost always conditioned the content. Now, if the elements and gear necessary to man's lifestyle could be designed according to the sole criteria of ease in handling, flexibility, and almost complete modularity, we could construct a dwelling system that could adapt to any spatial or temporal given... Once we have obtained a content that is perfectly suited to its function, we could cast the foundations for a more rational method of planning the container" (from the XIV Triennale catalogue presenting his "Flexible Living System" for La Rinascente).

This describes Colombo's philosophy in designing pieces of furniture, such as his "Combi-center" bookshelf and storage unit composed of stackable elements for Bernini (1964) or his "Triangular System," triangular storage units mounted on castors for Elco (1970).

In his interior design, however, the constraints of reality seem to have saved Colombo from his unfounded ideological fever, and he was finally able to give free rein to his creativity and skill in using materials, without overdoing it. One example of this was an apartment in Milan whose volumes he completely modified by means of raised and sunken levels. It had luminous dropped ceilings done in styrofoam sheets that hid fluorescent lighting fixtures; all the furniture, ranging from a bookshelf column to a flowerpot, was mounted on castors; and a dining-room table became a low coffee table when rolled over the raised platform.

Another example was a photographic equipment shop, where the equipment was gathered and protected under large plexiglass hemispheres, akin to great lenses. Then there was a casual-wear clothing store, where limited space spurred him to a series of innovative solutions: he devised five long metal tunnels, like suspension bridges over the empty ground floor, to contain the clothing collection, hung on a horizontal sliding rack.

Interestingly, in a *Domus* writeup of this interior (June 1965) the accent was placed on the technological functionality of the materials – metal, plastic laminate, and plexiglass: "It looks like and works like a mechanical device, a piece of

The three-bed room in the 49 $^1/_5$-square-yard (45 sq. m.) apartment decorated by Joe Colombo. The beds are simply two layers of mattresses resting on raised platforms. The steps in the background lead to the master bedroom.

equipment, with parts that can be assembled or dismantled..." Thus, materials that by the late Sixties had become popular for their looks, regardless of their functionality, here were exalted for their technological efficiency and resistance to wear.

In the first interior design presented here, Colombo uses remarkable invention to solve the problem of maximum occupancy (six beds) in a minimal space (49 $^1/_5$ sq. yds. [45 sq. m.]), breaking the interior volume down into various usable levels, that are made unitary and continuous by a single covering for walls, floors and ceilings: brick-red felt.

The different levels of the steps were made functional (seating, resting surfaces, work surfaces, etc.) through a three-dimensional use of space that comes closer to the nautical concept than that of building.

The entrance hall gives access to a three-bed room (for children or guests) in which the third bed is set higher, over the lowered ceiling of the entrance. The entrance itself leads to the pantry-kitchen and bathroom, set at the center and forced-air ventilated; and to the living-dining area from which, going up the steps (which provide additional "living" area for the living room), one arrives at the center of the mezzanine, which holds the master bedroom with dressing room and facilities.

An electric canal runs along the entrance, living room, and bedroom walls so that things can be plugged in at any point; other light fixtures are placed in niches or set into the floor.

There are few real pieces of furniture (all designed by Colombo), the same having been replaced in part by the interior architecture. The beds, for example, are simple mattresses resting on raised areas of the floor; there is a large central wardrobe unit that extends vertically and is accessible at different heights and from all sides. Thus, although the furniture is mainly fixed, the lifestyle is free-moving and variable, enhanced by adaptable uses of the different levels.

The second interior illustrates a few characteristic features of Colombo's work: the home is freed of conventional structural divisions; the environment is made unitary (here, by a blue moquette that rides halfway up the white walls, forming a distinct bivalve shell—the carpeted lower half, which holds all of the furnishing and objects for living, and the upper half, clean and uninterrupted); the space is recomposed by means of fixed utility blocks (that also camouflage the supporting columns) and movable all-purpose tower blocks, designed for Bernini and made up of combinations of various elements with different functions, stackable and rotating around individual axes. On the walls are the "Coupé" lamps that Colombo designed in 1970 for O-Luce.

The living area. Lamps and other appliances can be plugged into the continuous electric canal at any point along its course around the wall. Colombo designed the armchair and table for Kartell and Bernini respectively.

The living room of Colombo's second interior. The fixed and mobile utility blocks were designed by Colombo for Bernini.

VICO MAGISTRETTI

A pioneer in the fields of architecture, urban planning and architecture of interiors, Vico Magistretti is responsible for an output that ranges from a bookcase with adjustable shelves presented at the 1946 RIMA exhibition to the lamps and furniture he still designs today. He is represented by twelve pieces in New York's Museum of Modern Art. "Economy, practicality, and good taste were the aims," wrote Rogers on the architects who participated at the post-war RIMA exhibition. Since then, Magistretti has not lost sight of these goals.

The first of the images presented here shows a spacious vacation home in the countryside near Varese, freely laid out on three floors. On the ground floor are the service areas and garage. The first floor is completely dedicated to the living-dining areas, with a staircase leading to the night zone, which overlooks a roof garden corresponding to the living room roof. The materials used were pitch-pine for the living room floor, surface areas, and trim; white plaster for the walls; and exposed reinforced cement for the pilasters.

The second house was constructed in the pinewoods of Arenzano, a resort town distinguished by the illustrious works of a number of architects. The house's floor plans shows a net separation between the service areas and the main living quarters; the axis runs along an entrance porch, continuing through the foyer and the living-dining area with a fireplace opening onto another, larger porch overlooking the sea. From this portico a sweeping stepped ramp provides access to the roof of the house, which has been transformed into a terrace garden.

The furnishings are an integral part of the architecture: big cushions in black leather rest on white benches built into the walls in the area around the fireplace. Black-lacquered shelves are bracketed into the walls, forming a sort of dialogue with the biased checkerboard pattern of the floor, done in white Carrara marble and black slate.

In the third house, which is nestled into a hillside, the architecture provides a setting for the design pieces created by Magistretti for Cassina. It is a free arrangement of tables and chairs, unconditioned by spaces or structures. The walls are all white, with spacious picture windows veiled in white linen curtains.

The house is designed to permit great flexibility in furniture arrangements, even should new requirements arise. "Basically, the house is brought to life by spaces, patterns of flow, and volumes, so it is on these that the designer must focus his attention, and such spaces, which are the true protagonists of the home, must be able to contain furnishings that will change over time and according to individual taste. To choose series, and not custom-made (except in very particular cases), furniture is the method most consistent with our times to reflect our human condition in relation to contemporary society" (*Ottagono*, January 1967).

A living room by Magistretti in a villa near Varese. The curved banister of the stair leading to the night zone and the "Omega" lamp that Magistretti designed for Artemide share a common formal language.

The living room of the Arenzano house. To the left is a large brickwork fireplace between two low, projecting walls that can be used as shelves.

Magistretti's house in Carimate. Top: the part of the living room with picture windows that offer a view of the countryside. The sofas were designed by Magistretti for Cassina. Above: the stairway that leads down from the atrium to the floor where the bedrooms are located. Opposite page: the most intimate part of the living room, with fireplace and bookshelves.

VITTORIO GREGOTTI

Born in Novara in 1927, the recipient of a degree in architecture from Milan's Politecnico in 1952, Vittorio Gregotti from the very start of his career has occupied a central position, as designer and critic, in the ongoing Italian architectural debate. For many years he was the editor-in-chief of *Casabella* and later was *Edilizia Moderna*'s dossier editor.

In the decade we examined, his name came up frequently in relation to the neo-Liberty trend, and as contributor to "Nuovi Disegni per il Mobile Italiano" exhibition and the 1965 "La Casa Abitata" exhibition in Florence.

The house shown here was renovated by Gregotti for his own purposes and includes many of the pieces that appeared in these shows. "Few structural modifications accompanied by many contemporary ideas for an eighteenth-century dwelling," is how the April 1967 issue of *Abitare* described Gregotti's work on a wing of a neo-Classical, Settecento Milanese palazzo. The modifications involved the demolition of a stretch of the original load-bearing wall between the living room and hallway, linking them to the rest of the house. A partition wall was raised to separate off the pantry and cloakroom; a night zone was created around the concept of a generous private living space that went beyond the mere bedroom to include bath, dressing rooms, and a study.

The architect highlighted the atmosphere of a private living room by planning the purple-enameled bathroom as an extention of the bedroom, with a window and balcony, furnishing it with tables and chairs by Alvar Aalto.

In renovating this house, Gregotti implemented the proposal he had set forth in his presentation at the "Casa Abitata" exhibition, regarding the inclusion of the service areas in a broader concept of the home's lived-in spaces.

For a better understanding of Gregotti's work, it is worth quoting an interview published in *Espresso*, August 1970, on how to decorate the home of the Sixties. Gregotti advised emptying it. "To empty it means carrying out a two-phase operation. First of all, the importance of the object as a piece of furniture must be stripped down to zero, that is, the idea of its expendability must be wholeheartedly endorsed. But (second phase) one must ask oneself, what is there, then, that is lasting in a home, what can one grab on to, if the piece of furniture has gotten to be like a suit that one changes, discards, replaces?"

"Some years ago, I tried to identify this lasting element with a return to the modern tradition that for me was expressed in the so-called neo-Liberty style. It was a way to retroactively establish a tradition that in reality had never existed at all. But now I no longer believe that the lasting points lie in the furnishings: now I feel that they consist in the spatial layout of the house, in the attempt to make most of the furnishing built into the architecture, to fix an entire series of structures."

Left: living room with "Cavour" armchairs designed by Gregotti-Meneghetti-Stoppino for Sim.
The floor lamp is by Alvar Aalto.
Following pages: the neo-Classical wing of the eighteenth-century Milanese palazzo where Gregotti lives.

Top: bedroom with nineteenth-century bed in wrought-iron. Above: the large walk-in closet separating the studio and the night zone. Opposite page: detail of the bedroom showing wall decorations by painter Giosetta Fioroni.

ALDO JACOBER

In the 1960s Aldo Jacober was active in the fields of both design and architecture and was already well known for a best-selling folding chair, manufactured by Bazzani, that had won a prize at the 1966 Fiera di Trieste. In June 1969, *Casa Vogue* introduced three interior designs by Jacober with this note: "Floors that sink as deep as wells, walls that curve over into tunnels, wavy, palpitating ceilings, sinuous spaces, soft furniture: our lifestyle is getting closer and closer to that of Jonah in the belly of the whale." A marked preference for curved lines is evident in both his interior designs and the individual pieces of furniture he selected for them.

In collaboration with Fiorella Butti, Giuseppe Pagani, Mariarosa Rizzi, Aldo Jacober decorated this house for a person in the audiovisual field whose professional experience had gotten him hooked on the adaptable atmospheres of discotheques and the Piper clubs. It includes a control booth, similar to a disk jockey's, for regulating light and sound; the back wall of the living room can be illuminated by eight different colors. The structural surfaces are in motion, wavy, curving: the walls are done in glossy black plastic laminate, and the ceilings are a light fabric stretched over a wooden framework, creating concave and convex spaces lighted from behind.

Liberal use is made of two kinds of plastics, very popular in the Sixties—laminate (the walls) and methacrylate (better known under the trade names perspex, plexiglass, etc.). The soundproofing panels of the sound booth are done in methacrylate, with multifaceted decorations that take advantage of the prismatic effects on light typical of this material. Outstanding in the second interior is the curved wall of the dining room featuring one of Lucio Fontana's "slashes" (the only one he ever executed directly on a wall). Here, too, liberal use is made of materials and techniques much in vogue at the time: the glossy-white enameled walls; the dark brown wall-to-wall carpeting that rides up on the walls to form a homogeneous shell; the glossy black plastic laminate and plexiglass furnishings; the use of furniture as a continuation of the walls and floors, which in turn are treated as furnishings using the same formal idiom. The ceiling is in white fabric that screens the light sources, creating uniform, low-key illumination.

The cylindrical effect of the two arches marking the passages from the entrance hall to the living room and from the living room to the dining room is multiplied by the mirrors in the entrance hall.

The curved wall of the dining room, with a "slash" by Lucio Fontana (the only one he ever executed directly on a wall).
Opposite page: ceiling with white fabric stretched over a wooden framework that conceals the lighting fixtures and diffuses the light, reminiscent of the work of Pino Pascali and Enrico Castellani.
Following page: the living-room walls are faced with glossy black plastic laminate. To the left, a fireplace shared by the living and dining areas.

97

LINO SCHENAL

Architecture and interior design, exterior and interior, wrapping and content (where the content according to Renato De Fusco is a space, a room, shaped and delineated by the wrapping, that is, the walls or other architectonic elements that shape their contents): between these words, every type of union is possible.

On one hand, there is an architecture that is interior decoration—whose internal spaces are, in addition to being a logical consequence of the materials and construction techniques used, so intrinsic to the formal choices shown in the architectural design that the individual pieces of furniture serve only a subordinate function as bric-a-brac.

At the opposite extreme is this example by Lino Schenal—an artist who derailed from the school of easel painting to land on the track of plastic experience, of modeled spaces. His initiation to architecture may have come from Giò Ponti, who introduced Schenal's first "hanging composition" at the 1967 Salone Espressioni in Milan. This piece of design was a styrofoam cocoon inserted to function as a dwelling within a seventeenth-century building in Rome. The effect was an "architecture of interiors," meaning a true, proper architectural work set inside another architectural work (like Chinese boxes).

The house presented here is all in styrofoam, a lightweight material, easy to handle and dazzlingly white. Walls, ceilings, beds, tables, doors, and the kitchen are made of this single material, molded with virtuoso skill to meet a number of functions, in a way similar to what Piero Gilardi was doing in polyurethane foam or Mario Ceroli with untreated wood.

The designer's way of joining in a sculptural and undulating whole the ceiling, walls, and storage units for the bath and kitchen is interesting. They are carved out a single block of styrofoam, as if they were all-embracing packages for the tools of everyday life.

A sculpted styrofoam door opening onto the bedroom. In the background, a styrofoam stalactite that slides down the ceiling and along the wall.

Two sculptural pieces of styrofoam furnishings that become wrappings or containers for the tools of everyday life. Right: the living room.

THE **SEVENTIES**

The close of the Sixties corresponded with the twilight of the utopian dream of a new more committed and tolerant society. The failure of the "hot autumn" of 1969 to generate change led many of the protest movement's adherents to split up into various areas of political activity. Many extra–parliamentary groups continued to be an important forum for youthful encounter, and were primarily distinguished by their acceptance or not of the validity of the political struggle from within the parliamentary structure. Others, disenchanted, turned their backs on politics and settled into the calm of private life.

Under the spell of Marcusian theory, the Sixties generation had tried to find the way to reconcile subjectivity with social awareness, the drive for individualism with the need for group spirit. Many struggles—for civil rights, new divorce laws, the decriminalization of abortion, a new interpretation of mental illness—along with the women's and gay liberation movements, emerged in these years, born of a new subjectivity that upheld the struggles not in the name of class or of industry but in the name of a new type of body politic.

As Laura Balbo states in *Italia Moderna,* "In times of the harshest conflict, they will thus find themselves at odds with legislative proposals and political platforms, but also with a marked gap between world outlooks: one tending to give value to traditional principles and points of reference; the other committed to 'change,' no doubt underestimating resistance and costs, and dedicated to giving the most space to individual freedom, to overturning resistance and setbacks, to experimenting with transgressive and innovative behavior."

"Private life is political," was the attitude held by

"Basilica" table designed by Mario Bellini for Cassina in 1976.

many couples in those years. "This [is so] for two main reasons," continues Balbo. "[Because of] the central importance given to women's issues and demands, and because the private institution *par excellence*, the family and the relationships within it, decisions to live together, to procreate, to separate—day-to-day decisions—became public: they became political issues, the platforms of collective movements and institutions."

As the hope of finding the answers to these questions in the political and social arena faded, people rediscovered their "private lives"—not in the sense of a nostalgic revival but rather in a growing awareness of the gradual nature of change, of the necessity of personal commitment. The wish to change society had invaded the personal sphere: people started to examine closely their own lives, their bodies, their relationships with others. They sought to experience the present without putting anything off in the hope of a better tomorrow.

Erich Fromm's *To Have or To Be*, published in Italy in 1977, was taken as the symbol of this transition (in progress) from a structure of needs that was based on the need to be.

The economic hardships of these years were accentuated by the social roles inherited from the Sixties and by the government's weakness. The *coup de grâce* was Italy's high rate of inflation at this time, which was not entirely the fault of exogenous phenomena such as the explosion of petroleum products prices. It is more correct to see these price increases as having triggered a situation already loaded with inflationary prerequisites, as Italy's peak inflation figures—higher than elsewhere—confirm.

This gave rise to short-sighted, hysterical behaviors that were apparent in consumption patterns as well. People either put off buying (to mark time or to save) or accelerated their rate of purchase (to beat inflation). Demand was uncertain and erratic, peaking suddenly and then dropping off just as suddenly. Consumers tended to be more discriminating and more attentive to price-quality-service ratios and were slower to replace things. They tended to save less and to buy more on credit. The search for solid investments was on.

The atmosphere of uncertainty and instability undermined faith in socialization and government intervention in the economy. Between waste, social parasitism, government fraud, fiscal evasion, flight of capital and political clientelism, inflation in Italy had soared close to 20 percent, compared to the 6–7 percent rates of other industrialized nations. Individual and private initiatives were discovered as remedies to

Struggles over the great civil-rights issues (divorce, abortion, mental illness, homosexuality) left their mark on the Seventies, and the many movements and demonstrations of the decade gave rise to new forms of expression. Top: a theatrical performance produced by patients at the psychiatric hospital of Collegno (1973).

Above: huge polyurethane masks by the Turin La Comune collective (1977). Right: the punk look, born in England at the close of the Seventies, spread rapidly throughout Europe. Its very aggressive style aroused a sense of curiosity laced with fear. Opposite page, top: the cover design for an issue of the alternative review/comic book Frigidaire—a drawing by Aldo De Domenico, inventor of "rat art."

the welfare state.

The Seventies—which were also "Anni di Piombo," leaden years, for the Italians, ushered in by the 1969 bombing in Milan's Piazza Fontana on December 12, 1969 and culminating in Aldo Moro's assassination in 1978 by the Brigate Rosse— evolved into a contradictory reality that is still felt today and often bewilders non–Italian observers. On one hand, there is a nation that embraces many of the causes calling for social change; on the other, there is a political system that is impervious to these causes, and if and when it does adopt them, it is with minimal commitment and merely for the purpose of strategic maneuvering on the party gameboard.

Together with the revival of the private sector and the energy crisis, particular attention was paid in the Seventies to threats to the ecology and to personal health, and much energy was spent in the defense of the quality of life, in building personal fitness and in pursuing the free expression of sexuality. Parallel with a mounting distrust in the technocratic merit-system and the experts who were classed as "sellouts" there took shape a desire to discover and verbalize a knowledge that lay outside of the world of science. (These "sellouts" had their moment of glory and vindication, however, when on October 14, 1980, forty thousand Fiat employees, department heads and intermediate management, marched through the streets of Turin demanding an end to the strikes and repudiating the union strategies and pickets.) The language and purposes of culture were a crucial ground for contrast between the "creative" elements of the generation and the institutionalized political left. The various youth groups of this period (those that were not drawn into the black hole of terrorism) were tinged with shades of dada and futurism revisited, and they found expressive outlets in the music industry with new wave, hard rock or punk rock in the years 1977 to 1980. But the rock groups did not stop at making music: they produced an enormous volume of printed matter for informational and publicity purposes—the fanzines. The phenomenon spread throughout Italy, creating an aggressive graphic style with "tough and dirty" images that were fragmented and recomposed using the collage technique and photocopied or printed in offset. They were fraught with stylistic revivals and contaminations that by the beginning of the Eighties had broadened into the postmodern or the neobaroque, expressive currents which have touched on all fields from rock music to video production, to dance, art comic strips, and design.

In the first half of the Seventies, the return to nature

was channeled into an interest in physical expression, consciousness-raising and yoga groups, acupuncture, macrobiotic diets and alternative eating habits, and, in fashion, in the revival of old styles from the far West: flowered fabrics, checkered shirts, natural fibers, velvet, corduroy, patchwork, and natural colors.

Azure or blue plush carpeting, or, toward the end of the Seventies, expensive hand-knotted raw-wool versions of the poor man's carpet appeared in the home. In the wake of glass and chrome came the fad for wood—especially ash; its pale yellow blended well with the pallid "natural" foods from macrobiotic stores. In the case of seating (the seat of choice was the folding chair, as if all of Italy had been hit with a nomadic urge), wood formed the framework over which was slung raw linen or striped fabrics such as Buren's paintings. Leather and hide, in soothing beiges, creams, and browns, were the preferred upholstery for sofas. Treated to become as soft as fabric or left with its fur lining on in the country version, leather was proposed as an alternative to the patchwork quilt as a bedspread. Finally, the car called Panda, designed by Giugiaro in 1976 but not put into production until 1980 by Fiat, offered all the flexibility that this bucolic urge called for.

FASHION

At the close of the Sixties the innovative input of the Anglo-Saxon youth culture had created a new market that boosted mass consumption and had unwittingly laid the foundation for the look of an era. Industry was quick to grasp that "youthful unrest" could be transformed into a market that would generate a large amount of income. This underpinned all the creative endeavors over the next two decades, from music to fashions, fads and fantasies of the young. Youth was in the limelight and took a leading role in the "average consumer" category.

Until the 1960s in Italy, fashion production was channeled into two main sectors—haute couture and the ready-to-wear industry—which obviously corresponded to traditional social divisions. There was a third channel, closer in spirit to the first, which catered to an international market. This was the deluxe boutique, which in the Seventies experienced significant growth in its distribution of elegant, expensive designer-label accessories, such as Louis Vuitton's leather products, Ray-Ban eyeglasses, and, for the sports set, Lacoste T-shirts.

On the fringe of these, responding to the needs of the young, were a few boutiques managed by equally

young salespeople who understood the quick evolution of their clientele. Initially offering imported English or French clothing, they began to produce custommade articles and sold them under their own labels.

At the same time, small companies were starting to specialize in prêt-à-porter. All these market transformations contributed to the creation of a new role: that of the "stylist." Like the designer, this person was a freelance consultant (who could therefore work for a number of companies simultaneously), and he applied the same methodological approach to his job, taking his inspiration from the same sources (or, in any case, the differences were not great). The stylist, unlike the old-fashioned designer, did not own the factory that manufactured his models; instead, he acted as the interface between the technological and creative ends, and followed the product through each step of the production process, from conception to marketing. He had to create a strong image that stimulated the market to buy; to do this he no longer borrowed from the vernacular of industrial production, but rather from that of the mass media.

Walter Albini was one such stylist. With his French training and impeccable approach to design, he dominated the fashion scene throughout the entire 1970s. His drawings were at once fashion illustrations and technical designs. He also played an important role in the textiles industry, generously contributing to the realization of the fabrics he had designed for his collections.

Giorgio Armani was an innovative contributor to G.F.T. from 1975 on, and it was this large Turin-based textile group that created a fashion label image around his name. In a period of just a few years Armani was internationally known, and in 1982 *Time* magazine dedicated its cover page to him with the title "Giorgio's Gorgeous Styles". He was the inventor of a low-keyed, timeless style in dress, the "unstructured" look that was based on the English tradition of men's sportswear and adapted to the needs of a new, managerial female public.

Krizia, Mariuccia Mandelli's trade name since 1954, captured the Italians' imaginations and changed their dressing habits in the course of the 1970s with a collection that featured the very new, very short "hot pants," in contrast to midi- and maxiskirts. She had made a name for herself with award-winning apparel and a many-faceted œuvre that included a line of sweaters with animals embroidered on them and a children's collection.

The Missonis were famous for having introduced knitwear to the fashion scene. They were especially

The role of the stylist was created and gained importance in the Seventies, becoming increasingly similar to that of the designer. Opposite page, from top: two Giorgio Armani fashions for the 1979–80 season (photo Aldo Fallai); Gianni Versace fashion

show for the 1978–79 collection.
Top: a Missoni carpet for Saporiti (1974). The Missonis' collaboration with Saporiti's upholstery division gave rise to a lively new look.
Above: an advertising image by Barry Ryan for Krizia.

It did not take much to stay abreast of fashion. Tangas, hot pants and the nude look paid homage to sexual liberation, and along with the emerging figure of the stylist and the traditional ready-to-wear fashion industry, Fiorucci's brand of fashion-performance gained popularity. His styles' contrasts and contradictions anticipated the onslaught of postmodernism, and were particularly sensitive to trends in graphic design that arose out of the youth movements.

renowned for the fabulous colors of yarn that they used, and for their revival of decoration using a vast expressive lexicon whose sources ranged from Berber culture to the artistic avant-garde. They were the first to enter the race to export to the United States, an opportunity provided by an encounter in 1968 with Diana Vreeland, managing editor of *Vogue America*, who opened the wide golden doors of the RTW U.S.A. market to them. In 1973 the Missonis were the only fashion designers to be offered exhibition space by the Whitney Museum of American Art in New York City.

Versace, meanwhile, was experimenting with the sophisticated architecture of attire and with the application of innovative materials such as neoprene and metallic mesh in pursuit of a neoclassical vision. He replaced Albini as Callaghan's stylist, signed a contract as Genny's stylist in 1974, and in 1978 launched the Gianni Versace "Donna" line.

In the 1970s Milan took Florence's place as the fashion capital. Albini, Cadette, and Ken Scott held their fashion shows in this city for the first time in April 1972. It had become a point of reference for international buyers and generated a climate very different from that of Florence. The "designated space" for fashion runways no longer existed: hotels, cafés, restaurants, and circus tents were all possible venues for happenings flanked by fashion-spectacles directed at a well-defined public. In 1978 the Modit show (the women's ready-to-wear fashion salon) was inaugurated, uniting young and old talents at the Fiera di Milano under the direct sponsorship of the Italian knitwear and clothing manufacturing associations.

Along with the emerging figure of the stylist there appeared an alternative anonymous, ungovernable, child of the ecology movement and the return to nature. It made use of flower-print fabrics, checked shirts, natural fibers, jeans and T-shirts, western-style boots, and military belts. What was important here was that the clothing be "authentic," lived-in, that it have some story to tell. References from the theater, film, music, and news items past and present were all mined for their expressive potential, the only condition being that they were in tune with one's intended—or dreamed of—lifestyle.

The unwritten code allowed for everything and its opposite: the tanga and nude look paid homage to sexual liberation, and alongside them appeared chaste long skirts in flowered prints worn by the first feminists (who were considered scandalous for other reasons), the military attire of the urban guerrillas, and the "peace and love" symbols of the flower children. Fashion was no longer an imperative but rather a range of

possible alternatives from which to choose.

Practicality usually prevailed over aesthetics: there was the unisex style and the boom of anonymous jeans followed by their designer counterparts; and used-clothing stores were considered a viable alternative. Freedom from constraint meant freedom to compose on the score of one's own body; in these years the "casual" and "put together" looks blossomed, in a multilayered blend of styles and colors that Missoni was to put on the "official" fashion map as well.

The first one in Italy to pick up on the glitter of the new taste and its related lifestyle was Elio Fiorucci. Since 1967, working out of his store in the heart of Milan, he had become a driving force in fashion. Fiorucci was not a stylist in the true sense of the word: he had gradually developed a body of work, starting with articles purchased from others and employing a startling instinct for interpreting already existing things in new materials and colors (for example, his traditional military jumpsuit in shocking pink, or his machine-washable paper overalls). Another Fiorucci experiment was the Ufficio Dxing (1977), which he organized as a group for the continuing study of trends in fashion and the fantasies that created them; it was invited to exhibit at the 1979 Milan Triennale.

Fiorucci, supported by his creative staff, occupied himself not only with apparel but also applied his style to objects that unwittingly heralded the postmodern era. These were objects distinguished by a singular lack of "good design," made of humble materials such as plastic, cardboard, and cheap fabrics, and with excessive decoration, their surfaces invaded by outrageous hypercommunicative graphic designs and violent colors. Fiorucci's fame was a result of the skill with which he managed to link his products to current events and fads. Fashion magazines were hard-pressed to keep up with his stream of ideas, even allowing some delay, but talk about him they did, because he was major presence on the market.

With the passing of fashions, the useful life of shop decorations shortened. In this decade, the shops were beginning to upgrade their look to be in line with their products, comparable to what the Gavina or Cassina furniture showrooms represented in the Sixties.

On December 18, 1974, Fiorucci opened his store in Via Torino, in a renovated space on two floors, designed by Franco Marabelli and conceived as an image factory, an amusement park for pop fashion that precisely met the period's expectations. During the winter there was an atrium like those shown in photographs of New York skyscrapers, complete with waterfalls and real palm trees, a supercontrol booth where a

Six images from films of the Seventies in which the settings and the characters' lifestyles contribute to describing their personalities, to the point of becoming extensions of them. From top: Bernardo

Bertolucci's Last Tango in Paris *(1971), set design by Ferdinando Scarfiotti; Marco Ferreri's* La Grande Bouffe *(1973), set design by Michel Bodin; Luis Buñuel's* La Fantôme de le Liberté *(1974), set design by Pierre Guffroy.*

deejay made sure that the public was "music-conditioned." On the second floor there was an open patio, offering bar and restaurant services. The stores designed for Fiorucci by Sottsass Associati at the close of the Seventies, completely renewing the look of sales points, also attracted a great deal of attention.

At the end of the 1970s there came a strong tendency to reevaluate the idea of quality in general. Italians found themselves seeking to reestablish order, settling on a look of serious professionalism backed by an efficient and tested production sector. High-quality raw materials, careful workmanship and creativity were the ingredients that contributed to Italian fashion's success story. In March 1980 in the magazine *Donna* appeared these words: "Having served itself of the wave of spontaneous styles that inspired even the stylists themselves, fashion has gone back into their hands, it has gone back to being a studied affair, it evolves rather than being improvised, and professionalism is rewarded; the most successful articles are those conceived and constructed like pieces of design."

CINEMA

The confused and varied panorama of film in the 1970s offer clear evidence of a crisis, side by side with examples of renewal. This reflected the contradictions of the decade in general. A phase of growth rich in expressive, ideological, and industrial ferment was naturally followed by one of contraction, in which even progress and active initiatives took their meaning from the demise of preceding myths and values. In different ways, creators, styles, and trends seem to share the same attitude—disillusion and awareness that an era was coming to an end.

The identity crisis that prompted cinema to reexamine itself through the aesthetic of the revivals, quotations, and remakes (which in the Eighties converged into the postmodern trend) had its roots in this decade. Wim Wenders' *Kings of the Road*, for example, reflects on the end of the cinema of the past within the greater context of the difficulties of communicating and being.

The crisis in film was provoked by its competition with television, an ever-growing presence in the 1970s. Even the American film sector was touched by this competition and by film's diminishing role in the iconosphere. Italian cinema was particularly susceptible to the phenomenon, and within the overall context of an economic crisis there ensued a slump in production that was detrimental to debuts and experimentation. The industry concentrated on the production of *films d'auteur* (using directors of the previous generation) and box-office hits.

The sense of a mental, moral, and ideological void that accompanied the revisitation of the voyage theme also appeared in treatments of interpersonal relationships, introspection, and sentiments. The empty apartment with a few pieces of furniture covered with white dropcloths that appeared in Bertolucci's *Last Tango in Paris* (1971) was symbolic of the mental void of the film's protagonists. While in Antonioni's *Zabriskie Point* (1970) the power of the imagination could make the symbols of consumer society explode into a thousand fragments, this explosion also seemed to take with it many of the myths and ideals embraced in the slogan "Power to the imagination." The decline of a utopia of exchange between the public and private spheres seemed to translate into a problem-ridden recovery of private values, and in film it was reflected in stories and themes of "interiors" — mental, moral, psychological, and material.

In their very titles films such as Visconti's *Conversation Piece* (1974) and Woody Allen's *Interiors* (1978) allude to the term's many-layered meaning. In fact, in these films the settings and the dwelling models are the reflections and extensions of the characters themselves. In the first film, the clash between two philosophies of life and between different generations is embodied in the contrast between the two dwelling models: the aristocratic and traditional decor of the lonely old professor's apartment, crammed full of antique furnishings and objects; and the modern decor of his offbeat young tenants, which is minimal, with a few large sofas and pillows and some contemporary paintings that are like exhibitions of a certain look and status.

Characteristic of the homes of Allen's characters — and of those in *Annie Hall* (1977) and *Manhattan* (1979) as well — are furnishings in light-colored wood, natural fabrics, a few Oriental artifacts, and several more sophisticated design pieces together with simple objects for everyday use, made of wicker or common materials. On the walls, in addition to modern art, there may be some photographs, mostly black-and-white; books, records, and posters complete the portrait of the contemporary intellectual in crisis, as Allen presents him. In his *Interiors* the exploration of human psychology, individual neurosis, and interpersonal relationships is rigorously executed via interior shots that analyze and highlight the character-setting relationship through unusual angles and

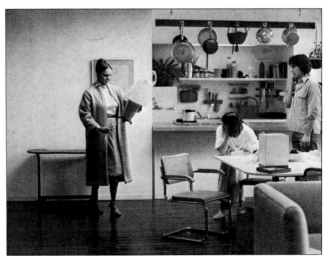

From top: Luchino Visconti's Conversation Piece *(1974), set design by Mario Garbuglia; Woody Allen's* Interiors *(1978), set design by Mel Bourne; Wim Wenders'* Kings of the Road, *set design by Heidi Lüdi and Bernd Hirskorn.*

lighting, with explicit references to Bergman. In fact, Bergman's interiors in *Scenes from a Marriage* (1974) were crucial points of reference. The analysis of the couple takes place in a specific setting in which the furnishings are completed by the meaningful presence of ordinary objects, as the character's attributes.

The vices, defects, and decadence of the bourgeoisie were symbolized more ironically and satirically by interior settings in films such as Ferreri's *La Grande Bouffe* (1973), with its overdone, kitschy villa and rambling kitchen that is the site of self-destruction; or Buñuel's *La Fantôme de le Liberté* (1974), with its inversion of the functional spaces of the home—the bathroom in the place of the dining room, the dining room in the private study.

Toward the close of the decade, the casual, put-together settings in disproportionately large places take on symbolic overtones; for example, in Wenders' *American Friend* (1977), the contents of the American's villa—recycled furnishings covered in nylon, neon signs, juke boxes, and leftovers from elegant decor—anticipate an iconography that would become commonplace in the following decade. Meanwhile, in reaction to impossible journeys and to the material or symbolic claustrophobia of the interiors, and perhaps as an escape from the *Anni di piombo*, the year 1977 gave rise to the fabulous science-fiction saga *Star Wars* and the exuberant *Saturday Night Fever*.

TELEVISION

Italian television underwent enormous development in the 1970s. One of the key points along the way was the advent of color television in 1976, though a first experimental broadcast had been aired in 1972, on the occasion of the Munich Olympic games. Furthermore, a legal reform divided the control of national television communications into two camps, whereby the public broadcasting company's first channel—with an audience of 20 million—was handed over to the Catholic, politically moderate element, and the second channel, with an audience of 2 million, was handed over to the laic-socialist element. A third public network was launched in 1979. The private networks entered the national broadcasting market in 1976. Their rise in influence has been continuous since then, capturing increasing shares of the market and naturally also contributing to great growth in TV advertising.

Technological innovations included videorecorders, video games, computers, and telematics. With the

Top: the eternally popular Rai broadcast Canzonissima, *in its 1972 season. This song-and-dance spectacular which is tied in with the national lottery, has dominated television's winter season since 1959. Its magnificent sets and costumes echo the style of Broadway musicals.*

Two sets (1978 and 1980) of Domenica In. This is a lengthy Sunday entertainment show that fills up an entire afternoon with made-for-television films, songs, guests, and sportscasts.

Above: the Kessler twins in Milleluci (1974). Participants in many television spectaculars, Alice and Ellen Kessler were a symbol of a new, more liberal atmosphere.

When they came along, TV's ban on legs and plunging necklines was lifted. The set employs giant posters of the show's hostesses.

introduction of the remote control a sort of video-restlessness set in, whereby in pressing a button one got a rapid succession of different, immiscible images —fragments that ranged from ancient Greece to spaceships.

The existence of past and future in the viewer's present led to a new type of visual and mnemonic construction, freed of the constraints of temporal or spatial coherence. This coincided with the recovery and juxtaposition of styles from different periods, and with a poetics of fragmentation that can also be seen in the buildings of the postmodern architects and in literary works such as Italo Calvino's *If on a Winter's Night a Traveler* or art such as Giulio Paolini's conceptual works.

Until the mid-Seventies, television advertising had been the exclusive privilege of the State, which in turn had handed it over on concession to the Rai company. The Constitutional Court, in a number of rulings between 1974 and 1976, put an end to this monopoly, thus legalizing the installation and operation of local radio and television stations. The effect of this liberalization was explosive: within a few months, time, Italy had been catapulted from a rigidly monopolistic situation into one offering a kaleidoscopic array of thousands of radio stations and hundreds of television stations whose survival depended solely and exclusively on their advertising clout.

Thus, the end of the state-run networks monopoly triggered an assault on the airways by privately owned stations. In their desperate need to attract audiences, the various broadcasting companies, both public and private, lowered their standards across the board. They offered no alternatives to the flat, homogeneous lifestyles that they already depicted. Thus, most television programs uncritically transmitted models of behavior that were characterized by lust for power, hedonism, and forced cheerfulness, the dangers of which, in terms of their power to condition the viewers' mentality are very much underrated. From its very inception, state television had been exceedingly careful about the use of advertising and the behavior models suggested, in order to avoid unleashing a wave of rash consumerism. RAI's editorial line limited the representation of luxury in both its programs and its commercials, barring from the screen any depictions of jewelry, fur coats, and even automobiles (which were not advertised until 1984).

The settings for dramas and mystery stories, the predominant genres in television's first 20 years, were modest but respectable in the early years, reflecting a simple, linear taste that left its mark on inexpensive,

Two of Franco Fiore's sets for the television serial La Carriera (1972). The décor of the show's settings changed from episode to episode, reflecting the characters' rise in society.

mass-produced furniture. For the first time millions of families had the opportunity to compare their situations with the one depicted by the television model, and to adapt their behavior and habits to conform with a model perceived as ideal. A show's setting took on more and more importance as television programming developed target audiences, and it eventually became the basic criteria used to identify an audience.

The setting, the "canned" room, was the sales pitch of many furniture stores, which were important advertising clients for the private networks. Their ads relied on the vernacular of a showman who is utterly indifferent to the historical, formal, or material coherence of the product offered. Kitsch, as Gillo Dorfles wrote, continues to be a very efficacious factor in advertising; which would not be so bad if it were used with a certain sense of humor and not merely to exploit the public's unsophisticated attitudes toward the home.

Some of the most popular programs of the Seventies were *Rischiatutto*, a quiz show hosted by Mike Buongiorno; *La Lotta dell'Uomo per la Sua Sopravvivenza*, conceived by Roberto Rossellini and directed by his son Renzo, examining the stages of man's evolution and *Domenica In*, a Sunday entertainment show initially hosted by Corrado and later by Pippo Baudo. This show devoted the afternoon to TV films, songs, guests, and sports notices, offering company to millions of Italian families who spent their Sundays at home in front of the TV, since fun on the town was a luxury that fewer and fewer people were willing to leave the safety and comfort of their homes for in any case. *Bontà Loro* was an Italian talk show hosted by Maurizio Costanzo, who was one of the first to propose this new formula of chat mixed with spectacle. Initially for Rai, it was later adopted by the private stations. *Portobello*, a family entertainment show hosted by Enzo Tortora, was based on the idea of promoting exchange of objects and services between the program's viewers and on the realization of dreams and sentimental aspirations, taking as its maxim "good will triumph in the end."

Over the course of the decade the networks also became producers of films, beginning, with Federico Fellini's *Clowns* in 1970, a series of high-quality productions. Outstanding examples of this series were Paolo and Vittorio Taviani's *Padre Padrone* and Ermanno Olmi's *Tree of Wooden Clogs*, winners at the Cannes Festival in 1977 and 1978, respectively.

INDUSTRY

Between 1964 and 1968 Italian industrial workers' real salaries were, with difficulty, kept on a par with increases in productivity. The production system had not been able to absorb the younger work force, nor had it established new, stable employment opportunities in the South. Public administration was crushed under the weight of managing an economy that over the past twenty years had shifted from an agricultural and rural base to an industrial, urban one.

The situation came to a head in the fall of 1969 when the unions intervened, thus becoming a powerful force in Italian society. The unions took on responsibilities that institutionally speaking were not in their realm of competence, but they claimed the right "by default." This resulted in many changes in the structure of industry: real salaries were significantly increased, modifying the nation's income distribution; salaries were established as a factor independent of productivity; pay scales were adjusted with egalitarian aims in mind; the work force lost all of its flexibility because the unions acquired the right to veto worker dismissals and the transferral of responsibilities or workplace.

The combined impact of the salary boosts, underdevelopment, and the energy crisis on Italy's petroleum-importing economy exacerbated the social strife. Between January and December of 1973, prices increased 25 percent; Italy's inflation rate was by far the highest in Europe. In the summer of 1974, eleven laws by decree were enacted, increasing the state's fiscal revenues by about 3 trillion lire. Small to medium-sized industries (which still represented 70 percent of Italy's work force, quite a large share compared to the rest of Europe) and small artisan's workshops were hardest hit by anti-inflation policies based on credit restriction.

The second half of the Seventies was marked by some degree of recovery in a few privileged sectors of Italian industry (fashion, interior decoration and so forth), and in limited geographic areas (in particular in the Po valley region, while the South continued to be excluded from any improvements), always on the fringes of the submerged economy that is one of the main factors underlying the 'Italian model's' at times inexplicable situation of relative stability" (Silvano Scajola, *Italia Moderna*).

The automobile. Auto production peaked in Italy in 1970 (1.7 million vehicles) and then endured a slump that lasted until 1983. The slump was caused, in large part, by the two great petroleum crises of 1973

The automobile of the Seventies: dream and reality. Stratos I, a smooth, aggressive wedge-shaped design by Marcello

Gandini for Bertone in 1970; Fiat 127, the first model to show a truncated rear end with hatchback opening.

and 1978. The inflationary spiral worsened. The first crisis had hit hard and unexpectedly, quadrupling petroleum prices and generating serious doubts as to the "automobile civilization's" chances for survival. Bicycles and even horses once again became viable means of transport; automobile use was restricted to alternate days, based on a system of odd and even license-plate numbers; people rediscovered the pleasures of spending weekends at home. The 1978 crisis caught the automobile industry in the middle of a twofold operation—reducing its workforce, and investing heavily in new technology in order to keep abreast of the progress that had been made in this industrial sector. Automobile designers were paying new attention to car interiors, closely watching developments in fashion and interior decoration. This approach arose from the need to achieve distinction in an industrial sector whose products were, at that point, for the most part undistinguished.

Wind tunnels, CX, strict safety standards, and fuel-consumption reductions were the order of the day for all car manufacturers, and the use of "computer design" left little room for formal innovation. Moreover, the energy crisis and the fear of showing oneself in a luxury car when the political climate was dangerously volatile contributed to the perception of the automobile as a functional vehicle and not as a status symbol. Many auto-body manufacturers closed down, and the role of the designer-manufacturer of auto bodies gave way to that of service-oriented organizations such as Giugiaro's Italdesign firm—a sort of R&D lab that produced the prototypes and planned the technological steps in the cars' manufacture.

Two projects of the Seventies represent these developments and confirm the shift of interest from the car's exterior (the auto-body) to its interior (the furnishings): Mario Bellini's Kar-a-Sutra (1972) made in collaboration with Centro Cassina, Citroën, and Pirelli and presented in New York at the Museum of Modern Art's exhibition "Italy: The New Domestic Landscape"; and the Panda designed by Giugiaro for Fiat in 1976 and unveiled at the Geneva salon in 1980.

Avoiding all reference to the usual mobile home (which, in Italy, was too often a grotesque miniature version of a vacation dream home), Bellini's project approached the problem of internal space in a new way. Reversing the traditional focus on mobility at the expense of comfort for driver and passenger, Bellini proposed a mobile space that was human, allowing for social interaction and alternative uses. The interior was decorated with "plastic inertia" cushions filled with styrofoam pellets that could be shaped according to

Mario Bellini's Kar-a-Sutra (1972), presented in New York at the Museum of Modern Art's "New Domestic Landscape" exhibition, demonstrated an alternative approach to the car interior.

Top: on the invitation of New York's Museum of Modern Art, Giugiaro invented a new model for taxis, focusing on the specific requirements of individual transport in an urban setting.
The vehicle's increased height enhanced passenger comfort and facilitated getting in and out.

Above: Fiat's new utilitarian model, the Panda, came to light after a four-year gestation. It represented the completion of Giugiaro's studies on the driving compartment, begun with his New York taxi and his Megagamma model.

their use. This material functioned like an elastic lung, and with the help of air valves could be expanded or flattened depending on the users' needs. This unusual solution made the vehicle's seating area into an "elastic field" that could be used for various activities, such as driving, talking, or sleeping.

The focus of this strange mobile object was being together, sharing, and group experiences—all concepts fashionable at the time. Its flexibility was enhanced by the pneumatically operated roof (23 $^2/_5$ in. [60 cm], which could be raised so that one could stand, walk around, and get in and out with greater ease. A second interesting feature was the option to open the automobile by lowering the windows, leaving only the center bar, the three verticle supports, and the windshield.

The Kar-a-Sutra remained at the prototype stage while Giugiaro in 1976 started a design project for Fiat that was to enter production as the Panda. It was a continuation on the path of the studies on experiencing the car interior as a living space that he had started with his taxi design for the Museum of Modern Art's exhibition "The Taxi Project: Realistic Solutions for Today", and with his Megagamma of 1978.

Designed to replace the utilitarian Fiat 126 (and, later, the 127) with a more competitive European-styled vehicle, the Panda overturned the traditional concept of the economy car. Instead of maximum performance in a minimum space, this project offered the maximum space for the minimum price.

As an economy car, the Panda did not attempt to miniaturize the services and accessories of more expensive models. Giugiaro's initial project offered a series of formal and use-oriented innovations that were so radical that they were not included in the production model. The seats consisted of an elastic cloth (offered in a number of shades and patterns) stretched over a tubular steel frame, free of old-fashioned springs, and easy to slip off. They could also be lowered to provide an emergency bed. The craftsmanship of the seats owed much to innovations in the padded-upholstery sector (see Lucci and Orlandini's 1974 "Vela" armchair for Elam). The sense of space and light in the interior was enhanced by a capacious open compartment with movable ashtray, which replaced the dashboard.

The car's height was another turning point in the automobile-manufacturing sector; the Panda's driving compartment was higher than those of other utility cars and a lot more comfortable. The lower side-trim in gray PVC, which served as protection from mud, salt, and corrosion in general, anticipated the high-tech look

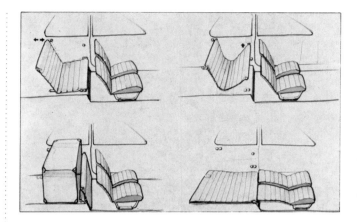

The Panda design started with the interior and moved outward. Notwithstanding its rather spartan look, the interior is in fact rich in innovations, ranging from the open dash compartment to the back seats, which could

be set in two positions depending on the amount of trunk space desired. The seats' upholstery owed much to innovations in the furniture sector, such as Lucci and Orlandi's "Vela" armchair (1974) for Elam.

and created an attractive line separating the area above and below the wheels.

The latest version of the Panda has moved from the young and spartan shine of its precursor in response to the recent conservative backlash and a slight tendency to conformism that conditions the automobile world. Taking its cue from the furnishing sector, it has replaced the folding chair, or *chaise longue* with the more traditional armchair.

The Fiat 127 was popular with Italian families throughout the 1970s. It was designed with important contributions from a young designer out of the Ulm school, Pio Manzù, whose premature death was an unfortunate loss to this industry. In enlisting the services of Manzù, Fiat embraced the design culture outside of its Centro Stile or the traditional figure of the auto-body maker.

The truncated rear end with hatchback trunk appeared in this car for the first time. More trunk space could be created by lowering the rear seat-back. It was a solution that was used in many other cars, even those of a larger size. In 1971, the first year of its production, 300,000 127s were manufactured, 30 percent of Fiat's overall production. The car remained one of Fiat's greatest successes throughout the entire decade.

The home-building industry. A safe investment *par excellence*, the home was and is the destination of an enormous slice of the national income. The building industry in the 1970s turned its focus to the home-ownership market, developing aesthetic models and features that were also transferred to the rental market.

These were active years for the real estate market; whole buildings were bought and sold, and subdivided; entire social brackets were evicted from neighborhoods, destroying the socio-cultural fabric, all for the single-minded purpose of income and profit. Apartment layouts underwent lasting modifications, mainly affecting the living-dining room area and facilities improvement.

Offers like the following frequently appeared in the newspapers: "Available: apartment, deluxe fittings, triple bath." It was a kind of wording that had long before fallen into disuse in ad campaigns for almost all other consumer goods; it is so elitist that in car or clothing advertisements it could have had a negative effect, but here it shows the social and cultural import of the house.

The bath facilities represented the last frontier in the demands of the affluent and reflected not only new standards of personal hygiene but also the desire to communicate and celebrate the move up and the change in status conferred by home ownership. In addition to allocating a larger area to the bathroom and exercising greater care in the selection of fixtures, designers sought new archetypes, which were inspired at times by Hollywood images and in any case involved a complex reorganization of the house's layout.

The remodeling boom of the Seventies led to the homeowner's increasing participation in the selection of the fittings and fixtures, from the doors and window latches to light switches and the type of sanitary facilities. This contrasted with the real estate speculation of the Fifties and Sixties, when the buyers were usually building contractors who paid more attention to the size and number of the rooms than to the quality of the fittings.

The demand for bathroom fittings and fixtures at first was met by manufacturers of accessories and decor, and then by faucet manufacturers. Color was an innovative addition to the products, and although its use was banal compared to developments in other home products, in this field it was revolutionary and made the fortunes of several companies. Later, tile manufacturers got into the act, demonstrating an amazing capacity to create new designs and glazes, whereas previously they had merely changed the serigraphic stencil from one standard floral pattern to the next. Italian floor and wall tiles became the undisputed heroes of such construction-industry salons as Saie of Bologna, Batimat of Paris, or Constructa in Germany. In the 1970s, with production exceeding 250 million square yards (equal to a 19 $^1/_2$ in. [50 cm] strip stretching from the earth to the moon), Italy became the world leader in tile production.

Furniture. At the start of the 1970s, the furniture-manufacturing sector consisted mainly of small to medium-sized companies, which were often specialized, technologically adept and possessed of an operating margin that allowed for marketing and advertising outlays. They were flexible and independent. The sector's steady growth (with a 60 percent increase in production between 1970 and 1974) had been accompanied by an increase in the number of businesses operating in the field. These were benefited by a demand that was markedly diversified, and their offerings were in continual evolution to keep abreast of the changing tastes of consumers who both expected and made possible a vast product range from which to choose. Furthermore, there were no significant barriers to entering the sector, in terms of either initial investments or know-how. The

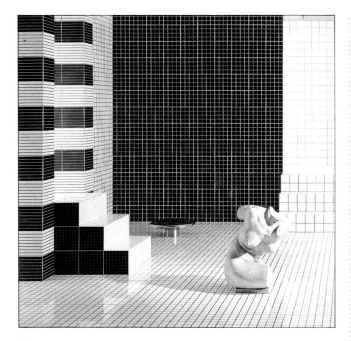

Above: tiles from Enzo Mari's "Elementare" series (1971).

Right: "Boma," one of the best-selling door handles in the world. Designed by Monti GPA in 1971 it comes in various shades of colored plastic.

Above: The new opulence of bathroom décor in the Seventies reflected not only new standards of personal hygiene but also a desire to celebrate the increase in status conferred by home ownership.

resulting highly differentiated structure of independent craftsmen was a crucial factor in the success of the Italian furniture industry.

Altogether this situation led a crowded supplier's market with the following characteristics: excessive production capacity, fierce competition, and competition among businesses with an industrial organization, whose costs were fixed, and other, more flexible "family-run" enterprises. Since demand was so diversified and mutable, standardized production was possible only to a limited degree, with few opportunities to take advantage of economies of scale. Furthermore, demand was such that the product lifespan was very brief.

Imitations were easy to produce, so product lifespans were further shortened by copies that saturated the market and quickly diminished the margins of the innovating companies.

In 1971 the number of furniture manufacturers with nine or fewer employees represented 88 percent of the sector's 1,700 firms and total work force of 90,000. Many of these small businesses (those with nine or fewer employees) were specialized in manufacturing furniture parts for the larger businesses, including frames for the upholstered pieces sector, drawers in general, wooden doors for kitchen units, and lathed parts and decorations for period-style furnishings. This gave rise to the structure of intermediate suppliers that was so crucial to the success of the Italian furniture industry.

By the close of 1974, the sector's total ex-factory sales, including exports, reached 1,500 billion lire. It was not until 1975 that this sector began to show signs of a slump that was already anticipated by other industrial sectors. In particular the housing-construction crisis (the same that in the Sixties had set many architects on the road to furniture design) had robbed the furniture industry of an important stimulus. The reduced availability of new dwellings and the smaller number of family units negatively affected furniture sales.

To compensate for flagging domestic demand, the sector turned to the export market, which required a different approach and knowledge of foreign products, their quality and cost. At the end of the Seventies, the furniture industry's balance sheets registered a sharp increase in exportation. In 1978 the furnishing sector reached a peak of 1,138 billion lire (in 1984 it has settled back down to 238 billion), versus imports of only 43 billion; 168 billion lire in lighting fixtures were exported versus imports of only 26 billion. The two sectors combined had therefore totaled a surplus balance of 1,237 billion lire. As a source of foreign cur-

In the Seventies many companies turned to the production of modular furniture. Its parts permitted the furniture to dominate every room in a number of different versions.
Top: the "Fiorenza" series designed by Tito Agnoli for Molteni (1970).
Above: the "Carioca" series designed by Pamio and Toso for Stilwood (1971).

Top: the "Piper" in ash or with lacquered doors, designed by Adalberto Dal Lago for Misura Emme (1972).

Above: the "Linear System," designed by Rodolfo Bonetto for Bellato in 1973, is distinguished by its rounded edges and compact volumes, finished on both sides.

rency receipts, the furniture industry stood immediately below the automobile, mechanical equipment, and the shoe and sheet-steel industries, on a par with the jewelry and knitwear sectors. Its products were mainly exported to the Common Market nations, and they were not limited to what the *New York Times* called "Italo-Milanese design" pieces by Bellini and Magistretti, or by the Kartell and Cassina companies; they could also be imitations of exogenous styles, such as the "made in Italy" German rustic that was all the rage in Germany, or Louis XV and XVI in France.

It is important to realize that Italy's substantial penetration of the foreign markets was a projection of what had already happened on the domestic market, since in few other economic sectors is a shift to dependence on foreign trade so clearly determined by the market situation at home as in the case of interior decoration products. And it is also worth recalling that although Italy had benefited by a wide margin from low labor costs during the Fifties and the first half of the Sixties, other factors (aside from formal innovation) that could guarantee a net commercial advantage were totally lacking. Italy had no situation like that in West Germany, where the availability of resins and intermediates at prices lower than other countries was guaranteed by the powerful chemical industry established there. Nor could Italy rely on abundant forest resources. Thus the Italian furniture industry was forced to specialize in strongly innovative products aimed at the upper crust of consumers.

It is interesting to look in hindsight at the editorials published by the review *Abitare* (under the editorship of Piera Peroni and with the assistance of architect Eugenio Gentili Tedeschi) on the growth of the furniture industry. They clearly illustrate how objectives changed in the course of the decade: how the analysis of the problem of producing in quantity while maintaining high standards of quality passed from a perspective of social commitment to one of a purely disciplinary interest.

"Meno mobili per favore" (Less Furniture, Please) was the title of the article on the Salone del Mobile show of January 1970. Its author deplored "the fragility of a system built up on the wave of success, unable to respond to the true needs of a society torn by contradictions, but whose right to improve its knowledge and lifestyle certainly must be recognized." He also deplored the high prices of design products and the failure of design to meet the needs of the "human masses...who continue to fill their homes, whether in the overcrowded cities or the countryside afflicted by rampant urbanization, with furniture of an indistinct

Top: the "Hilton" system of modular storage units designed by Giotto Stoppino and Lodovico Acerbis and manufactured by Acerbis (1978). The sliding door panels could be folded back into the units, and internal lighting fixtures could be applied to the glass cases.

Above: the "Zibaldone" bookcase with vertically sliding glass doors, designed by Carlo Scarpa for Bernini (1974).

style produced by the wagonload and sold at the same prices, equally unjustifiable, as modern pieces."

The debate continued in even harsher tones the following year (January 1971) when *Abitare*'s cover featured a frame from Michelangelo Antonioni's *Zabriskie Point* depicting the explosion in the desert of society's countless useless consumer items, with an article entitled "Per favore, mi dai un cerino?" (Anybody Got a Match?). The article asked "Where can this insanity lead if not to the desire to blow up this mountain of futility? A single product of top quality would be far better than infinite mediocre products, sapped of their vitality and therefore with little hope of a lifespan of any duration, making their prices doubly scandalous."

Designers and entrepreneurs had their say on these topics in the March 1971 issue of *Abitare*, in which they explored the future of an increasingly complex product. Mario Bellini, one of the participants in this debate, pointed out that the absence of industrial and environmental conditions comparable to those in the Scandinavia could not be offset by force of will. He argued instead in favor of the designer's right to freely explore his interests and of the value of pure formal experimentation, because only in this way would new experiences come to the fore.

In its December 1970 issue, the review *Ottagono* published an article entitled "Design: la Fine di un Mito?" (Design: The End of a Myth?). This piece unleashed another hot debate on the Italian design situation and the profound metamorphosis it had undergone in the previous decade (with particular reference to 1954, the year in which the Compasso d'Oro award was inaugurated, as the start of an important phase of design study in Italy). The article also discussed the change from a situation that had made possible a craftsmanlike relationship between designer and manufacturer to that in which the public now seemed bombarded by a volley of incomprehensible forms that were often uprooted from the social and economic realities and environment in which they should have been anchored.

In the role of design-critic, Gillo Dorfles also took part in this debate, analyzing the diminished importance of the prestigious object—whether museum piece or Compasso d'Oro award-winner—and the diffusion of forms (or, often, antiforms), whose lifespans were considerably reduced by the fact that they immediately became commonplace. He attributed these phenomena in design to the shift in emphasis from crafts production for an elite to mass production for many.

Further consequences of all this were the crisis of the object as object and the crisis in the interior decoration industry which increasingly turned away from fixed notions and inflexible and definitive production equipment.

The Flos showroom in Milan, designed by Achille Castiglioni. Each lamp has its own exhibition space.

FURNITURE STORES

Distribution structures in Italy are traditionally weak in the interior-decoration sector, and retail outlet networks are very fragmented. A census in October 1971 registered 12,773 retail furniture outlets, an increase of 60 percent over the figures for 1961. When the number of other retailers authorized for the sale of furniture is added to this figure, a total of about 26,000 outlets is reached. The disproportion of this number of outlets is easily demonstrated by comparing it with the number of Italy's licensed dairy shops, that is, stores handling a broad spectrum of products classed as basic necessities, which must have a fairly dense geographical distribution for consumer convenience. The exact number of these in 1972 was 28,301, versus 26,047 licensed furniture stores.

In the Seventies the evolution in furniture styles from period-style to contemporary design reached its summit, and the conversion was so complete that it is now possible to speak in terms of a "design style."

The number of sales outlets increased from 43,393 with 108,649 employees in 1971, to 60,482 with 142,043 employees in 1981.

During these years the old conception of the furniture salesman as simply someone who sells furniture increasingly gave way to that of the interior decorator, and the old conception of the vast furniture store, with hundreds of room settings deployed on several floors of a building, ceded to that of a smaller, more rational structure, characterized by the coordination between the internal and external images of the showroom and the products on display.

The careful selection of the furniture series, with the market neatly divided between period-style and contemporary furniture, suggested smaller displays within the showroom, so that the relationship of the container (the showroom) to the content (the collections presented in arrangements of easily interchangeable elements and no longer in complete room settings with rigidly interlocked pieces) favored the cityward migration of the showrooms.

The figure of the salesman-interior decorator was

Elegant craftsmanship characterizes the various pieces of the "Artona" *series designed by Afra and Tobia Scarpa for Maxalto (1975).*

gaining in importance; this was the person who knew all the ins and outs of the trade, the one who could weave his way knowledgeably between a vast and continuous supply of products and the problems of dressing the exhibition space, able to offer services and advice to a clientele that was day by day growing more culturally aware.

At the same time, the sales outlets were gaining influence over the production sector, which paradoxically in this period of crisis continued to grow in an amoebic way, chasing the carrot of exposure in a qualified store (and, if possible, in the storefront window) in a harshly competitive situation.

In this period, the sales outlets played a growing role in business strategies, which tended to be "marketing oriented" and to make use of such devices as sales accounts and bonuses.

FURNITURE

In the first half of the 1970s, riding on the swell of the previous years, furniture production experienced a period of expansion that saw various parallel trends. Side by side with objects that had no future were others that, through a combination of technical, manufacturing, and distribution factors, took hold. They were the offspring of the new creative ferment—expressions of reality, of ongoing trends and changes in lifestyle, qualities that often distinguished Italian-designed products from those of other countries.

After a decade of steel, glass, and plastic, wood stole the show: light-colored wood, such as ash, with clear varnish or glossy polyester lacquer, or domestic walnut—anything sold as long as it was wood and offered a sense of solidity and safety to anxious buyers in an age of socioeconomic instability.

During these years many companies exploited series production to its maximum potential, by relying on "modular" furniture—that is, a limited number of mass-produced basic units that could be assembled in different combinations. With the introduction of interchangeable elements, such as various types of doors, shelves, and internal accessories, modular furniture had come to dominate every room, from the living room to the childrens' bedrooms. For the master bedroom there was a series of 23 $^2/_5$ in. (60 cm) -deep all-purpose modular components that could be lined up along the room's walls to serve as wardrobe, bureau, and night table. Worthy of mention among the many variations on this idea are: Tito Agnoli's

"Fiorenza" series, manufactured by Molteni (1970); Pamio and Toso's "Carioca," manufactured by Stilwood (1971); Adalberto Dal Lago's "Piper," manufactured by Misura Emme (1972); Angelo Mangiarotti's "L 12" system, manufactured by Lema (1972); Rodolfo Bonetto's "Linear System," manufactured by Bellato (1973); Antonia Astori's "Oikos," manufactured by Driade (1973); Palange and Toffoloni's "Slim," manufactured by Malobbia (1974); and Lodovico Acerbis and Giotto Stoppino's "Hilton," manufactured by Acerbis (1978).

By the second half of the 1970s, a few companies (Driade, Estel, Lema, Misura Emme, Molteni etc.)—the largest in terms of output and organization—no longer produced closed units to be set up side-by-side; rather, they turned out more flexible systems based on the concept of load-bearing uprights and a greater range of modules. Stilwood, for example, presented the "Acquario" system in 1978. Designed by Pamio and Todo, it could be assembled three-dimensionally and included, in addition to the usual storage units, platforms and stepped areas that could be finished either as seating arrangements or beds.

For various reasons—not the least of which were the significant investments necessary for production, for warehousing, and for spare parts of the modular pieces, the cost of providing the client with the services necessary for such systems, and the expressive *ennui* that is inherent in mass-produced pieces (the design stage was often limited to the problem of the knob) —other companies returned to the production of finished pieces of furniture. Here, rather than renewing tried-and-true typologies, the designer's focus was on the size and the surface finish of the pieces. Examples of "closed" pieces are: Giuseppe Raimondi's 1973 "Caravan" and "Brunelleschi" for Tarzia, both of them variations on historically well-established forms; Carlo Scarpa's 1974 "Zibaldone" bookcase, with latching glass doors for Bernini; Afra and Tobia Scarpa's 1975 "Artona" series for Maxalto, making use of elegantly crafted wood in the tradition of the lutemakers; Giotto Stoppino and Lodovico Acerbi's 1977 "Sheraton" storage units, with unusually large doors that could be opened thanks to a unique combination sliding and hinged mechanism, winner of the Compasso d'Oro in 1979.

The modular concept was also applied to seating arrangements. Over the course of the decade this contributed significantly to breakthroughs in the polyurethane technology, both foamed and block-cut, and in different densities, which led not only to a renewal of the traditional living-room typologies but also to the

Three highly expressive polyurethane pieces manufactured by Gufram in the early Seventies.

From top: the "Bocca" sofa and "Capitello" armchair designed by Studio 65; "Pratone" by Ceretti, Derossi, Rosso.

127

discovery of unique objects that offered completely new ways of sitting and acting.

In the 1970s the upholstery sector went through a phase of great expansion, due in part to the ease of production, which was feasible on a small scale as well. Many new firms sprang up and the most popular models were copied endlessly. As a result, the market became greatly inflated. Noteworthy among the upholstered modular systems were De Pas-D'Urbino-Lomazzi's "Carrera" for BBB Bonacina (1969); Mario Bellini's "Camaleonda" for B&B (1971); Citterio and Nava's "Baia" for B&B (1975); and Vico Magistretti's "Fiandra" for Cassina (1975).

In discussing armchairs and sofas, it is useful to remember that at the beginning of the 1970s "when designing an object, there were two approaches from which to choose: the first was that of an object so laden with form and expressive power that it could have been mistaken for a symbol, a banner or a pop monument—an object that shouted out what it intended to represent. The second was that of letting the object speak more softly." (Isa Vercelloni, "1970–1980—Dal Design al Post-Design," *Casa Vogue*). Examples of the first tendency are the pieces selected for display in New York at the Museum of Modern Art's 1972 exhibition "Italy: The New Domestic Landscape" on the basis of "their sociocultural meanings" and their formal traits derived from the "rhetorial manipulation of conventional objects": De Pas-D'Urbino-Lomazzi's "Joe" armchair for Poltronovo (1971), in polyurethane foam shaped like a baseball glove; and Ceretti-Derossi-Rosso's "Pratone" for Gufram (1971), which reproduced, in a flexible synthetic material, blades of grass that one could stretch out on, as its name—translated as "Big Meadow"—suggests.

Studio 65's pieces for Gufram also had a powerful expressive charge: the "Bocca" sofa (1971), taking Dali's giant lips as its inspiration; and the "Capitello" armchair (1972), in the shape of an Ionic capital, anticipating the postmodern idiom. In 1971 Simon International presented its "Ultramobile" collection, organized by Dino Gavina, with the "furniture of poetry," pieces conceived by Man Ray, Meret Oppenheim, Sebastian Matta, Novello Finotti, and Mario Baruch.

After 1973, Italian design changed direction. Formal discoveries abated, and the pieces took on a more practical look (De Pas-D'Urbino-Lomazzi's "Centopercento" for Zanotta dates to 1973; it is comprised of sofas and armchairs with completely removable, washable, or replaceable slipcovers). The marketing surveys showed a demand for more reliable objects with longer lives, for things that came under the category of du-

On these two pages are pieces representing various trends in furnishings of the early Seventies. Opposite page, from top: the calm, bourgeois serenity of the "Bonheur" sofa, designed by Ammanati-Vitelli for Brunati; the baseball-glove-shaped "Joe" armchair, clearly of Pop inspiration, designed by De Pas, D'Urbino, Lomazzi for Poltronova; the subtle and irresistible

appeal of Meret Oppenheim's table for Simon.

Above: two pieces manufactured by Cassina in 1973: Vico Magistretti's "Maralunga," whose inclining headrest renewed the traditional sofa typology; and the Archizoom group's "AEO," a look that was fresh and technologically sound.

rable assets, a category conditioned by its high costs. There was a return to the traditional parlor set with armchair, two-seat sofa and three-seat sofa. The soft and inviting shapes of Mario Bellini's "Bambole" series for B&B and Cini Boeri and Laura Griziotti's "Strip" for Arflex (both 1972) appeared prior to this trend. The latter especially enjoyed great commercial success for the soft, fresh look captured in its polyurethane foam structure, which contained no rigid elements and was upholstered with quilted material that recalled a sleeping bag or ski jacket.

On the other hand, under the banner of "progress without mishaps" and well-ensconced in the groove of tradition were armchairs and sofas (almost always upholstered in brown leather) that for the bourgeoisie represented a safe harbor in a world in tumult. Examples are the living-room sets designed by Ammanati and Vitelli for Brunati "Bonheur" and "Paros"; from the 1960s, the "Simona," by Ferdinando Buzzi, one of the firm's best-selling articles; Cini Boeri's "Bengodi" for Arflex; Alberto Rosselli's "Confidential" for Saporiti; and Afra and Tobia Scarpa's "Erasmo" for B&B.

At this time the buying public was divided into cultural compartments, no longer according to census statistics. This is demonstrated by two products, both launched by Cassina in 1973: the "Maralunga" by Vico Magistretti and the "AEO" by the Archizoom group. They reflect two completely different philosophies and two idioms. The first was an instant success because it gave a novel twist to a traditional typology: it introduced an adjustable headrest that crowned the sofa back, so that the center of gravity could be raised or lowered as one wished—a variant that numerous firms adopted in its wake. The "AEO" (in which the influence of Paolo Deganello, one of the founders of the Archizoom group, is clearly evident) marked a turning point in the design of the soft, overstuffed chair. Its look was a new departure—discordant, but of a flawless construction logic; it was an armchair that functioned as a sort of stage curtain, an anticipation of better things to come. A taut canvas web suspended by a metal frame gave the chair its shape; here the inspiration was drawn from the familiar design of the fabric-and-wood folding chair. The "AEO" also represented a meeting of two industries: attire and furniture. The problem of the jointures of the back, the armrests, and the seat—that is, the critical points in the design of an armchair, comparable to the sleeves and the neckline of a jacket—was handled here in the cut and the seams of the upholstery.

The success of the "AEO" came far after its release on the market, but the finest examples of pure styling

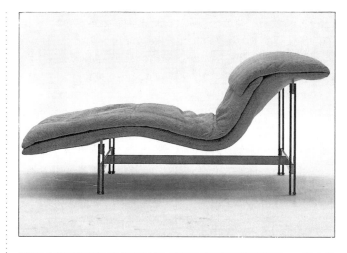

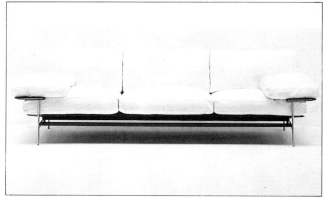

From top: "Wave", designed by Giovanni Offredi for Saporiti (1978); "Diesis," designed by Citterio and Nava for B&B (1979). The exposed framework and seeming suspension in air of these pieces marked a turning point in the design of upholstered furniture.

came even later: Giovanni Offedi's "Wave" for Saporiti (1978), and Citterio and Nava's "Diesis" for B&B (1979). The latter, in particular, exalted the role of the structure that supported the cushions, giving more emphasis to the technical scheme than to the upholstered finishing touches. Its carefully designed, cast light-alloy framework, painted or nickel-plated, was exposed, with the steel back and armrest panels covered in leather. Following the example of Franco Albini, the "Diesis" was an elegant interpretation of a style imported from the United States: high tech. The publication of a book on industrial decor by two *New York Times* journalists, Joan Kron and Susanne Slesin, had contributed much to the success of this trend. They pointed out the tendency to use, in home decor, robustly constructed, functional metal products conceived for the factory or the office by anonymous designers—metal chairs, workbenches, sheetmetal storage units with tool drawers, etc. The pieces' predominant lead-gray, aluminum, or zinc-plated tones were well-suited to another trend in urban lifestyles: loft living, which involved the conversion into spacious apartments of industrial spaces with painted concrete floors, left free by the flight of many businesses from the cities.

Seen in the context of Italian design, high tech, as it was, was in reality neither a great stimulus nor a great innovation; the adjective "hard" perhaps describes its product's technological look better than "high." It was influential inasmuch as it promoted an interchange between the two sectors, home and workshop (or, generally, collective) decor, offering new stimuli to both.

Reinterpreted and enriched, high tech introduced a new preference for use of metal products in the home, for their greater practicality and sturdiness (necessary in products destined for collective use). By the same token, domestic design introduced to the "collective" sector a new attention to the product's look, thus enhancing the permeability between these two product sectors.

The following is a quick review of products of the Seventies, selected at random from the vast range of a decade of production.

After the rationalist current, glass was given a broad range of new applications in the early 1970s, in combination with metal frameworks (Carlo Scarpa's "Doge" table for Simon of 1969 anticipated this trend, though here the glass played second fiddle to the design of the framework supporting the surface), or as an integral part of the structure, as in Marco Zanuso's 1970 "Marcuso" table series for Zanotta, in which

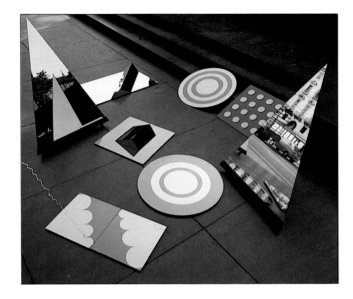

Top: decoration made a comeback in this series of mirrors designed by Raimondi for Cristal Art in 1970. Above: Superstudio's

"Monumento Continuo" and "Quaderna" tables, in which the group reproposed the grid-pattern design of its architectural utopia for domestic use.

glass was welded to metal bottoms (a technique already used in the automobile industry) to create a logical system of tables of various sizes, in which the glass is no longer simply one layer resting on top of another but becomes integral to the architectural equilibrium of the piece and its simplification of construction. In other works, such as those of Giuseppe Raimondi for Cristal Art, the material itself—transparent or mirror-finished glass—was the focus of a study that aimed to give it new expression outside of the rationalist or functionalist canons. Favored at one time for its transparency, its "invisibility" compared to the framework that monopolized the designer's attention, or for its reflective function when mirror-finished, in these works glass became a presence, thanks to partial silver-coatings that "decorated" it and called attention to its use. Mirrors thus regained their importance as objects, establishing a curious reciprocal relationship between user and object.

The recovery of certain forms of craftsmanship can be attributed to the vogue for cane and bamboo (launched in 1972 in Rome by Vivai del Sud and Arpex International), Valentino's naïf objects and flowered fabrics, and Tommaso Barbi's objects, which introduced the thrill of kitsch to Milanese design. In this period "scenographic" pieces started appearing on the market. Using Cinecittà craftsmen who were unemployed because of crisis of the film industry, the furniture industry rediscovered the lure of the dreamlike, with products rich in volutes and lamé or beaded decorations, and pillows of every shape and size, aimed to please the Arab or international jet-set markets. Products designed by film or fashion personalities such as Pierre Cardin, Willy Rizzo, Pierre Balmain, and even Alain Delon (who in 1978 lent his name to products marketed by Sabot) fall into this category.

In response to external insecurities in the 1970s there was a revival of more traditional domestic lifestyles: sitting together at the dinner table recovered its ritual importance, and tables once again became the focus of designers' attentions. They were momentous tables for their size, and the materials used were solid and of antique tradition, such as marble and solid wood. Superstudio and Angelo Mangiarotti designed two very different tables, both dating to 1971, which share a tendency to achieve an archetypical status; they should be considered pieces of architecture rather than of design.

Superstudio's "Quaderno," manufactured by Zanotta, is the reduction to domestic scale of the "continuous monument," a utopian vision of "total urbanization" by means of a single architectonic object. Winner of the Graz international "Trigon 69" award, this plastic laminate table featured a silkscreened grid pattern that could stretch to infinity, a motif that became a sort of trademark distinguishing Superstudio's other work.

Mangiarotti's marble "Eros" tables, initially conceived for Brambilla and later manufactured by Skipper, were more than just tables; they were a masterly structural invention in the harmony of their proportions and the underlying logic of the juncture between the tabletop and the cone-shaped supports that penetrated its limits. Other imposing tables of the Seventies were Carlo Scarpa's "Valmarana" for Simon (1972), with a solid ash structure and stone top; Mario Ceroli's "La Rosa dei Venti" of his *Mobili nella Valle* series for Poltronova (1973), in untreated Russian pine; Enzo Mari's "Frate" for Driade (1974), with a wrought-iron structure linked by a beechwood beam and a top surface in glass; Mario Bellini's "La Basilica" in ash or walnut and his "Colonnato" with a marble base and a glass or marble top, both designed for Cassina in the period 1976–77.

Although tables and armchairs abounded in the 1970s, no chairs emerged that could represent the era as had happened in the 1960s. Except for the following, the Sixties' innovative drive in design and technology had fizzled out by the 1970s: Castelli's "Plia," which was unveiled at the 1969 Salone del Mobile; Bellini's "Cab" for Cassina (1977), in which the leather combination sleeve-and-structural element offered an innovative look; and Anna Castelli's stools for Kartell (1979), which achieved a remarkable variation of the high-tech look. Instead, designers resurrected the folding-chair motif in a few clever variations on the film director's, military camp, or garden chairs (for example, Paolo Pellion's 1977 "Ripiego" for Art&Form, and Achille Castiglioni's 1978 "Celestina" for Zanotta).

At the close of the decade, Ettore Sottsass toppled all these pilasters, debunked the codes on which they rested, and introduced uncertainties even in the presence of marble tables with five legs.

Toward the end of the 1970s the Flos company was founded. It arose as a manufacturer of a specific product—the bed—based on a precise production technology: the fully removable, machine-washable overall slipcover. Its most famous product, which put the company's name on the map, was the "Nathalie," designed by Vico Magistretti in 1978 and featuring a down spread and an upholstered headboard with pillows fixed by bows at the sides; it was a bed that offered

Above: Marble "Eros" tables designed by Mangiarotti for Skipper (1971).

Right: detail showing the notch in the tabletop where the cone-shaped pedestal fits in.

Below: the "Colonnato" table, with marble base and glass or marble top, designed by Bellini for Cassina (1976–77).

its users a soft, warm niche. With the "Nathalie" Flos launched the vogue of the "textile bed," that is, a bed whose look and feel made it stand out from the other furniture in the bedroom. A rich array of slipcover fabrics to choose from offered consumers a new flexibility in choosing the desired style. This was a departure from the usual business strategies of the furniture sector, which considered the bed to be an object of secondary importance, a complement.

With the introduction of the "textile bed," the role of fabrics—already important in armchairs and sofas—was given a boost, to which the textiles industry responded with a continuous flow of new textures and patterns. Star, the textiles trade fair in Milan, became a not-to-be-missed annual date for designers and manufacturers Italian as well as foreign.

As dwelling models had remained substantially unchanged, the kitchen-furnishing sector offered no important developments. Rows of upper and lower cabinets remained the standard, with slight modifications in size to accomodate electrical appliances. The only area in which designers could make changes was in the graphic design of the blocks, by focusing on the accessories, knobs, colors. By varying such elements, the look of the kitchen changed from that of an "abstract laboratory for food preparation" clearly separated from the rest of the house, into one of a space in which one could also eat and spend time. To get away from the repetitiveness of styling, some designers turned to technologically more complex projects, a clean break from the commonly accepted "American-style" kitchen scheme. These had no follow-up, since they required a complete revision of residential typologies. In this respect, in addition to such proposals of the Sixties as Joe Colombo's 1963 "Mini-kitchen" for Boffi, along with the 1966 kitchen block that he designed for the Eurodomus exhibition, and Masanori Umeda's mobile block, winner of the 1968 Braun award, and manufactured by Mesaglio in 1971, Joe Colombo and Ignazia Favata's "Toral Furnishing Unit" was of particular interest. It embraced in a single block a lavatory, a kitchen, storage units and beds. Fabrizio Cocchia and Gianfranco Fini's "Cubolibre," presented at the 1972 Eurodomus 4 in Turin, was based on a similar concept.

A few designs showing the great leaps made in kitchen technology and design in the 1960s were put into regular production. These were Alberto Salviati and Ambrogio Tresoldi's "Isola" block for RB in 1971; Salvarani's 1973 "Longline", the first kitchen with a continuous plastic laminate surface area up to six-and-a-half yards (six meters) in length, with housing for

From top: Anna Castelli's stools with lacquered iron framework, polypropylene seat, and polyurethane foam backrest, manufactured by Kartell (1979); Magistretti's "Nathalie" bed for Flos (1978)—the best-known and most-imitated textile bed; the "Longline" kitchen, manufactured by Salvarani (1973)—the first kitchen with a continuous surface, reaching up to six yards (six m.) in length.

Above: Designed by Achille Castiglioni and Pio Manzù (Flos, 1970), the "Parentesi" featured total flexibility in positioning the lamp's height and direction.
Right: the "Hebi" table lamp designed by Isao Hosoe (Valenti, 1970).

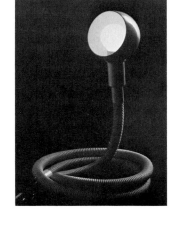

Right: the "Tizio" table lamp, halogen bulb, and extensible arm, designed by Richard Sapper (Artemide, 1972).

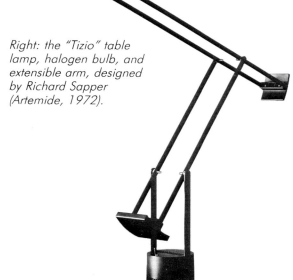

electrical appliances on the surface areas or in the cabinets; Makio Hasuike's "Osa" for Ariston, 1976, offering a perfect balance between electrical appliance and storage area, with highly flexible, three-dimensional assembly possibilities; and Claudio Salocchi's "Metro Sistema" designed in 1978 for Alberti, a wall storage unit with sliding doors that was suitable for homes, community homes, or residence hotels.

Lighting fixtures. The lighting sector underwent such growth in the 1970s that beginning in 1976 a trade fair specific to it was held as an offshoot of the Salone del Mobile, contemporaneous with it. The new accent on flexibility that had appeared in other sectors emerged in the lighting field as well, with directional, portable, optional battery-powered, track, and interchangeable models.

One of the handsomest of these was the "Parentesi," designed in 1970 for Flos by Achille Castiglioni, based on Pio Manzù's original idea (1979 Compasso d'Oro). It featured a light that could be moved up and down and 360° around a cable stretched from ceiling to floor. Another highly popular lamp was the "Hebi," manufactured by Valenti on Isao Hosoe's design. Its extremely coherent design represented the maximum achievement in the flexible tube line of table lamps, where flexibility became a sort of *raison d'être*.

Richard Sapper's world-famous "Tizio" table lamp for Artemide dates to 1972 (Compasso d'Oro, 1979). Its highly innovative look, strongly characterized by a technical line, with 50-watt/12-volt halogen light bulb, has all the airy appeal of a Calder mobile. In 1974, Artemide produced its "Area" series of lamps, in table, floor, and wall versions designed by Mario Bellini. Here, the technology of the materials (a sheet of flame-retardant synthetic fabric stiffened just enough to give it shape, pressed between two curved pieces of the light-bulb socket) creates a soft lighting effect that recalls a form well-established in our memories: the classical lampshade.

Two very interesting and very different lamps date to 1977. The first is Vico Magistretti's "Atollo" for O-Luce (Compasso d'Oro, 1979), an enameled metal table lamp accurately described as a "furniture personality," since its proportions make it an imposing presence in spite of its simplicity of line. The second is Ettore Sottsass' "Valigia" for Stilnovo, a table lamp in sheet metal, full of an ironic inventiveness that heralded the new postmodern idiom.

The use of the 300-500 watt halogen light bulb led to an eclipse in the importance of the central lighting fixture and the hanging lamp (one of the last of these was Achille Castiglioni's "Frisbi" for Flos), favoring, as halogen bulbs did, floor models in which the light reflected off the ceiling. Among the many that were launched in the late 1970s, two are outstanding for the understated elegance with which they employ halogen technology: Tobia Scarpa's "Papillona" for Flos (1977) and Gianfranco Frattini's "Megaron" for Artemide (1979).

EXHIBITIONS

Italy: The New Domestic Landscape/Achievements and Problems of Italian Design. This exhibition, organized by Emilio Ambasz for the Museum of Modern Art in New York City, contributed much toward making 1972 a landmark year for Italian design. On one hand, it confirmed the triumph that this creative sector had enjoyed in Italy; on the other, it provoked a critical reexamination of the phenomenon, taking stock of the lasting cultural values, versus those that were merely transitory, that it had introduced. It consisted of a collection of 160 objects for the home that had been produced in the previous decade, broken down into three groups based on: the coherence of technology and form with production processes (for example Piretti's "Plia" or Zanuso and Sapper's "Doney" television); the sociocultural implications underlying formal choices (for example, Ceretti-Derossi-Rosso's "Pratone" or Raimondi's mirrors); the objects' flexibility in use with reference to their functions (for example, Becchi's "Amfibio" sofa-bed or Munari's "Abitacolo." A second section consisted of twelve rooms designed expressly for the exhibition. The participation announcement requested "proposals for micro-environments and micro-events, the design of spaces and articles that singularly or collectively represent home lifestyles, and the demonstration of ceremonial and ritual models to which they might apply." The opportunity to propose environments for no precise client induced many of the participants (who in general could be classed as designers and counter-designers) to plan hypothetical living situations unlikely to correspond to reality, freed of the constraints of the Italian design context that many of them had contributed to making.

With particular reference to uses and typologies, the installations were conceived for two different lifestyles: some focused on fixed pieces, others on mobile pieces. Joe Colombo, with the contribution of Ignazia

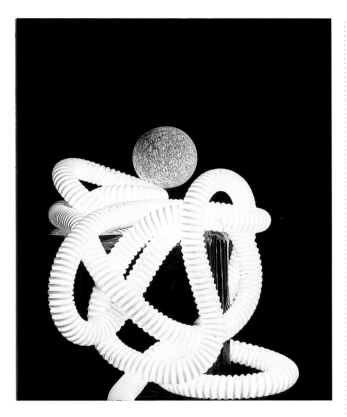

From top: the "Boalum," a "boa of light" designed in 1969 by Livio Castiglioni and Gianfranco Frattini, using a string of five-watt bulbs inserted into a flexible tube of transparent plastic; the "Atollo," designed by Vico Magistretti, and manufactured by O-Luce (1977); the "Frisbi" hanging lamp offering direct, diffused, and reflected light, with diffuser in opalescent methacrylate suspended from three very fine steel wires, designed by Achille Castiglioni and manufactured by Flos (1978).

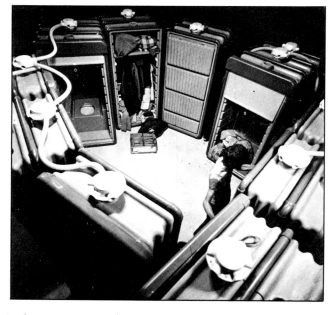

In these two pages, four settings designed for the exhibition "Italy: The New Domestic Landscape."

Top: the "Total Furnishing Unit" by Joe Colombo and Ignazia Favata, a series of pieces of equipment assembled in blocks that satisfied a wide range of living requirements.

Above: Ettore Sottsass' proposal, a series of plastic containers mounted on castors that could be mixed and matched to create different living areas, from the kitchen to the bedroom.

Favata, designed the "Total Furnishing Unit," that is, a series of block structures equipped as kitchen, lavatory, living room, and bedroom.

Ettore Sottsass proposed a system for community living that was not closed behind definitive walls but rather was open to new and changing configurations. The idea of the house as a cemetery of family memories was rejected outright. It was a series of mobile modules—plastic containers mounted on wheels—that could be opened and arranged according to the user's wishes, to be mixed and matched to enliven different areas: kitchen, living room, shower, bookcase, closet, or jukebox. Thanks to the units' mobility and flexibility of arrangement, the traditional roles assigned to domestic spaces became irrelevant; it was the user who indicated, through the arrangement he selected, his psychological state. Sottsass insisted that the form of the object and the compositions that could be generated were purposely ungraceful, in order to combat the sense of ownership and object fetishism: "I was not the least bit interested in making elegant or graceful objects, and even less so in designing silent things that leave the viewer secure in his psychic or cultural status quo. The idea was to be able to make furniture in a sort of orgy of applications for plastics that leaves one with a sense of detachment and perhaps indifference.

"These pieces, which become vulgar containers, just ordinary boxes, hold all the other elements conceived to meet the traditional list of domestic needs that mass-production society has formulated bit by bit. Depending on the ethnic culture of the user of these units, the needs list grows longer or shorter, but the containers themselves remain impassive; they are formally exonerated from the ethnic state of ownership, and the solution to the problem becomes a question of quantity and not of quality." (Ettore Sottsass, 1972).

Gae Aulenti proposed an interior conceived as an urban space in which the furnishing elements appeared as buildings. Great red fiberglass pyramids made up of three distinct elements—one linear and the other two angular—created concave and convex multipurpose spaces. A few articles designed by Aulenti were included in the environment: a table, a chair and a lamp. For the rest, the flexible elements could be adjusted to form a bed, a bookcase, a sofa. A quote from Borges, repeated in the film illustrating the project, highlighted the elegant illusionism of the invention: "Nothing is built on stone, it is all on sand, but we must build as though the sand were stone".

In his installation Gaetano Pesce set the scene for the archaeological recovery of a piece of an underground city built after the great atomic catastrophe of the year 2000 and discovered by survivors from other areas one thousand years later. It was the reconstruction of a habitat from which only large spaces in nonbiodegradable materials (rigid polyurethane) remained. These spaces suggested the existence of minimal communities whose members isolated themselves in womblike niches, on shapeless, all-enveloping mattresses. The dwelling had a 5 $\frac{1}{4}$ yard (4.8 meter) square floor plan, 3 $\frac{9}{10}$ yards (3.6 meters) high, designed for a couple belonging to a twelve-person commune. Access was provided by a ladder, and the dwelling stretched along a diagonal axis: the walls and fixed furnishings were built-in blocks of rigid and semirigid polyurethane; the seats were of flexible polyurethane. A gloomy, tomblike geometry dominated in all the rooms, which the photographic "documentation" showed to be inhabited by sleeping nude figures. A great funerary pyramid of industrial design and contemporary society, Pesce's environment suggested a design that identified totally with the figurative arts and instead of offering products proposed apocalyptic messages about its own condemnation and death.

Archizoom Associates, refusing to "pronounce from on high" and present preconceived living situations, presented an empty gray room. Inside, a speaker suspended from the ceiling broadcast the voice of a little girl describing a bright and colorful domestic space. Thus, the group rejected a single vision in favor of the many that would be created, uncontrollably, in the minds of all the people who listened to the little girl's voice. Not a single utopia, therefore, but as many as there were listeners who imagined the space. "In place of the complex technology of living spaces that gave rise to improbable theories on the future of housing, the group preferred to leave it up to the public to imagine, stimulated by a vague account, its own home. Our motto at the time was 'Living is easy,' and by it we meant to sum up the efforts that were necessary to get free of the constraints of the formal avant-gardes, which all over Europe continued to turn out machines for living, with the motto to remind us of the simple right to freely experience one's own domestic space" (Andrea Branzi, *La Casa Calda*).

Closely linked to the idea of the mobile home was Alberto Rosselli's project, with Isao Hosoe, of an aluminum dwelling unit for five or six people, that was portable and expandable. The project took into consideration the two different aspects of a mobile home: ready to travel, at its smallest and most compact; and parked, when the needs of living require expansion and the use

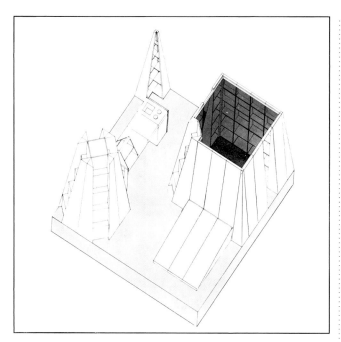

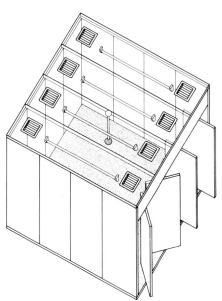

Top: the interior conceived by Gae Aulenti as an urban space. The furnishings consisted of great red fiberglass pyramids—archetypical shapes that could be assembled in different combinations—that punctuated the space cleanly and precisely.

Above: the Archizoom group elected not to present a "real" setting, opting instead for a "conceptual" room that would stimulate the visitors' imaginations.

of all available space.

It was a project that upset traditional conceptions of the mobile home, which tend merely to miniaturize and reduce things to a meaner scale—to treat the home as a container. Indeed, all the furnishings of Rosselli's mobile home were contained within it during transport, and its dimensions were kept within the limits fixed by the highway laws then in force in Europe. Closed, in its traveling format, it occupied 10 $^9/_{10}$ square yards (10 sq. m.) of space; fully open, it reached 30 $^2/_3$ square yards (28 sq. m.), with kitchen, double bed, and wardrobe, and its walls could be dropped to become part of a patio.

Marco Zanuso and Richard Sapper's project proposed a new use for large transatlantic shipping containers. Conceived of not so much as a vacation-home unit but more as an emergency refuge in times of calamity, or temporary housing for communities outside urbanized territories, it could be expanded and grouped. It was made up of stockable units whose outer surfaces provided a ready protective wrapping for storage and transport. Inside, there were two large "pods," one for the bed and the other for the kitchen, with lavatory and wardrobe to the sides, which slid out toward the exterior once the container's hatches were opened. The hatches themselves functioned as an adjustable-height platform on which the pods rested.

Mario Bellini's "Kar-a-Sutra," described in the section on automobiles, was also presented at this exhibition.

The Eurodomus exhibitions. The third Eurodomus, a pacesetting exhibition dealing with the modern home and organized by the *Domus* review, took place in Milan at the Palazzo dell'Arte May 14 to 24, 1970. Open to the public at large—unlike the Salone del Mobile which was restricted to those active in the sector—it was well-attended with 85,000 visitors, including 26,600 foreigners.

Within the context of the general show Eurodomus had invited a few graphic and experimental artists to participate, including Livio Castiglioni, Giulio Confalonieri, Ennio Lucini, and Pino Tovaglia.

In the large, open dark space over the grand staircase, Castiglioni achieved with the simplest of means a surprisingly luminous and sonorous effect: the "action" of electrical energy on metal wires suspended from wall to wall across the void heated the wires to the point of incandescence. Luminous and vibrating, they expanded and dropped, tipping off mercury switches that cut off the current. Immediately cooling, the wires contracted and rose, bringing the switches back to their normal

Alberto Rosselli and Isao Hosoe's project for "Italy: The New Domestic Landscape," a portable aluminum dwelling unit that expanded from its traveling format of 10 $^9/_{10}$ to 30 $^2/_3$ square yards (10 to 28 sq. m.) when fully open.

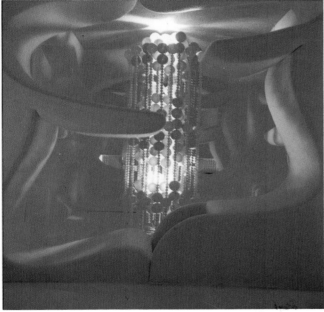

The Third Eurodomus, Milan (May 14–24, 1970).

Top: Gio Ponti's "La Casa Adatta," a dwelling whose spaces could be extended due to folding wall partitions. Ponti also designed the handy folding furniture.

Above: Bayer presented Varner Panton's "Visiona Due," a sort of soft cavern with dralon-lined walls. The overall effect was enlivened by seating arrangements at various heights.

position, starting the whole process over again. Speakers placed to one side transmitted the amplified sound of the wires' vibration into the air.

In the park, inside a large pressurized cupola designed by De Pas-D'Urbino-Lomazzi, was a "Telemuseum" display. Twenty televisions lined up along the walls continually transmitted tapes of artistic events. It was the first exclusively video display in Italy for a nonspecialized public and anticipated the revolution that was soon to take place with the videocassette. The participating artists were Vincenzo Agnetti, Gianni Colombo, Gino Marotta, Fabio Mauri, Henry Martin, Michelangelo Pistoletto, and art critic Tommaso Trini.

A proposal for a dwelling called "La Casa Adatta" was drawn up by Giò Ponti for the event. Its layout was based on the extension of usable spaces with fully retractable, folding wall partitions (a solution that Ponti had already tested in a number of his interior-design projects). In this case, an 87 $1/2$-square-yard (80 sq. m.) dwelling could be expanded another 65 $2/3$ square yards (60 sq. m.) by opening the folding partitions. "A new idea for the home," wrote Giò Ponti in *Domus*, "that answers the requirement of not wasting space (lower costs, easier to maintain), but which at the same time is big and versatile for living: an invention where 'less is more', to quote Mies Van der Rohe." The folding pieces of furniture, occupying little space and easy to move, were designed by Ponti specifically for the project, and they were an airy addition to this all-white installation that was filled with the light that came through its large windows.

This exhibition also featured Bayer's "Visiona Due," conceived by the famous Scandinavian designer Varner Panton. It was a single environment, sculpted like a soft cavern, rich in color, and enlivened by seating arrangements at various heights, wrapped in a single covering of red dralon.

Poltronova, using Ettore Sottsass' design, displayed a living, dining and bed space, taking the occasion to present the new "Mobili Grigi" collection in molded fiberglass on a design by the same architect.

The fourth and last Eurodomus took place in Turin, May 18 to 28, 1972. To avoid duplication with respect to the Salone del Mobile, and to highlight the experimental nature of this exhibition, Giò Ponti promoted two guidelines: "a new way to conceive of the dwelling," and "mass production that answers to these basic cultural assumptions." The industrial sectors therefore participated on two fronts: with projects for environments and with objects of their own production.

"The house must be a simple affair," Ponti wrote in *Domus*. "We would like it if the architect, designer, or

The Fourth Eurodomus, Turin (May 18–28, 1972). Top: Cesare Casati and Emanuele Ponzio's project for a 5 ¹/₂ x 8 ³/₄ yard (5 x 8 m.) dwelling for a couple, completely finished in Print plastic laminate and with floors rigged out as containers. Above: "The House of the Five Senses" presented by the French review La Maison de Marie Claire: five environments, each dedicated to a different type of sensory stimulation. The photograph shows the "tactile" zone, where visitors were invited to enjoy the soft, pleasant-to-the-touch material that shaped the space.

artist's effort could be always be gauged, in the case of home construction—even at the industrial level—by the *degree of enchantment* one feels when looking at it from the outside, and by the *degree of enchantment* one feels when living inside it."

To illustrate the dynamics of the relationship between the entities that designed, constructed, and lived in the house, and to determine whether there was effective exchange of ideas, Eurodomus launched an experiment called "Codice: Incontri e Scontri sulla Casa" (Code: Agreements and Disagreements over the Home). An architect (Angelo Mangiarotti for the design), a family (the user, represented by a working-class family) and a Turinese furniture retailer (Galliano) were invited to realistically plan two dwelling models on the basis of precise requirements and economic means (70 square yards [64 sq m] and 12,000,000 lire to spend for remodeling and furnishings). Both professionals had at their disposal two sceneshifters and movable wood panels that served as internal walls and partitions. The family was given furniture catalogues to consult, with addresses of Turin-based stores where they could go to pick out their articles. The results were then compared and discussed.

Expanding on the theme of dwellings to that of the neighborhood, the same experimental procedure was applied to a second operation: groups of youths were asked to offer a critique of their neighborhood and suggestions for improvements. In both experiments, the events were videotaped and provided the visual material for the public's participation in the discussions between designers, family, and experts. Among the numerous proposals for living that arose out of the fourth Eurodomus were two involving prefabricated models: Fabrizio Coccia and Gianfranco Fini's "Cubolibre," an all-purpose plastic laminate cube measuring 2 ³/₄ yards (2.5 m) per side, which embraced in its basic modular form all the fixtures for living; and Cesare Casati and Emanuele Ponzio's project, which used floors rigged out as containers. The use of a single material throughout, Abet's pink plastic laminate, gave it a uniform appearance.

The French review *La Maison de Marie Claire* constructed "The House of the Five Senses" to remind visitors and designers that in the domestic environment all five of the human senses receive stimulation: at the end of a dark hall was a room frescoed in different shades of color to gratify the sense of sight; moving on, the "hall of temptations" stimulated the sense of taste by means of a system of mirrors that reflected an infinity of images of foods; touch was called into play by the passage between walls lined with fabrics pleasant to

caress; smell by a room transformed into a stretch of seacoast, with images of the sea and marine life projected onto the walls, soft rocks to sit on, and the pungent odor of a storm at sea permeating it all; lastly, the sense of hearing was stimulated by a hilly environment with the sound of a waterfall in a forest.

Studio 65's display "Babilonia 72" stood out for its originality. This group broke the spell of the furnished home by presenting the large base of an Ionic column, broken in two (it was a funerary symbol as well as an oversized toy). Entering, the visitor found an interior invaded by objects aimed at expressing very playful dwelling metaphors: the central block kitchen became a huge, well-equipped brazier, the living room a rubbery sofa of acanthus leaves, the bed an altar for "offering sacrifices to Venus."

Il Design Italiano degli Anni '50. This exhibition was organized by Kartell's research center, Centrokappa. It ran from September 26 to October 30, 1976, and offered a broad overview of the design culture of the 1950s, highlighting its developments in the fields of graphics, objects, textiles, fashion, and interior decoration. With a vast array of objects on display and accurately detailed reconstructions of a few settings, it was the first and up to that point the most eloquent testimony to the creative vitality and the social and moral tensions that characterized the years prior to the consumer boom of the 1960s.

The Fifties marked the postwar socioeconomic transformation of a nation that was laying the foundations for its industrial development. They were the years in which Italian design came into its own, emerging from an indistinct hash that mingled graphics, advertising, furnishing, and other fields.

This exhibition also had the merit of reviving interest in some of the great Italian architects and design pioneers (the extraordinary Mollino, for example) and in the style of the 1950s, with its delight in overt structural play, the use of metal rods, and Giò Ponti's and Fornasetti's decorative imagination.

The Triennales. After repeated postponements the XV Triennale finally opened on September 20, 1973, under the direction of painter Remo Brindisi. The most interesting changes evident were in the distinction between architecture and design, and the lack of a preordained theme. The international architecture section was headed up by Aldo Rossi, while that dedicated to industrial design was under the direction of Ettore Sottsass. The designers participated on invitation, submitting not objects but videotapes that were run contin-

Above: the large base of the Ionic column presented at the fourth Eurodomus by Studio 65, with the acanthus-leaf sofa in painted polyurethane.

Right: a beechwood chair sculpted by Carlo Mollino, one of the leading figures in the "Italian Design of the 1950s" exhibition.

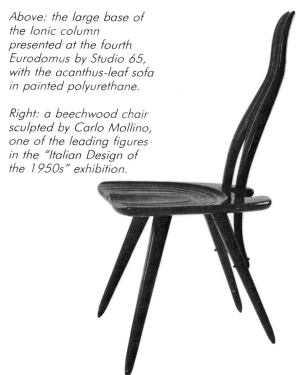

XV Triennale (1973).

Top: Two works presented at the "Contatto Arte-Città" event organized by Giulio Macchi: Alberto Burri's concrete-and-steel theater, as notable as the artist's more famous compositions; Giorgio de Chirico's "mysterious bath," a translation of one of his famous paintings into three dimensions. Colorful statues swim in a marble pool; a cabin on stilts stands in contemplation of the scene.

Above: the Italian section organized by Eduardo Vittoria and Roberto Guiducci.

uously on a lineup of television sets. There was also a sector dedicated to "national sections," organized by individual participating countries, and an "Italian section," organized by Eduardo Vittoria and Roberto Guiducci. The theme shared by these two sections was the dwelling and the relationship between architecture and the city, touching on land-use planning issues. There was one more exhibit, dedicated to Mackintosh chairs and Joe Colombo's work.

The most popular event took place in the park: it was "Contatto arte-città," organized by Giulio Macchi with the participation of various artists. Arman had conceived a theater-seating tier with iron chairs in all styles rising from concrete steps that engulfed them like limestone fossils, Alberto Burri presented a concrete theater with painted steel stage wings, Giorgio de Chirico created a "mysterious bath," a transposition into three dimensions of one of his famous paintings: marble statues and colored animals swam in a marble swimming pool with a painted "parquet" floor, and a cabin on stilts in one corner of it. Gino Marotta participated with an "artificial Eden," featuring marble benches and pink plexiglass animals that children could climb up on and play with.

Apart from rare bright spots, this Triennale was rather uninspiring and unfocused in its aims. It had been undermined by a slipshod approach in general, and by an inability to communicate ideas. The organization had also been burdened for some time by the problem of the renewal of the institutional structures, insufficient funds, political indecision, and divisive leadership.

By the time a new board of directors for the XVI Triennal, was appointed to manage the organization, the situation was a shambles. To this group, headed by Giampaolo Fabris, goes the credit for having launched a renewal program that transformed the Triennale from an episodic exhibition at three-year intervals into a permanently active "museum of progress" that was more attuned to the present social context, one that had undergone profound changes since 1923, the year of the first exhibition.

It was an initiative that was not limited to merely intensifying the rhythm of exhibition events, but supported the traditional shows with research, workshops, and the like.

On December 15, 1979, after much debate and indecision, the XVI Triennale opened its doors with a first cycle of exhibits. The design sector was broken down into three exhibitions that bore witness to the innovative ferment just then emerging. The first was "Inizio di un Censimento" (Beginning of a Census), dealing with the poetics of some of the most famous Italian designers; the second was "La Casa Decorata," (The Decorated Home), where the latest generation of designers (Michele De Lucchi, Martine Bedin, Sauro Mainardi, Paola Navone, et al) were invited to participate in a revival of the decorative idiom, as part of an international competition on the theme of "the home, after the functional" in which creative examples in the postfunctionalist era were examined; and the third was "Paesaggio Casalingo" (Home Landscape), sponsored by home articles manufacturer Alessi, organized by Alessandro Mendini and with installation by Hans Hollein.

Among the young designers Michele De Lucchi stood out (we shall meet with him again in the 1980s, working out of the Memphis group); he showed a series of models for "small, colorful, idiotic" electrical appliances; they were reassuring machines, even without their instructions for use. Another very important novelty was fashion's debut at the Triennale, which confirmed its cultural influence and presented it as a new environmental discipline. A multivision display designed by the firm Eleonora Peduzzi Riva highlighted the links between fashion and history over the past thirty years.

An additional section, the "Galleria del Disegno" (Drawing Gallery), was dedicated to the solo exhibition of a young architect named Mario Botta. A unique figure in the field of architecture, in the Eighties Botta shifted his focus of study to the design of tables, chairs and lamps.

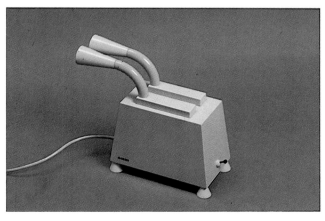

XVI Triennale (1979).

Top: the room presented by Paola Navone at the "Decorated Home" exhibition. The floor was silk-screened black and white in imitation of composite concrete tiles; color slides of decorative

studies by Abet Print were projected onto the furnishings, which consisted of a door, a curtain, a cupboard, and a small table.

Above: Michele De Lucchi's model of a toaster in painted wood.

THE COMPASSO D'ORO AWARDS

Following the tenth presentation of the Compasso d'Oro in 1970, nine years passed before it was given again. In 1979, the twenty-fifth year since its foundation, thanks to the financial support of the City of Milan, this important initiative was resumed. To make up for its absence, it was decided to assign forty-two Compasso d'Oro awards taking into consideration work done between 1970 and 1979, subdivided as follows: thirty-five to products and work in the field of graphic design; three to companies or organizations that had distinguished themselves for their overall activity in the field of design (Olivetti, Kartell, Rome's Istituto Superiore per il Disegno Industriale); and four to the most important efforts in the fields of original design and design promotion.

INTERIOR DECOR REVIEWS

With the furniture industry's growth in the 1970s, a number of interior-decoration magazines were born. The year 1971 saw the founding of *Casa Amica*, a monthly supplement to the Rizzoli editorial group's magazine for women, *Amica*. It achieved great success among millions of reader-consumers who appreciated "its thorough coverage, the style that characterized its choices, and the practical spirit that determined them..." And the Rizzoli group came out with *Brava Casa* in 1974, offering columns on subjects ranging from furniture to gardening and do-it-yourself activities.

Mondadori, which had always shown interest in home issues, started publication of *Casaviva* in 1972, announcing in the pilot issue, "It is our hope that in time this review will become a habit for everybody who loves his own home, and most do; for young couples, fine families with two or three children, singles who do not feel alone because they live in a comfortable environment and at home always have something to do... *Casaviva* will be concerned with interior decoration, but also with home economy."

Over the decade great changes took place in the architecture reviews in the oldest tradition—*Casabella* and *Domus*, which together with *Modo* (a new monthly design review, founded in 1977) were all at one time or another under the editorship of Alessandro Mendini. Since Mendini worked with Studio Alchemia beginning in 1976, the reviews that he directed gave ample coverage to many of the radical design experiments, conceptual art, postmodern trends, and to the renewal of the design idiom in general.

ART SHOWS

As part of the ideological thrust of the late 1960s, the Venice Biennale came to be challenged and boycotted by artists as an obsolete institution. Compounding its troubles was a statute inherited from the Fascist era that provided for commissions whose task seemed to be to identify "masters" of an extreme rightwing political bent. In the course of the 1970s, however, many of these protesters who worked with metaphorical representations of the contemporary world and of opulent society got over their doubts, fears, and self-censureship about the politicizing of art, and suggestions for overcoming this cultural impasse and for developing a keener recognition of individual

In 1979, after nine dormant years, the Compasso d'Oro award was revived, accompanied by an important display that offered a historical overview. Among the award-winning products was the "Strip" line of soft chairs and sofas (top) designed in 1972 by Cini Boeri and Laura Griziotti for Arflex, and the "Osa" kitchen block (above) designed in 1976 by Makio Hasuike for Ariston. In the furnishing sector, the Compasso d'Oro was awarded to Bellini for his "Bambole" armchairs,

manufactured by B&B; to Magistretti for his "Maralunga" sofa (Cassina) and for his "Atollo" lamp (O-Luce); to Bruno Munari for his all-purpose "Abitacolo" piece (Robots); to the Castiglionis for their "Parentesi" lamp (Flos); to Salocchi for his "Metro Sistema" kitchen (Alberti); to Mari for his "Delfina" chair (Driade); to Stoppino and Acerbis for their "Sheraton" cases (Acerbis); and to De Pas, D'Urbino, Lomazzi for their "Sciangai" clothes stand (Zanotta).

poetics came out of the creation of *arte povera* and conceptual art in the 1960s.

The freeing of the expressive medium from social constraints, the lack of interest in formalizing it into objects, and the revival of theatrics in many of the performances and happenings that took place in the galleries or at large (picked up in the plays and productions of such avant-garde theater groups as the Bread & Puppet Theater, Magazzini Criminali, etc.) led to an attenuation of the climate of exchange that had existed between the sector producing interior-decoration articles and the world of art in preceding years.

In the early 1970s, a new generation of artists was born. They were not easily labeled as a single group or trend, being oriented more toward individual experiments aimed at discovering new approaches rather than at formulating new images. On one hand this reestablished the "heroic stature of the artist" (as Achille Bonito Oliva wrote), but on the other it laid the groundwork for a stretching of art's boundaries. In Italy this second effect became evident in the use of unusual, untried materials (with the accent on the process leading up to a finished product rather than on the work itself), and in the contemplation of the properties and pecularities of art as communication, as a profession, and as history.

The decade was most marked by the artists of *arte povera* (Merz, Anselmo, Boetti, Penone, Zorio, Calzolari, Pistoletto, etc.) and by the international trend of minimal art, so named for the attention its adherents (Morris, Judd, Flavin, Serra, Sol Lewitt, Andre) give to the study of basic structures; and conceptual art, in which the creative principle is based on the visualization of a word or a sentence, or the linguistic definition of an object reproposed independent of its utilization (sometimes only as a memory of a real or potential experience, or as a citation from art history) and whose practitioners include Paolini, Beuys, Weiner, Kosuth, Barry, Huebler, and Wilson. Although in the 1960s items such as polyester and computers were used by progressive artists as expressive media, and were, in themselves, the message at one time (a section of the 1970 XXXV Venice Biennale was dedicated to the art-technology connection), in these newer art forms the medium seemed to have lost its importance. "Faith in the artistic process has taken the place of faith in technology," according to Harald Szeemann; and this new faith found its key spokesman in the German artist Joseph Beuys. Those artists who had identified with *arte povera* continued a conceptual, but ineffectual dialogue with that trend, isolating themselves from the ideals that had originally bound the group together.

Top: Michelangelo Pistoletto, The Sacred Conversation *(1973). Mirror-polished stainless-steel plate with silkscreened images*

by Zorio, Anselmo, and Penone.

Above: Mario Merz, Double Igloo *(1979).*

There was a renewed interest in the human physique and its expressive possibilities; these years gave rise to performances labeled "body art" or "behavioral art," which through the medium of the artist's body and behavior tended to involve the spectator, sometimes in a way that recalled the ambiguity of an "s&m" show (Gina Pace, Urs Lüthi, Herman Nitsch). The 1972 XXXVI Biennale dedicated to the theme of "Art or Behavior," introduced several young behavioralist artists including Bendini, De Dominicis, Fabro, Merz, Olivotto, and Vaccari, and contrasted their works with that of the post-informal naturalists of twenty years before (Morlotti, Moreni, Guerreschi). The Austrian povilion exhibited the work of Hans Hollein, an architect, designer and interior decorator of international fame, known also for his work in collaboration with many Italian furniture manufacturers. The work presented here was entitled "Opera o Comportamento—Vita o Morte-Situazioni Quotidiane," (Work of Art or Behavior—Life or Death—Daily Predicaments), and showed an example of how an elegant shape can be given to a space using just the constructive elements of architecture.

From a broader perspective, starting with *arte povera*, the interest in the medium and its transformation at the hands of man or of time (or even of the atmosphere, as in Walter De Maria's work), and the interest in a "natural" medium as opposed to the "artificial" media that pop art had explored, gave rise to a series of artistic initiatives that were closely aligned with the conceptual and which took the name of "land art" or "earth art." This art could be furrows carved into a frozen river, like those Richard Long did, or stones thrown into the Great Salt Lake to form a gigantic spiral, like Robert Smithson's work, or the packaging of landmarks, like Christo's. The environmental artists saw in these ephemeral ideograms an experience of nature that was an alternative to and a reaction against the hyper-urbanization of contemporary society. The vehicle used for the diffusion and sale of many of these works of art were photographs, personally autographed by the artists; it is uncertain how tongue-in-cheek the artists were about doing this, but it no doubt made a mockery of collectors who invest in "artist goods."

These experiments were shown at the 1976 Venice Biennale in the Visual Arts and Architecture sector, under the direction of Vittorio Gregotti. Richard Long, representing Great Britain, showed photographic documentation of his stone trails, *Line in Ireland* (1974) and *Line on the Himalayas* (1975). The Italian section offered works dealing with the environment (social, urban, extraurban), ranging from murals to solutions to

Top: Luciano Fabro, Feet *(1969–72). Silk and Portuguese pink marble.*

Above: Alighiero Boetti, Planisphere *(1973). Embroidery.*

From top: Nicola De Maria, Not Having Traveled by Sea *(1978)*; Pierpaolo Calzolari, Painting and Fire-Eater *(1980)*; Giulio Paolini, The Swan's Exile, *installation ot the Venice Biennale (1979–1984).*

the housing struggle and executed by various artists and culturally involved people, such as Ugo La Pietra, Riccardo Dalisi, Ugo Nespolo, or by groups committed to community experiences. The exhibition "Ambiente/Arte," organized by Germano Celant, was a clever retrospective, starting with the reconstruction of rooms designed by artists of the early twentieth century (Kandinsky and Mondrian) and concluding with the work of contemporary artists such as Mario Merz, Joseph Beuys, Bruce Nauman, Jannis Kounellis, Daniel Buren, Maria Nordman, Sol Lewitt, and Robert Irwin who had adopted the environmental experience as the force behind their work.

While the Biennale was offering its summary of the situation, a new climate was already forming that would propel us toward the 1980s. Young artists from various schools appeared on the horizon: Remo Salvadori and Marco Bagnoli, continuers of the conceptual approach; Sandro Chia, Francesco Clemente, Mimo Paladino and others, promoters of a return to the painted work of art, to figurative art understood as a revival of the painting medium ("Transavanguardia" was the name applied to this movement by Achille Bonito Oliva). It was the start of a schism, accompanied by heated debate, between what the Sixties and Seventies had proposed and the pictorial vision that this generation offered. This schism marked the transition into the Eighties, which had been anticipated by postmodern architecture and design and which became official with Paolo Portoghesi's "Strada Novissima" at the 1980 Venice Biennale.

Worthy of mention among the art shows of the decade was "Contemporanea," held in Rome in the underground garage of Villa Borghese, designed by Luigi Moretti. It ran from November 30, 1973 to the end of March 1974 and was organized by the Incontri Internazionali d'Arte group. The aim of this large international show was to demonstrate, through an interdisciplinary presentation, the opportunities for interaction among the various idioms of the artistic avant-garde. The show's different sections (art, film, architecture, design, photography, music, dance, alternative information, and so forth), each with its own curator, made it possible for those who attended to grasp how many new things had emerged, and not just in the field of art, between 1955 and 1973. Alessandro Mendini organized the architecture and design section (one of the most thought-provoking of the whole show) and invited the participation of representatives of radical architecture such as the Gruppo Strum, Ugo La Pietra, the Ufo group, Riccardo Dalisi, Ettore Sottsass, and Andrea Branzi.

INTERIORS

CARLA VENOSTA

Carla Venosta lives and works in Milan, and has carried out most of her work in the furnishing and industrial design sectors. She has won two Compasso d'Oro awards, one in 1979 for a computerized electromedical device and another in 1981 for an integrated dropped ceiling. Her focus of study and her accomplishments show her readiness to implement formal solutions that offer a new style to dwelling models, often based on a large open space shaped by raised platforms and dropped ceilings. She replaced the static space with one full of cadenced movement by means of a coordinated series of images, later adding single functional utility blocks for the kitchen and lavatory.

The house shown here designed by Venosta for Caterina Caselli, a famous singer of the 1960s, is characteristic of her work on interiors. The entrance is telescopic, with inclined walls in highly polished white stucco. The floor is graded slightly upwards, covered in black moquette, and interrupted at regular intervals by fissures of light that mark the passage, turning it into a colorful kaleidoscope that unexpectedly opens into a large, well-lit living room. Here the dynamic of the hallway walls is repeated in the planes of the floor and the ceiling, which are raised or lowered to create specific zones, dividing the dining area from the conversation area. The result is a space whose volumetric definition is enhanced by the two colors used, the white of the walls and ceiling and the black of the moquette. To this Venosta added a few elements that she had designed: the pyramidal sculpture-lamps in strawberry-pink plexiglass, and the pyramid-shaped display case, done with mirrors and plexiglass, to hold a precious jade sculpture.

The Egyptian tone is offset by the "Soriana" armchair and sofas designed in 1970 by Tobia Scarpa for Cassina. Their soft, imprecise forms contrast with the faceted walls of the house and its glittering lights and seem to welcome the visitor.

Preceding pages: in a villa by Gae Aulenti, high-angle view of the living room furnished with pieces by Le Corbusier.

Left: the apartment decorated by Carla Venosta for Caterina Caselli. The entrance, with inclined walls in white stucco, leads to the luminous area of the living room, furnished with "Soriana" armchairs (Cassina) upholstered in striped fabric.

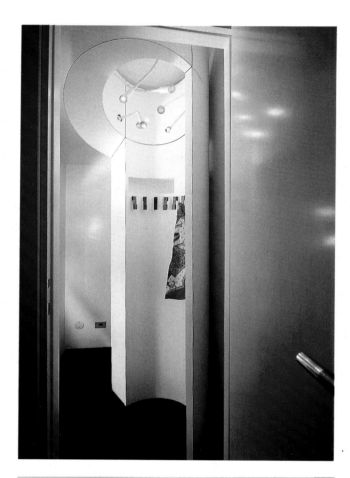

Left: the dressing room. Right: view of the conversation area with, in the foreground, a unit containing hi-fi equipment and, to the right, a display case with precious jade pieces, and a pyramid-shaped lamp, both designed by Carla Venosta.

NANDA VIGO

In 1959, having taken her degree at the Lausanne Polytechnic and completed her apprenticeship in various architecture studios in San Francisco, Nanda Vigo launched her career in Milan. Venturing into the realms of art as well as architecture, she participated in the construction of environments with the likes of artist Lucio Fontana and architect Giò Ponti. Over the years, working alongside of Le Parc, Castellani, Uecker, and others, she explored the kinetic potential of visual-temporal perception. She was at various times a member of the Gruppo Zero, the Aktuell Gruppe, and the Gruppe Licht und Bewegung of Berne; she participated in the XIII Triennale of 1964, the XV Triennale of 1973, and the Venice Biennale of 1982.

Two of Nanda Vigo's interiors, done in 1970–71, are presented here. In the first—the home of an art collector—the task was not to decorate the spaces with works of art, but rather to create a single environment using various different works. The rest of the great collection was housed separately in a cellar-gallery.

The decor is based on two different types of visual and psychological perception. On one hand a sense of "immobility" is created by the use of a single color (electric blue) to dress the walls and the storage units, stripped to their essentials by means of the "metaphysical" chairs by Ceroli in the dining area and through the overall lighting, accomplished with exposed fluorescent tubes. On the other hand, a sensation of "mobility" arises from the shifting reflections of the mirrored surfaces that involve every facet of the room: the ceiling, with a work done in mirrors by Enrico Baj; the walls, with their "chronotopes," overlapping panels in reflective glass by Vigo, and with a "sheet metal" piece by Lucio Fontana; and the floor, with its long table in mirrored, sapphire-blue glass.

In the second house, the night area and facilities are set distinctly apart from the central entrance/living-room area, from which all the other areas are reached. The floors are carpeted in electric-blue acrylic moquette, except the facilities, which are in blue and white ceramic tiles. All the furniture is an integral part of the apartment's structure, placed along its perimeter, leaving most of the space available for the client's personal touches. The single color of the walls and storage elements gives prominence to the works of art. The "functional" furnishings are done in mirrored blue glass with anodized aluminum and steel profiling. A diffused lighting effect is achieved using fluorescent tubes behind a perimetral molding.

In the living room/entrance/conversation area, at the edge of a raised platform is a central block with mirrored blue surfaces holding the bookcase, bar, and stereo, which also acts as the backrest to the long sofa, whose individual seats can be moved about.

In the children's rooms, the closets and ceilings are lined with Print plastic laminate in a striped or checkered blue and sky-blue pattern.

Left: the living room with a "sheet metal" piece by Lucio Fontana and two "Chronotopes," overlapping panels, by Nanda Vigo; a work made with mirrors, by Enrico Baj, decorates the ceiling. The low table is the architect's "Essential" model for Driade (1971).

Following pages: dining area with Mario Cerioli's chairs (Poltronova) and paintings by Piero Dorazio.

Left: the dining area of the second house, enclosed by sliding glass and mirrored panels. The "Blok" table (Acerbis) and the chairs upholstered in imitation monkey fur were designed by Nanda Vigo.

Above: a child's bedroom furnished with a central bed-storage unit in sky-blue and navy Print plastic laminate.

GIORGIO PES

iorgio Pes was born and lives in Rome, where he studied at the Accademia di Belle Arti, specializing in set design, interior decoration, and antiques. At one time he owned an antiques gallery in Rome, which deepened his knowledge of art and of historic homes (he also renovated a fifteenth-century Venetian building overlooking the Grand Canal). For many years he worked in the film industry, collaborating with Luchino Visconti, working on the furnishings and historical documentation for *Gattopardo* and *Boccaccio '70* as well as furnishing the homes of Visconti himself.

The home shown here is an apartment in Rome, done by Pes with Roberto Federici. It holds one of the most extraordinary collections of American art in Europe (there are works by Hans Arp, Louise Nevelson, Andy Warhol, César, Roy Lichtenstein, Lucio Fontana, Frank Stella, and Victor Vasarely, as well as four marvelous Canalettos, an eighteenth-century bronze horse, and more). A landscape unfolding in generous and suggestive rhythms was created as a backdrop to these works of art, in perfect harmony with the splendor of the building the apartment occupies. In order to avoid

the effect of a house-museum, the works were made an integral part of home life; they are distributed throughout the house, from the dining area to the bedroom and bath. Some of them contribute in a striking way to the decor, and were conceived and executed for this purpose by their famous creators. Beverly Pepper designed the dining-room table base, which is a bent iron band, projected toward infinity; Jean-Claude Fahri created the handsome living-room doors, in brown plexiglass with iridescent patches in relief, and the guest-room decorations; Salvatore did the study doors with their gold and silver linear patterns.

Many works of art and few pieces of furniture, therefore, were planned to avoid the interference of other presences and other colors. The living room's conversation pit is done in the same beige as the moquette that rides up the seats and onto the backrests; the pillows pick up the dominant colors of the works that hang on the walls. In the bedroom, the setting is made uniform by finishing everything in the same shade of brown (including a brown fur bedspread), the better to set off the aggressive sensuality of Tom Wesselmann's *Mouth with Cigarette* and Fontana's *Red Slash*.

Left: detail of the living room with a work by Roy Lichtenstein. The brown plexiglass door with iridescent patches in relief was designed by Jean-Claude Fahri.

Overview of the living room with, from the left to right, works by César, Robert Motherwell, Louise Nevelson, and Andy Warhol.

Above: dining room with a long table supported by an iron sculpture by Beverly Pepper. In the background, a painting by Frank Stella; to the left, a Pop canvas by Tom Wesselmann; to the right, above the long travertine shelf, a painting by Victor Vasarely.

Top, right: bedroom with Fontana's large Red Slash *and Wesselmann's* Mouth with Cigarette. *On the table at the foot of the bed, a Lichtenstein piece and a sculpture by Giò Pomodoro.*
Below, right: a detail showing Beverly Pepper's sculpture/base of the dining-room table.

ROBERTO MONSANI

Architect Monsani of Florence started his career in 1957, working in the fields of architecture and interior design. From 1982 he has designed all of Salvatore Ferragamo's shops worldwide. Some of his ideas, such as the furniture designed specifically for the two interiors examined here, were produced in series in 1974 by the Acerbis firm under the name *Life Collection*.

The first home is set in a renovated monastery on a hill near Florence. On the ground floor, beneath the portico, the entrance, living room, library, and dining area face one another. The upper floor houses the bedrooms, which open out onto a large terrace set over the portico. The restoration of the rooms and their interiors has preserved the sense of religious tranquillity transmitted by the large spaces with their cross vaults and high ceilings.

Contributing to this special atmosphere are the wooden door, with its light-filtering grid pattern that opens onto the portico, the living-room wall unit, with its overhanging volumes and suffused lighting effects created by plexiglass spacers set between the wall and the unit, and the roughly knotted mats that cover the floors. Large tables and low sofas, with transparent methacrylate bases that participate in the chiaroscuro play in which all the furnishings take part, rest on these mats without interrupting the horizontal flow of the floor plan.

The second apartment, remodeled by Monsani, is in a nineteenth-century *palazzo* overlooking the Arno river. The architect retained the ceiling height of 5 $^2/_3$ yards (5.2 m.) that he had inherited from a prior restoration, organizing the space around it so as to exalt its unusual dimensions. The entrance is centrally located between the living and dining rooms. Its ceiling consists of a series of horizontal panels that drop down one yard, leaving, however, the original ceiling in sight, and providing the house with a double ilumination effect, both direct and indirect, by means of recessed lights. In the living room is a loft designated as the play corner. The materials used here are the same as in the interior described above, arranged in a graphic cadence of blacks and whites. Stairs, mezzanine, and tabletops are in black plastic laminate; the Belgian marble used for the living-room fireplace is also black. The plastic laminate walls and the moquette in handwoven natural wool are white, as is the leather upholstery of the armchairs (which were also designed by the architect). Accents of methacrylate, both transparent and luminous, reinforce this graphic layout; this material was used in the back wall of the dining room (where the perforations of the white plastic-laminate panels are plugged with methacrylate disks to allow the passage of light from fluorescent tubes set behind them), and for the bookcase shelves.

The suite of rooms separated by sliding doors finished in plastic laminate and illuminated by small spotlights mounted on metal tracking. In the foreground, a madonna and child by Jacopo del Sellato; in the background, the living room with furniture from Monsani's "Life Collection" (Acerbis).

The living room with its high, cross-vaulted ceiling and shadow play on the expanses of wall. The armchairs and sofas were designed by Monsani.

Top: the dining room. Above: the staircase linking the day and night zones.
Right: the dining area of the second apartment. The back wall is in perforated white plastic laminate to create a luminous and decorative effect.

Left: the loft designated as the "play corner" exploits the height of the ceilings. The table and bookshelf make up part of the "Life Collection" series.
Top: the living room with a marble fireplace and methacrylate bookshelves.

Above: the black plastic laminate sliding door separating the entrance and the dining area.

The living room illuminated by a wide, arched window overlooking the Amalfi sea.

GAE AULENTI

Gae Aulenti was quite young when she completed her studies and started to work on *Casabella-Continuità*'s editorial staff (her stint there coincided with the years of Ernesto Rogers' editorship, 1955–65). From that time up to the present, she has pursued an extremely full career as an architect, designer, and set designer (earning along the way the title of chevalier of the Légion d'Honneur, bestowed on her by French President François Mitterrand for her restoration of the Gare d'Orsay in Paris). Reviewing her works, we can start with the neo-Liberty debate and the bookcase she presented at the 1960 "Nuovi Disegni per il Mobile Italiano" exhibition; then comes the splendid "Arrivo al Mare" installation for the 1964 Triennale, inspired by the women inhabiting Picasso's works, cut in large silhouettes and multiplied by the mirrored walls. In 1966 she did the Paris Olivetti store, in which the exhibition space was shaped as if it were a freestanding object, with no separation between furnishing, walls, and ceilings. It all evolved out of a single material—white plastic laminate—shaped in a continuous line, no longer as a mere backdrop to objects on display but instead practically competing with them. Breaking every purist or functionalist rule then in vogue, the volumes and multiple levels became exhibition platforms as well as seating, like steps overlooking a piazza. In a masterfully dramatic ploy, Aulenti placed two symbolic entities in sight of the street in order to arrest the attention of even the most distracted stroller along the Faubourg Saint-Honoré: a large wooden African statue—an archetypical personality—who gazes curiously at the machinery of the future, powerfully represented by the second entity, a red spaceship-shaped column set in the center of the store as if it had come in for a momentary landing.

She also did a number of installations for Fiat and for the Knoll stores in New York and Milan. Her contribution to the 1972 exhibition in New York was an installation vibrant with historical references, ambiguous and complex, yet not complicated. She invented extraordinary scenic machines for Luca Ronconi's theatrical productions and in 1986 remodeled the Palazzo Grassi as an exhibition center. Finally there are two pieces among the many she did for series production that we feel represent her highly personal design approach, independently of scale: the "Pipistrello" table lamp for Martinelli Luce (1969), used in the Paris Olivetti store; and a table for Fontana Arte (1979), a sheet of glass suspended from freely moving industrial castors.

The interiors shown here were selected from among the many that Aulenti has executed because they represent two contrasting design situations: that is, one where the structural elements of the interior were preexisting, and the other where the architect designed both structure and decor.

In the first interior, the structure is a natural grotto in Amalfi overlooking the sea, enlarged to make it habitable. The rapport established between "natural" nature and "artificial" nature is very clear: a precise geometrical shape, shiny, smooth, and tiled in pink ceramic, unfolds to perform several different functions without blending into the rough vault formed by the rock. It is the floor, step/seat, table, bar, kitchen, and dressing room, but it is also an evocative reconstruction of waves in a grotto, thanks to the play of pinkish light reflected up from the "sea bed" floor onto the vault.

The living room, situated a few yards higher, is quite luminous thanks to the wide arch-shaped opening that overlooks the sea; it adopts the panorama as a part of its decor: the azure of the sea is picked up by the lacquered pieces of furniture and dissolves into the white of the fabrics lining the sofas and the natural color of the woven raffia fiber moquette.

The second dwelling is a single-family house in Pisa, designed in 1973. The architectural style is based on the idea of walls and on the potential shades of meaning that different types of openings in them could assume. These built-in stage wings, perforated, permeable, and placed parallel to one another, delimit the flow patterns and the shifting gradients of light that are possible between interior and exterior.

"My advice to whoever asks me how to make a home," stated Aulenti in an interview in 1970, "is to not have anything, just a few shelves for books, some pillows to sit on. And then, to take a stance against the ephemeral, against passing trends, against anything that lasts just one day, and to return to lasting values.

"All I care about is to describe a space, to define a structure that is already so complete in itself that entering into these empty rooms, they already seem perfectly filled and resolved, so that one could live happily in them. Then, naturally, one makes his personal contributions, bringing his own objects with him, and the home is defined by whoever lives in it. However, the structure keeps the upper hand" (from an interview with *Vogue America*, July 1970).

This house is consistent with these statements: everything is made to last. The furniture itself, taken from Cassina's "I Maestri" collection, is understated and classic (tables and chairs by Rietveld, sofas and armchairs by Le Corbusier). It is almost a suggestion for a lifestyle rather than a collection of mere objects that can be replaced by the apartment's occupants.

The grotto's pink-tiled floor rambles over several different levels to perform the functions of seat, table, bar, and dressing room.

Above: two views of the Pisa home, with built-in stage wings, walls that establish a sort of permeability between interior and exterior.
Right: the dining room (with tables and chairs by Rietveld), the living room (sofas and armchairs by Le Corbusier), and the study furnished with family heirloom pieces all flow together in a single large space.

GIANCARLO LEONCILLI MASSI

efore taking his architecture degree in Rome in 1968, Leoncilli cultivated a number of additional interests, including painting, sculpture, theater, film direction, music, and politics. Architecture was the main focus of his life, however, and he went on to become a professor in architectural composition at the University of Florence, after having taught in Venice. In 1985 he participated in the Venice Biennale by invitation of Aldo Rossi. These multifaceted interests often resurface in his installations, as they did in his work for the "Venezia e lo spazio scenico" exhibition (1979), in his set designs for Spoleto's Festival dei Due Mondi (for example "Ezra Pound in Concert," 1980), and in his restoration or construction projects for historical city centers, such as the portico of Spoleto's Duomo (1980) or Perugia's Palazzo della Provincia.

The house shown here is the Palazzo Zacchei-Traviglini, today a national monument in Spoleto's city center. It was begun in the sixteenth century and underwent continual transformation up to the close of the eighteenth century, when the architect Bandini made it a pivotal point along the city's main axis. In 1975 Leoncilli started to renovate the top floor for his own personal use. The building's state of decay made this difficult. An earlier subdivision into several apartments had obliterated the original decorations and frescoes. The building had suffered the violence of successive domestic invasions: the Allied command, evacuated families, a series of tenants, and so forth. The restoration was therefore not only structural but also decorative and stylistic. The problem was to make the building into a functional modern home without betraying the bygone times. The interpretation of the dialectical relationship between modern elements and the antique parts that were uncovered bit by bit as the restoration work progressed, was fundamental to the project. Apart from the stylistic and structural renovation of the floor structures suspended from large beams, this dialogue between old and new can be seen in the original use of glass bricks in the division between entrance and studio and between waiting room and cloakroom; in the striped decorations, which anticipated Botta's or Pedrecca's work, in the spaces linking the dining area with the kitchen; and in the juxtaposition of new and antique decorations, reflecting a studied choice between unity and dissonance, between the projected layout and the recovery of memories.

Left: a glass-brick partition wall framed by an open cement structure separates the entrance from the studio.

Following pages: the pink ceiling with its late nineteenth-century decorations inspired the rest. The armchairs and sofas are Bellini's "Le Tentazioni" models designed for Cassina in 1973.

Top: the bedroom with decorated ceiling by Serafino Cioti in 1788. To either side of the bed are spacious walk-in closets.
Above: mirror-play creates a sense of space in the bathroom, done in yellow Siena marble.
Right: the dining room. The black bands of the marble floor continue up the wall partitions. The table is Scarpa's "Doge" model for Simon; the chairs were produced from a design by C. Mackintosh.

BRUNO SACCHI

A graduate of the University of Florence in 1963 and a founding member of the architectural studio Forte 63, Bruno Sacchi works mostly in Tuscany in the construction and interior decoration sectors. For years he worked in collaboration with one of Italy's greatest architects, Giovanni Michelucci. His work includes the Memorial to Michelangelo in Carrara (1973), the spa in Massa (1980), and the Marino Marini museum in Florence (in progress).

The work shown here is the recovery for private use of a medieval "lord's estate": a turret and the two outbuildings at right angles to it, which were later surrounded by other, lower buildings with courtyards and transformed for use as a rural habitation.

Faced with the tower and group of low stone buildings (small blocks of limestone and sandstone with smooth riverbed stones interspersed) with brickwork arches and pilasters, Sacchi decided to keep the new construction work detached from the preexisting wall structures, giving it its own autonomous life. None of the new floor structures touch the old walls; the only points of contact are the iron girders that support them and the lighting fixtures that have been placed in the resulting interstices. The beams of light grazing over the irregular surface exalt the stone. On the ground floor Sacchi worked freely to overcome its architectural constraints. He allowed the spaces to slide into one another, arriving finally at the large living room and fireplace and opening onto the medieval court with its stone paving and lemon trees, which form a green hollow, the silent heart of the house.

The arches of the portico, which had been closed during a later period, were returned to their original state, with full-length windows, conserving the primordial sensation of space under the arches. Sacchi did the living-room floor in slate (a material foreign to Tuscan tradition, but used here in place of terra-cotta to accentuate the new), with an ample travertine shelf running along the room's perimeter, within reach of the armchairs (Arflex's "Strips" model). The wood ceiling is original and is interrupted at a point about three-quarters into the room, creating a vertical shaft around the fireplace that reaches up to the ceiling of the room above. The dining room is on the ground floor and is accessed through the medieval court, by means of a small slate bridge. Its walls hold what remains of the fourteenth-century decorations.

On the upper floor—once completely separate from the ground floor—the floor structure had been damaged by a fire. In his restoration, the architect decided to leave this void, designing for the master bedroom a balcony with a glass parapet and heating radiators that serve as balustrade, overlooking the living room. In this room as well, a large part of the fourteenth-century frescoes was salvaged.

The solution adopted for the children's room is interesting: the architect conceived a box for living—a room within a room, complete with bath, wardrobe, bookcase, desk, and beds in the upper area. It is done completely in pine and suspended from two iron beams to avoid overburdening the floor structure and to keep the new structure separate from the original, according to the architect's plan.

Left: the restored portico of the medieval structure, tranformed into a living room.

Following pages: the living-room floor is slate; travertine shelves run along its perimeter. The sofas and armchairs are from Arflex's "Strips" series. The picture windows are fixed, and ventilation is provided by means of opening behind the pilasters.

Right: a glass parapet in the master bedroom, which directly overlooks the living room on the lower floor.
Above: for the children Sacchi designed a room within a room, which enclosed the bathroom and wardrobe and had bookshelves along its exterior and, on top, beds.

CLAUDIO DINI

Claudio Dini took his degree in Milan in 1963 and started his design career with an editorial post and consultancy work on industrial design problems, covered in a number of publications. Since 1970 he has worked for the large construction company Edilnord S.p.A., for which he designed many interior decor projects for the new residential districts of Milano 2 and Milano 3. He was also heavily involved in the renewal of vast areas of the city and of other townships of the hinterland. In 1982 he was a member of the commission on the fixtures and furnishings for the Milan subway system's third line, whose fourteen stations he also designed. The first interior shown in these pages in one Dini created in 1973 for Edilnord, out of a lot of ten model apartments of different sizes, ranging from a one-room studio to a duplex apartment in the residential complex of Milano 2. The furniture—almost all of it executed on design—was considered not as "accessories" but as basic elements of the plan: the wall partitions provided closet space; the dining table was designed as an element both separating and linking the kitchen area with the living room; the baths were separated into "functional areas," permitting their contemporary use. The choice of materials ranged from plastic laminate to the most valuable types of wood—or, in the case presented here, in anticipation of high-tech fashion, a system of metal nodes and chrome tubes (the USM Haller model).

The second interior was designed for an eighteenth-century Lombard structure with the main building in the center of a large C-shaped courtyard. Nearby is a lovely park, and annexes serving as stables, stock areas, and facilities. This job took place in two phases. The first, begun in 1975, focused on the design for an outbuilding to serve as the guesthouse (a small, completely autonomous apartment) and as the area designated as the owner's private study.

The second phase started in 1982 and carried out in collaboration with architect Umberto Capelli, concerned the design of the villa's private gymnasium by transforming an adjacent rural building linked to the main building by an underground passage. Inside is a swimming pool and above it a steel framework supporting the glass floor of the gym. Distributed at different levels are the various facilities (sauna, Turkish bath, massage room). The owner, a professional in the field of television production, is able to stay on the job even in moments of relaxation, thanks to the installation a large television screen. A squash court completes the gym's facilities. The entire structure was finished with paneling and floors in planks of teak, the same material used for the furniture.

Left: like the rest of this interior, the kitchen is constructed using the metal USM Haller system, whose nodes and wide range of tube formats makes it possible to create a number of elements.

Following pages: the night zone viewed from the dining area, also showing the outline of the facilities. Drawers slide neatly under the bed by means of wheels mounted to the frame.

The second interior by Claudio Dini in an eighteenth-century villa.
Above: the studio with (at right) a chimney lined with brushed steel. A night zone was carved out of the double height of the structure.
Right: the private gymnasium and swimming pool, with wall facing and floors of teak planks.

Following pages: the central hall—formerly a ballroom—with a grand piano, located in the restored wing of the building.

THE EIGHTIES

The legacy of the Seventies—a situation of economic and political crisis—weighed heavily on the nation at the start of the Eighties. The crisis involved the entire industrial sector, and political tensions ran high. Things had come to a head in 1978 when the President of the Republic, Giovanni Leone, resigned; and due to terrorist acts the climate had become almost unbearably strained.

These dark beginnings notwithstanding, the overall situation by the close of the Eighties could be considered positive. The country's new president, Sandro Pertini, was a moral figure with whom the entire populace could identify, and although the nation was torn by internal strife, it had finally proved equal to the task of mounting a united front against terrorism. And if the Seventies' inflation had compounded the existing problems, the Eighties' technological improvements helped the economy back on its feet. The upward spiral of prosperity that occurs when a new demand is met with a new supply, a key factor in the growth of the Sixties, was repeated—in qualitatively different terms—in the Eighties. Other phenomena also contributed to this positive economic trend—phenomena such as a general improvement in educational levels, an increase in life expectancy and in geographical mobility, and the progressive internationalization of the nation.

As the Eighties dawned, a phenomenon that previously had barely been hinted at emerged forcefully: the replacement of the shrinking industrial sector by the services sector. Public opinion and the media followed

Alessandro Mendini's adaptation of a Louis XIV table for the Paola Rosella Colombari gallery (1987).

with interest the modifications in production technology and the new professional roles that emerged with the many new "trades."

The decline of leadership in industry was hastened by both new awareness of ecological issues and the shrinking role of the working class in the economy. Over time, disclosures of environmental accidents set off a critical revision of the previous passive acceptance of the industrial point of view. The environmentalist Green party succeeded in rallying to their cause political forces outside the traditional party affiliations, and so became an authentic political voice during these years.

The transition to a post-industrial society (at the cultural, certainly not economic, level) brings several issues to the fore. In a clearly hierarchical system, the process of observing and analyzing reality reflected internal structures analogous to those of the reality observed: there were privileged vantage points for observing the world, and preferential axes along which to organize it. With a crisis in the hierarchy among the production sectors and among the various social brackets, these preferential vantage points lose credibility. The subject of knowledge (and of activity) becomes minutely fragmented or miniaturized. In philosophy this is recognized as the awareness of the end of all certainties, even at the level of itineraries/procedures. In every field—science, the arts, morality, politics, and last but not least architecture—after the strong theories of the modern age came the weak theories of the postmodern age.

The overall picture of change was further dominated by the enormous growth of the middle classes: "In any case, it must be recognized that class differences and the heterogeneity of the middle class, as well as historically determined distinctions, are growing weaker; among the positive consequences of this is a certain attenuation of the conflicts; and among the negative consequences is the leveling out of culture" (Sylos Labini, *Le Classi Sociali negli Anni '80*).

In the work world, the figure of the manager came to the fore. The quest for innovation and the zeal with which many Italian businesses leapt into the international limelight were accompanied by a rediscovery of enterprise, a zest for risky economic initiatives, and an acceptance of uncertainty as a normal condition (viz. the widespread speculation in the stock market). At its worst, the figure of the manager almost paralleled that

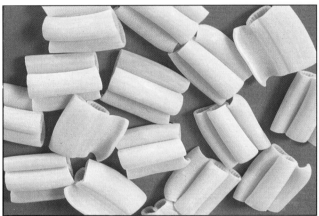

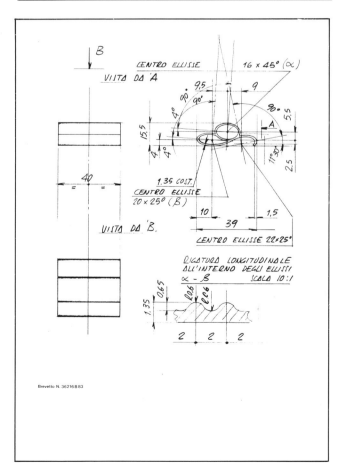

Automation in industry changed production processes, thus creating a new technological culture within the business environment, and in the Eighties it generated various forms of patronage outside this environment (top: robot by the Comau company, in Fiat's plants; opposite page: stand designed by Frank O'Gehry for the G.F.T. group). The designer phenomenon permeated everyday existence, extending to the most commonplace products ("Marille" pasta designed by Giugiaro for Voiello), as well as to the physical person, who could be redesigned through bodybuilding.

of the social climber—the yuppie—whose drive for success was fueled by designer-label consumerism. The rich—what they do, where they go, how they dress—generated such interest as to justify the creation of a new magazine genre represented by, among others, *Capital, Class,* and *Il Piacere*. Not until the end of the Eighties did a reaction to this philosophy of life, this idea that politics and the economy are a thing apart from morality, start to take shape. Francesco Alberoni and Salvatore Veca's book *L'Altruismo e la Morale* discusses this change in public opinion, this need to retrieve from the wreckage of ideology the concepts of commitment and of individual and social responsibility, and proposes a new enlightenment based on altruism and rationality.

In fashion, as in interior design, the Eighties saw the formation of a large "new majority" distinguished by its cultural approach to consumption. What established and motivated these people was an aesthetic logic that substituted for religion, morality, politics, and ideology. This "skin-deep" population (in the majority more by virtue of its visibility than its actual numbers) had as its rallying points ordinary modes of expression: fashion, mass media, advertising. The social transition was made from a silent majority to a majority that at all costs must talk, come forward, show off: a clamorous majority. The youth culture, which at one time had voiced dissent (ideological in the Sixties: behavioral in the Seventies), gave way to a series of majoritarian youth cultures, from one that embraced the fashion myth, sun-lamp tans, and fast food, to one of mindless aggression, the fruit of urban alienation. In these forms of deliberate exhibitionism the body played a decisive role: it became a façade to be constructed through body-building or make-up and clothing, a personal promotional campaign.

In the interior design field, the codes were not as clearly identified as those in attire. "The equation social status = attire is mathematically certain, while that of status = interior décor is more approximate," Cristina Marozzi correctly observed. The Eighties thus gave rise to myriad products aimed at vast market segments. Industries built up broad and safe product terrains, each with its own marketing mix. Along with these, as early as the late Seventies, a series of trademarks emerged that offered a number of different typological options (precisely because they were free of production or technological problems), based more on the overall value of the trade name than on that of the individual product. The advent of the postmodern era injected new vigor into the by then hackneyed stylistic lexicon of the International Style. A few designers made *objets d'art* sold as such, and some artists turned to producing functional works of art. Big industry was very alert to all this, ready to implement what it could, just as though it were coming out of an enormous research lab. A "modern antiques" market started to flourish as the supply of usual antiques dwindled and as modern products became obsolescent at an increasingly rapid pace.

FASHION

Research, study, quality, the capacity for mass-production, and the flexibility of artisan production were the ingredients of the "made in Italy" success story. The reason for the widespread diffusion of fashion and the importance it assumed in the Eighties, however, are perhaps more to be found in the fundamental changes in consumer habits, particularly those involving fashion.

Fashion's sphere of influence became comparable to what had once been exercised by ideology and morals. In our time, fashion became a conveyor of values and a reference point for a new majority of people who expressed themselves through physical display of external traits that attested to a wealth or poverty that may not have been backed by the facts. People no longer bought solely for reasons of status; prestige was no longer the driving force behind purchases, and fashion no longer concerned just an élite: it became the domain of the masses. Fashion became commonplace, also in great part thanks to the "secondary lines" (apparel designed by famous stylists and distributed in mass quantities at accessible prices). The designer's *griffe* became the craze and spread to furniture, tiles, washing machines, bicycles, eyeglasses, and telephones. Trussardi, for example, designed a bicycle, a new driving compartment for the Mini Morris car, sofas for Busnelli, tiles for Rex, and a telephone; Krizia undersigned kitchen blocks for Salvarani and tiles for Edilcoghi; Versace applied his neoclassical motifs to tiles for Cerdisa.

The phenomenon was so widespread that there was a risk of oversaturation; paradoxically, fashion was

Top: Fashion show presenting Gianni Versace's 1986–87 collection.

Above: haute couture fashion by Gianfranco Ferrè.

Opposite page, from top: one of Giorgio Armani's spring-summer fashions (1986); an advertisement for Krizia, with Mario Botta's "Seconda" chair (Alias).

in jeopardy of falling out of fashion, of losing its allure, its aura, its magic. Toward the end of the Eighties the first counter reactions to this process of excessive mass production began to make themselves felt. Not by chance did people begin to talk of High Fashion, exclusiveness, the tailor-made.

Giorgio Armani was a landmark figure during these years. Known for his rigorous, no-frills lines, he invented a type of woman that had no historical precedent—the working woman. A winner, even at times yuppie-ish, she freely borrowed styles and fabrics from the male wardrobe.

The Japanese stylists (Rei Kawakubo for Commes des Garçons; Issey Miyake; Yohji Yamamoto) held shows in Paris for the first time in 1981. They challenged the classical canons of dress, and this was an important stimulus to Italian fashion as well. Their austere, ascetic clothing was a middle ground between the Orient and the Occident, but utterly devoid of revivalism. At the beginning, its dominant features were the use of the color black, geometric cuts, and articles of clothing designed independently of the body, which served merely as a support. Using an idiom that in time also absorbed Western influences, especially turn-of-the-century fashions, the Japanese stylists immediately won over the young avant-garde, rock stars, and furniture designers. (Paolo Pallucco, designer and manufacturer of a number of interesting pieces of this period, was the driving force behind this trend in Italy.)

Gianfranco Ferré, an architect by training, applied this discipline's quest for harmony and proportion to his design work, unfurling volumes and structures from his fabrics. His collections were not revolutionary nor an affront to classical fashion values: his clothing is perfectly balanced, and even when exaggerated it maintains an equilibrium that is achieved through dynamic asymmetry. Ferré also designed, with Paolo Nava, the "Gli Abiti" series of sofas and armchairs for B&B, in which the "bodies" of the chairs could be dressed in different styles, making a seasonal wardrobe change possible, or even chair attire for special occasions: for summer, winter and the evening.

A new personality that came to the fore during these years was Franco Moschino, whose extremely ironic creations made light of fashion. He defines himself thus: "I do not consider myself a stylist, but a serious and capable designer...I am not, nor do I wish to be, an inventor; it's as if I had a great wardrobe trunk full of all

the theatrical and private life costumes of all peoples, of all epochs, to draw on." For Moschino, everything could be recovered from the past; his way of re-presenting it constitutes the newness of his styles. When he presented his first collection, in 1983, Moschino immediately became famous for the unmistakable style that projects him beyond the usual parameters of the rigorous or the baroque. His work is a journey through the collective memory, a dreamlike juxtaposition of absolutely antithetical values, in the manner of the Surrealists, that likens it to the experiments of the postmodern designers.

Romeo Gigli was the creator of another myth that dominated the second half of the Eighties. After spending a few years as a consultant for a number of firms, Gigli came out with his own label in 1981. He invented a style that has been defined as "minimal"; its formal purity, naturalness, and modesty offers an apparently fragile, childlike image of the woman. There are some parallels between Gigli's style and that of the Japanese, even if his is more tied to the Western traditions. He upholds the classical stylistic lexicon and adheres to the most traditional sartorial rules, moving away from them only to achieve new effects of volume. The press, especially the foreign press, contributed in great part to Gigli's success.

Fashions for youth that appeared during this period, including the punk, dark, *paninaro*, and yuppie looks, decisively influenced the official fashion world. The punk look dawned in Great Britain at the close of the Seventies and rapidly spread throughout Europe. It combined several elements of the most important postwar youth subcultures (leather jackets, straight-legged trousers, brightly colored socks, amphibian boots, s&m belts, colored locks of hair, safety pins) in an aggressive style that simultaneously roused curiosity and fear. The dark look, also English in origin, reflects some aspects of Japanese style—the use of the color black—and took a few elements from the world of black magic (long, dissheveled hairstyles, heavy make-up, crucifixes, long fake fingernails, black nail-polish and lipstick). The punks were the latest expression of a transgressive political message (anarchy) and values (always negative); the darks confined themselves to a pure image—a single somber color, free of ideology.

The *paninari* were a patently Italian phenomenon. The nucleus of this group first formed in 1981, in a coffeeshop in downtown Milan. From the start, their

Top: Benetton, known the world over, is the largest Italian manufacturer of Italian knitwear and young fashions, with a retail network that, although franchised, presents a consistent image of the firm.

Above: fashion's appeal struck many avant-garde interior design groups,

drawing them into the world of "dressing design," as with these decorated shoes by Mendini (1983).

Opposite page: fashion show (1988–89), and a minidress with appliqués by Franco Moschino, a stylist whose originality links him to the postmodern designers.

philosophy was superficial: they were not against anything, they had no political ideology. For them, fashion had become religion, true and proper, with precise rules of conduct. Whoever did not follow these rules was automatically excluded from the group. Their symbols were the Montcler ski jacket, Timberland shoes and boots, the Henry Lloyd jacket, Armani or Levi jeans, RayBan sunglasses, etc.; what counted was that the clothes were costly and that they smacked of the United States. Their meeting point was any downtown fast-food establishment, and their favorite rock band was Duran Duran.

The yuppies (a name coined in 1983 by journalist Bob Green) were a phenomenon that originated in the United States. For the American yuppie, dress was very important, since success depends on one's personal look. Their ideal home was the loft, and they abhorred plastic furnishings; the Breuer chair, Le Corbusier chaise longue, Jacuzzi tub and personal computer were all *de rigueur*.

CINEMA

At the start of the decade, the introduction and diffusion of powerful new technologies such as videotape and the electronic image seemed to herald the doom of traditional cinematography, both as a medium per se and as entertainment. The sector was indeed in crisis at both the production end and the box office, especially in Italy. Notwithstanding however, its significantly diminished role in the contemporary iconosphere (what with the advertising images, video-clips, high-definition television, and video-decks that brought the show into the home), and notwithstanding a general change in attitude toward spectacle (which involved such disparate spheres as fashion, art exhibitions, society events or cultural appointments, and so forth), film did continue to occupy an important position in the public imagination.

Whether superficial or deeply innovative, the film proposals were many, and about midway through the decade the cinemas enjoyed a renewed popularity. In Italy, the young in particular started to crowd into the new multiplex cinemas that had replaced the second-run and revival houses founded in the early Eighties. The strategy for winning over the young audiences relied heavily on special effects, which, thanks to great technological advances made in these years, were truly extraordinary, and on the assimilation of fads, tastes, and trends from the culture and the formative years of the newest generation. There was thus a return to spectacular formats, an introduction of new themes and new social models. In general, between its special effects, changed narrative expectations, and the introduction of the latest trends, the cinema of these years offers powerful images, and its framing and at times convulsive rhythm of montage bring characters to life in well-defined contexts.

Although films of fable and fantasy, of the Star Wars or Indiana Jones genre, were upheld by their special effects, it was the suggestive power of the images and the richly decorated sets in Ridley Scott's *Blade Runner* (1982) that presented an anguished, apprehensive vision of the near future. In Syd Mead's sets for the film, neon lights, demolition sites, and postmodern hybrids created a troubling urban universe, a megalopolis in which old and new overlap and diverse styles cancel one another out. Juxtaposed with scenes of a Los Angeles of the future are entire sequences filmed in a neo-Victorian building of the 1920s (the Bradbury building), and architectural confusion reigns supreme throughout the film, a highly personal mix of reality and fiction that had many imitators later on, even in advertising.

Other evocative images of the future as a Babel of archaeological finds and arcane sources are seen in Terry Gilliam's *Brazil* (1985). Its setting, a low-cost housing-project building (the Palacio de Abraxas by Catalan designer Ricardo Bofill, 1983), together with various references and direct quotations from the Fifties and later, made *Brazil* a postmodern cult film.

A postmodern mood permeated many French films of the Eighties. In the neo-*noirs*, for example, improbable, somewhat mannerist vagabonds and antiheros run aground amid nocturnal atmospheres. Jean-Jacques Beineix' *Diva* (1981) is a good example of the postmodern pastiche with its overlapping of diverse idioms (advertising, video-clips, references to *Métal Hurlant* comics). The cold colors and self-indulgent play of the camera over the spaces of the enormous loft, a mixture of the baroque and the high tech, became a commonplace in many later films. This type of large, unitary environment, unhampered by the walls or precise functional zoning of a bourgeois home, endowed the film characters of the Eighties with the

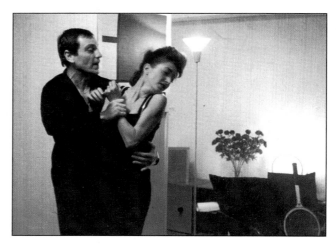

Three cinematographic interiors of the Eighties. From top: Michael Cimino's The Year of the Dragon *(1985), Detail showing the apartment furnished with Italian design pieces; Danny De Vito's status living room in* Jerry Zucker, Jim Abrahams, and David Zucker's Ruthless People *(1986), furnished entirely in pieces by Memphis; Eric Rohmer's* Les Nuits de la Lune Pleine *(1984), whose protagonist is a designer of postmodern lamps.*

ability to live chameleon-like existences. The interior decor was more a matter of primary design elements (lighting, sound, ornament, color, and so forth) than actual furnishings. This was a far cry from the public or open "on the road" spaces of the films of previous years such as *Zabriski Point, Strawberry Statement*, or *Easy Rider*.

In *films d'auteur* outside of the mainstream as well, particular attention was paid to the backdrop and settings, especially the furnishings and design, which were decidedly contempoary. In Marco Ferreri's *I Love You* (1986), set designer Jean-Pierre Kohut-Svelko built an enormous loft with all the trappings of the modern lifestyle: exposed brick walls, Sony TVs, hi-fis and compact-disk units, together with recognizable design objects and the ever-present glimpses of the urban periphery.

In Martin Scorsese's *After Hours* (1986), a Soho loft with plaster columns, furniture finished in nylon, and papier mâché sculptures renders the postmodern nightmarishly grotesque in the eyes of the unsophisticated yuppie who finds himself face to face with it. For Michael Cimino's *Year of the Dragon* (1985), a team of designers decorated a spacious, luxurious apartment in which the distribution of functional areas and the arrangement of the furniture and the picture windows that offer a view of Brooklyn Heights (pure imagery, in living color) create a sense of solitude, inconsistency, and urban void.

In Adrian Lyne's *9½ Weeks* (1985), the protagonist's apartment is like an advertisement from the pages of an interior-design review; in *Le Nuits de la Lune Pleine*, acutely and subtly directed by Eric Rohmer, the relationship between the home décor of the protagonist (who designs lamps in the Memphis style) and the urban backdrop create a rapport between the characters and the setting that serves to explore human behavior.

In a different vein, in Italy the comic genre was often tuned in to the fads, the tics, the neuroses of our era, providing precise, at times scathing representations of postmodern lifestyles. Moretti's and Nichetti's post Sixties-generation characters (the latter's *Ratataplan* of 1979 deserves mention) offset Carlo Vanzina's farcical characters (*Yuppies*, 1986). The following year Vanzina depicted the world of fashion and top models in his mystery *Sotto il Vestito Niente*, which showed how fashionable fashion really was in the Eighties.

From top: two distributing visions of the near future that reflect the postmodern mood of the early Eighties: Terry Gilliam's Brazil *(1985)* and Ridley Scott's Blade Runner *(1982)*.

Above: American dwelling models in the French neo-noir genre: the large, baroque, high-tech loft in Jean-Jacques Beineix' Diva *(1981)*.

Top: return to the
neoclassical in
Jean-Jacques Beineix' The
Mirror of Desire (1983), a
reconstruction in Cinecittà
of an entire waterfront
district.

Above: the "Cités-Cinés"
exhibition in the Grande
Halle de la Villette in
Paris, which displayed
cinematic interiors and set
designs.

Finally, the great interest filmmakers took in interior decor and architecture, even at a historical and theoretical level, was confirmed by the important exhibition "Cités-Cinés" that took place in Paris at the Villette through February 1988. Using up-to-date technologies, it recreated film's most evocative and important set designs, architecture, and cities.

TELEVISION

The Eighties was the decade of the video image, at home, at work, and during leisure time. Per capita television viewing hours rose significantly, from two-and-a-half hours per day, in the Seventies, to four hours a day. The computer with video screen moved out of the workplace and into home, and involved each member of the family. Children and adults alike played videogames; the personal computer was a valid means of keeping order in one's bank book or kitchen pantry; the television had a place not only in the living room but also in the bedroom (and, with the advent of morning programming, in the kitchen and lavatory). Thus a new type of audience targeting—by room—was activated.

In the near future we may witness high-definition televisions with bigger and flatter screens that can be hung from the walls, like paintings; but today's market already offers a wide range of high-tech products able to meet a multiplicity of uses and settings. For those who prefer the comfort of home to the movie theaters, there are wide-screen televisions; portable sets of various dimensions meet every other need, whether perched on movable carts or on the built-in shelves of bed units. For travel, there is the miniature version that can be tossed in the bag along with one's toothbrush and calculator. And just as one's daytime occupation requires increasing interaction with videoterminals, in the evenings there are the new videomania bars, clubs and discoteques where the TVs are no longer relegated to a stand in the corner, but instead dominate every inch of the walls.

The debut of the videotape-deck allowed the viewer to staunch the endless flow of television broadcasts, to freeze the images, to create his own show. And this applied not just to films made by others but also to one's own films. With the advent of the videocassette, the nature of audiovisual communication changed:

material could be stored, consulted, or catalogued like a record or a book, and it thus shed the hitherto immaterial quality of film or television. And one could enjoy seeing his own and friends' images on the screen, just like that of his favorite TV personality.

As far as television programming is concerned, it should be noted that by 1980, Rai-TV's monopoly had been replaced by a mixed system of public and private television networks. In 1979 a census revealed that in Italy there were about three hundred private broadcasting stations. Rome was at the top of the list with twenty-nine "free" stations, but there was not a region in the country that did not have at least ten of them.

The private networks set out to profit by the nighttime void left by public television and thus contributed to a change in Italians' habits of television consumption. TV ceased to be a mass-communications medium, offering instead a multiplicity of messages broadcast by different channels, each in search of its own, clearly individuated audience. The game was no longer to be innovative (and thus risk being tuned out by one's target audience) but rather to consolidate one's position step-by-step with well-defined fields of reception.

In 1980, Canale 5 was born. Owned by Silvio Berlusconi, a self-made businessman with fingers in many pies, it soon became state television's main rival. In 1981 it captured an audience of ten million people with the *Dallas* series, but in short order it was producing and distributing its own shows. It absorbed all its major competitors almost as soon as they appeared, and went on to conquer the rest of Europe in 1986, inaugurating the first private French TV network, La Cinq, and establishing a network that could broadcast to Germany.

What dominated the airwaves were American serials and South American soap operas constructed around almost identical story lines based on love and hate, and distinguished primarily by the socio-cultural contexts as expressed by the set-furnishings. Fashion had never been so fashionable as in this decade, and provided the material for a number of talk shows. The postmodern viewpoint was also adopted by television; spectacular daily broadcasts such as *Quelli della Notte* and *Indietro Tutta* (of which we will speak more) introduced vernaculars (from radio shows and variety-show curtain-raisers) that had existed prior to the advent of television, but laced with heavy irony vis-à-vis the

From top: Mister Fantasy, *a sophisticated 1981 music program, hosted by Mario Luzzatto Fegiz and Carlo Massarini;* Pronto Raffaella, *midday broadcast hosted by Raffaella Carrà from her* living room, characterized by opulence of the most banal kind; a model used in the production of Giulia e Giulia, *the first high-definition film, directed by Peter Del Monte and with sets by Mario Garbuglia.*

power of advertising. Experiments in design received in official recognition in Giuliano Ferrara's *Il Testimone*, the scenario of which had been designed by Mario Garbuglia using Gaetano Pesce's "Cannaregio" and "Feltri" armchairs for Cassina. Never before had television been so attentive to interior decoration, and as a result, the best of Italy's sofa and armchair production made up part of the nation's daily video-fare.

With the rise of the commercial television networks, Italy became one of the countries most heavily bombarded with advertising messages. For the country's advertisers, investment required to reach the potential consumer was one of the the lowest anywhere. Italians were subject to about 500,000 advertisements per year, 3 trillion lire's worth.

In October 1980, Pippo Baudo took Corrado's place as host of *Domenica In*, transforming the Sunday variety show format into a sort of cultural notebook (there were discussions of theater, cinema, books). Thanks to Baudo's talent as a host (a role that he occupied until 1985) the show captured a weekly audience of 6–7 million viewers, or 50 percent of the public.

At noon on October 3, 1983, *Pronto Raffaella* was launched. Hosted by Raffaella Carrà this "living room" style show offered various studio guests and many viewer participation telephone games with prizes.

On October 14, 1983, Berlusconi's Italia 1 launched a variety show that shot to the top of the popularity charts: *Drive In*. A program that attracted over 10 million viewers, it was at times boorish and vulgar, but highly popular with the young—who quickly absorbed its vocabulary—for its irreverent irony, for the buxom "fast-food" girls who pranced through each scene, and for the show's fast gag pace.

On April 9, 1985, to combat the reign of the private networks during the evening hours, Rai launched a program that will go down in television history: *Quelli della Notte*. It was hosted by Renzo Arbore, an ex-disk jockey, singer, and musician, but above all a man endowed with a charge of subtle irony and extraordinary appeal. Joined by his "New Patetic Elastic" [*sic*] orchestra, and an entourage of new personalities, he discussed serious issues in a surreal key, in a setting that looked like his own living room.

Three years later, in 1988, Arbore's new show *Indietro tutta* met with equal success. Borrowing from the radio-show vernacular and located in a ship's-deck

Top: set by young designer Massimo Josa Ghini for After Hours, *with the armchair he designed for Moroso.*

Above: set of Il Testimone, *decorated by Mario Garbuglia with "Cannaregio" and "Feltri" sofas and armchairs by Gaetano Pesce for Cassina.*

Above: Renzo Arbore in the 1988 TV spectacular Indietro Tutta, *which in a setting inspired by the*

allegorical floats of folk festivals imitated old-time radio music programs.

setting, Commander Arbore chatted with Master of Ceremonies Nino Frassica, who moved about on a sort of parade float whose iconography recalled the decorations of town celebrations for patron saints.

Two programs dedicated to interior decoration and sponsored by Assarredo (a national association of furniture and decoration manufacturers) were launched in 1987: *Qui Casa* and *Il Piacere di Abitare*. *Qui Casa*, first aired on September 20 by Canale 5, was a Sunday morning show aimed at women and furniture retailers with sections dedicated to do-it-yourself ideas, home decorations by architects, interviews with designers, and so forth. *Il Piacere di Abitare*, broadcast by Rai 2, starting November 4, was marked by a monographic style, with thirty shows aimed at disseminating ideas on lifestyles proposed by the leading figures in architecture and interior decoration at the time.

INDUSTRY

In terms of both demand and supply in the advanced technologies sector, Italy stood among the top European nations as it prepared to meet the new demands that would be placed on its economy with the creation of a unitary European market in 1992 and complete deregulation of trade. Microelectronics and information technology, biotechnology, automation, and new materials were in the vanguard of this industrial revolution.

New markets (for example, telematics) were created, and others (such as the automobile or television industries) were built up ex-novo. New, previously unimaginable, standards of price, quality, efficiency, flexibility and rationality were set and surpassed at a surprising rhythm.

The automobile. In recent years, demand in the automobile sector has continued to enjoy worldwide growth. World production went from 27 million vehicles in 1982 to about 34 million in 1988. In the same period production in Italy went from 1,297,000 to 1,700,000 vehicles. The industry recovered brilliantly from the slump of the Seventies, when the petroleum crisis and its effects on the world economy made people talk about the "impending and inevitable end of the automobile."

The extraordinary evolution in auto production

during the past decade involved not only production technology, but also people's behavior with respect to the automobile. Fiat, following its purchase of Lancia, bought out Alfa Romeo as well in 1986. It reorganized its productive structures with automated processes to reduce the number of laborers. The first results of this were crowned with success: the Uno of 1983, of which 3 million were produced over the course of five years. In 1988 came the Tipo, which was manufactured according to a new industrial process called C.I.M. (Computer Integrated Manufacturing). The first fully automated production line in the world (with 403 robots), C.I.M. offered guaranteed quality and production flexibility; different models or variants of a single model could be produced on the same line. This concept had already been explored at the prototype level with Fiat's VSS, which was developed by the I.DE.A. institute in collaboration with Renzo Piano.

To understand the new rapport between user and automobile that appeared toward the end of the Eighties, it is necessary to take a step back in time. In the Fifties, automobiles represented for many an inaccessible object of desire: automotive forms were charged with a level of expression that was often verging on kitsch. Later, during a period of crisis that inhibited any form of exhibitionism, the automobile became austere, a functional tool. At the close of the Eighties, the automobile started to recover its role as an object of desire (the Ferrari F 40 released in June 1987 typifies this type of love). The new style of auto design takes for granted advanced aerodynamics and safety features, but also goes a step further: it takes on a sculptural shape, exemplified by the Saguaro, a Ghia prototype unveiled at Geneva in 1988, in which the body is modeled along natural, almost biomechanical lines. It is a multipurpose volume with space for seven passengers. Its line is patently carlike, as shapely as an athlete's physique, nothing like that of a van. The interior was designed to function as a sort of psycho-ergonomy—that is, an ergonomy that is not only nominally scientific but which, in addition to communicating its functional traits, makes itself clearly present in the vehicle's comfort and "user-friendliness," thus making a transition from high tech to "high touch."

Another car that made its mark in the Eighties was the Renault Espace. Midway between the traditional auto and the motor home, it was a container that reproposed, on a larger scale, the functionality of the

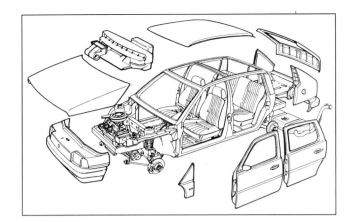

A rationality in production and the rediscovery of their emotional appeal mark the automobile designs of the Eighties. Top: Fiat's VSS experimental vehicle, designed in 1977 by I.DE.A., conceived for production as subsystems in plastic to be mounted on a load-bearing framework, so that a variety of models could be obtained with the same structure.

Center: the Tipo, released in 1988, adopted this philosophy. It is the first of five models soon to be put in production.

Above: the Ferrari F 40, a high-performance sportscar designed by Pininfarina.

Panda, the Kar-a-Sutra and some of Mitsubishi's experiments.

It was precisely a car of this type (imported from Japan for assembly in the U.S.) that, under the guidance of Lee Iacocca, lifted Chrysler from the jaws of bankruptcy. When the Chrysler Voyager and the Dodge Caravan debuted on the American market, there was nothing to rival them. They were compact, all-purpose vehicles whose structure, based on front-wheel drive, allowed for a spacious interior. Giugiaro's and Bertone's proposals at the Turin Salon of 1988 confirmed just how winning and ahead of its time this structure was.

Giugiaro designed a high-performance vehicle, the Asgard, that had room for six adults and two children. Its body, no longer the smooth surface of the past, showed the marks of a new functionality (ranging from the battery-run lug wrenches for changing the tire to the fuel gauge to hydraulic jack for raising the vehicle).

Bertone's Genesis retained the shape of his fabulous sports cars (such as the Miura or the Countach) which had space for only the driver and one passenger, but underneath a new concept. This new vehicle still carried within its streamlined monostructure the powerful 12-cylinder Lamborghini motor, but its positioning was subordinated to the aim of creating a spacious, flexibly organized interior. In fact, the car holds five passengers who can stay in contact with the outside world by means of the telephone, computer, and telefax on board.

Plastics and new materials. An exhibition organized by Montedison Progetto Cultura entitled "Gli Anni di Plastica" (The Plastic Years) at the Villette Museum of Science and Industry in Paris, closed on January 4, 1987. Its original approach recalled the 1968 exhibition "Plastic as Plastic" at New York's Museum of Modern Art. It is interesting to see synthesized by these two exhibitions the evolution of plastic over the intervening twenty years. The first exhibition bore witness to the end of plastic's imitative phase, during which it had tried to capture the superficial appearance of materials that were considered more "noble." The second demonstrated not only the importance of plastics in our everyday lives but also the aesthetic and logical coherence in all of plastic's multifaceted applications, and the broad range of solutions it had provided in industry's commercial and produc-

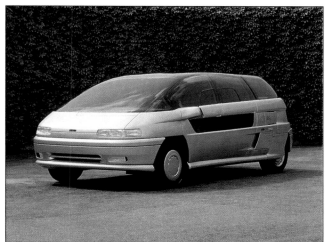

Top: Ghia's Saguaro and Giugiaro's Asgard, two 1988 examples of the sculpural trend in auto-body lines.

Above: the interior of Genesis presented in 1988 by Bertone—a roomy sports coupé in which the back seats were shifted slightly to the center relative to the front seats, an assymetry that enhanced the field of vision through the windshield.

tive strategies.

In the meantime, the accelerated cultural sedimentation of our era had seen the birth of the modern antiques, which included plastic objects. In the Eighties plastics made a comeback in the interior-design scene. The rather naive plastics boom in the Sixties has witnessed a number of incorrect applications, leading in part to the rejection of plastics in the Seventies. Plastics are materials in constant evolution that offer divers combinations of qualities. Few plastics achieve the durability of special steels, the lightness of certain wood types, the elasticity of natural rubber, or the transparency of glass, but only plastics are simultaneously resistant, lightweight, elastic, and transparent. Polymers in particular have undergone vast development over the past years, resulting in high-performance mechanical, technological, and chemical products.

The most innovative applications, however, can be seen in the field of fiber technology. Composite materials have been devised that combine at the microscopic level two or more materials that, when united, retain all the special qualities of each of the components and compensate for each others' negative qualities. Carbon fibers offer the most potential, combining as they do mechanical resistance and lightness, meeting many needs in structural applications in the aerospace industry (Boeing 767 or Airbus A 310); the sports industry (skis, tennis rackets); and furniture industry (Alberto Meda's "Light-Light" chair for Alias).

Two materials had already found broad applications in the Sixties: plastic laminate and polyurethane. The former enjoyed a second youth in the Eighties, because of its decorative potential, in Alchimia's and Memphis' furniture. Polyurethane in semirigid form (as in automobile armrests), press-molded for the desired finish, had applications not only as a structural detail, but also as a primary component, for example of chairs manufactured by Alias, Bontempi, and Zeus. Another application of this material was in surface covering—such as in Limonta's products, which were in fashion and interior design—where the polyurethane was calendered onto cotton or polyester substrates.

The home-building industry. The housing crisis of the Eighties arose out of a cumulative effect of negative economic and financial trends (lower family savings, mounting difficulties in traditional systems of credit) and a relative maturation of demand, since at

Plastics, neglected in the Seventies, made a comeback in decorative objects in the Eighties. Top: Abet's new "Straticolor" laminates, in different layers of color.

Above: Alberto Meda's "Light-Light" chair in carbon fiber, for Alias (1987).

Top: clocks with ABS housing, designed by George Sowden and Nathalie du Pasquier for Lorenz in 1986.

Above: Kartell's "4310" tables, constructed in various plastics for their responsiveness to specific requirements (table top in polymer, pedestal in ABS, base in reinforced nylon).

the close of the Seventies 60 percent of the families owned their own homes and 13 percent owned second homes.

The statistics for homes designed between 1980–81 speak for themselves: there was a reduction of 14.2 percent. This was a phenomenon that in the next years showed a strong dichotomy: on the one hand, there was the "post-primary" demand (that is, not related to the "absolute" need for housing, but a relative need for domestic and/or territorial mobility for families that already owned or rented their homes); on the other hand, an unsatisfied primary demand, on the part of both those without a home (young couples, for example) and the "potentially excluded" (the retired, low-income families under eviction).

As for trends in housing of the Eighties, focusing on the metropolitan areas, one notes a general disappearance of rooms dedicated to a single household function; these were replaced by all-purpose spaces. The kitchen, the lavatory, and, in part, the bedroom were greatly influenced by changes in behavior that took place.

With frozen and prepackaged foods, microwave ovens, and food processors, the preparation and consumption of food have undergone change, as have family structures, which now include a minimal nucleus—singles or noninstitutionalized groups who pattern their lives on different schedules and rhythms. Consequently the use of the kitchen and its role in the home environment changed. Market researchers noted a progressively less formal attitude toward mealtimes, which in Italy were, traditionally, daily rituals with precise rules, and were now being replaced by quick and irregular consumption of snacks.

Although food preparation was becoming simpler, and the number of meals consumed outside the home was on the rise, the pleasures of food were rediscovered: dinner was becoming a gastronomic experience to be shared with friends, where the host could demonstrate his expertise. More was demanded of kitchen furnishings compared to when the kitchen was merely a "cooking corner" relegated to a few square meters of space. It continued to be a super-equipped, rational and functional space (preparing the way for the telematic house), but its look ranged from that of a high-tech industrial kitchen to an old-fashioned kitchen, loaded (in spite of the efficiency of the electrical appliances) with "warmer" values resulting from

Examples of the two main trends in kitchen furnishings during the Eighties: high tech and the extension of the living room, in which certain traditional value were recycled through the use of natural materials such as wood and marble.

Top: Paolo Piva's "Diva" for Dada (1988), a rectangular island with two measures of depth and doors that could be

opened from either side. In the center was the cooking block underneath a steel structure that supported glass shelves or cabinets.

Above: the "Contralto" model in wood; in the corner, cooking and food preparation areas with a continuous countertop in granite. Design by Giovanni Offredi for Abaco (1988).

the use of classical materials such as wood or precious materials such as marble and lacquer suitable for cooking and for entertaining friends.

The lavatory has also followed this social-minded trend. In the past it was a room closed to outsiders, neglected in favor of other domestic spaces; today, it stands on equal footing with the rest of the rooms. It has almost become a recreation room, a space in which a person may legitimately spend time alone, dedicating himself to his personal care. Furnishings have conformed to this trend, taking their inspiration from a nostalgia for the splendors of the past (Cesame's "Belle Epoque" washbasin) as well as from the latest electronic discoveries (hydromassage tubs have enjoyed great success, and remote controls for carrying out a number of activities from the tub are already on the market).

The bedroom, because of its symbolic content, was the most resistant to these changes, although it too slowly evolved during this period. First it underwent a drastic reduction in size to make room for the home's "public" spaces—the living and dining rooms. The bed was gradually stripped of its monumentality, becoming a sort of aseptic low platform to be used exclusively for sleep and for gathering one's strength for the next day. The next transformation made the bedroom more like a living room, a space for working, television viewing, telephoning. No longer a private sanctuary, it is now shown to guests as part of the home tour, establishing with them a less formal, more intimate rapport.

Furniture. In the last chapter we saw how the sector's manufacturing structure was based on a myriad of small and very small firms with a craftsman-like approach, concentrated in Lombardy, the Veneto, and Tuscany (these regions alone accounted for 55 percent of the production and employment in the sector). In the Eighties the sector continued to be highly fragmented, with a low growth rate. Between 1981 and 1983, structural phenomena—for example, inflation, the building crisis, and the rising cost of labor per product—furthered this fragmentation. Lasting changes in consumer tastes and habits caused a drop in demand, with lower profits and reduced investments contributing to a general slowing of the industry's growth.

A few firms diversified their product ranges, seeking their own distinct target groups and relying heavily on product design and company image to stand out from the competition. Although diversification could not ensure a solid advantage (given the ease with which products can be imitated), it became an increasingly decisive factor in a firm's success. With a market of such variegated needs, thousands of smaller businesses were able to carve out their own well-defined niches. Other firms relied on low diversification (whether technological or in design) and a low competitive edge, occupying an area characterized by more risk and tougher competition, but also higher production volumes.

The public tended either to buy lower-quality products when furnishing non-representational spaces or second homes; or—on the contrary—it sought out products of outstanding quality, no longer sold in sets but as single elements, for a personalized touch that could enhance the entire room. The companies hit hardest by this new attitude were those that had aimed at the middle bracket, offering complete sets with middle-range prices and quality.

Aggregate data compiled by the Ufficio Studi Federlegno-Arredo in 1986 show that the Italian furniture sector was subject to three-year cycles between 1972 and 1980. These cycles were made up of subphases of approximately one year's duration: the first year saw expansion; the second, further expansion but usually at a more moderate pace; and the third a more or less abrupt drop. In 1980, however, this pattern was interrupted. From 1981 on, the furnishing industry entered into a downward spiral that in 1983 saw industrial production descend to levels only a little above those of 1978. This drop, unlike previous ones, signaled a structural shakedown rather than a periodic adjustment to the market conditions. In 1984, after three consecutive years of decline, the sector started its recovery with a slight handicap compared to the level it had reached in 1980, and is presently making a slow comeback. This is due to improved domestic demand, which, following years of recession and stagnation, has shown clear signs of improvement.

As a counterpoint to this, growth in the export sector has weakened, partly because of setbacks in the economies of some Western countries that imported Italian products—especially furniture—as well as because of changes in the foreign currency market. Overall, Italian furniture exports in 1986 amounted to 4,272 billion lire, compared with imports worth 264 billion lire.

With the advent of electronics within the home was born a new scence: "domotronics"—the research and development of telematic houses.

Top: Carlo Urbinati's "Viana" hydromassage tub (Jacuzzi).
Above: three versions of "Modulus," a domestic robot designed by Isao Hosoe for Sirius in 1984.

FURNITURE STORES

The close of the Seventies signaled a spreading crisis in this sector as well. The lack of housing, fewer marriages, inflation that discouraged people from saving money or spending it on their homes, as well as the flight of capital goods or services considered more gratifying or prestigious (travel, cars, clothing) accentuated the problems of distribution and cut its profitability. Some large stores in the north (Aiaz-zone, Grappeggia, Centro Convenienza) turned to the mass media to draw people to their sales outlets. Relying on a marketing mix based on products with ambiguous formal aspect, low quality and low prices, but paired with a strategy of financial services and huge advertising and promotional campaigns, these organizations succeeded in attracting numerous consumers. In fact, their operations aggravated the crisis of the small- to medium-sized stores serving the middle brackets. Consequently, the system of distribution began to change, offering improved services and product quality that characterized the Eighties. On one hand, the small and medium-sized dealers abandoned the middle range to focus on the upper-middle to upper range of the market, at the same time seeking to expand their services beyond mere installation and adaptation. On the other hand, the traditional furniture stores catered to the middle bracket, and the large outlets served a broad sector of the market, predominantly its lower-middle and lower brackets. The large outlets made intense use of the mass media to broadcast messages based on prices and terms of sale (very long-term financing); this, however, greatly confused the public, which often could no longer distinguish the qualitative value of the products. A leveling of quality and a proliferation of low-cost "copies" occurred. Alongside of these outlets, quality stores (restricted to local markets) started to appear, offering and upholding design pieces. These exposition center-boutiques were not always able, however, to achieve the volume of sales, necessary to finance the advertising that was needed, both to make the public aware of the products' quality and to improve services such as the design and personalization of the interior-design projects.

During these years, the quality industry (high value pieces) for the first time moved to back its own distribution systems with nationwide advertising mass-media campaigns (newspapers, reviews, television, and so

Memphis products.
Top: the "Carlton" unit in
Print HPL laminate
designed by Ettore
Sottsass (1981).

Above: the "First" chair in
metal and lacquered
wood, designed by
Michele De Lucchi (1983).
It was the Memphis
collection's best-selling
chair.

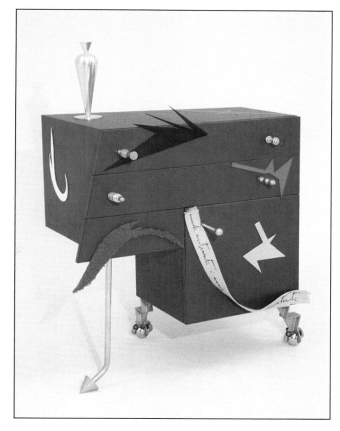

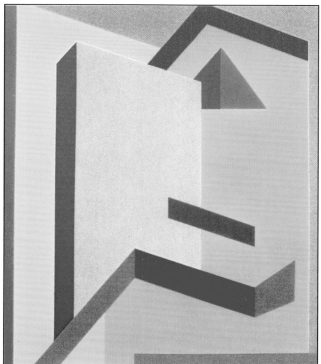

*Alchimia products.
Top: a drawer unit of the
"Mobilie Infinito"
developed in 1981 by a
variety of designers and
made up of an indefinite
series of elements that
could be freely mixed and*

*matched due to
decorations in magnetic
laminate created by
transavanguardia artists.*

*Above: "Finestra," a
carpet design by
Alessandro Mendini.*

forth). Of particular importance were the campaigns launched by Scavolini, Fantoni, Castelli, B&B, Lema, Berloni, and Febal, to name just a few. This gave rise to another phenomenon that in these years characterized distribution: the selection of series presented in exhibitions. The manufacturing companies' advertising campaign required in fact a greater concentration of sales volumes in few expositions: in exchange for the sales outlets' exclusive right to sell their well-advertised products (and related services), the industries exercised a strong contractual hold on the outlets, as long as new trade names that could erode market shares were barred. This created the need to specialize for lifestyles that ran a complete gamut of typologies, but with few or no alternatives within each furniture typology—unlike what took place in the Seventies when the broad product ranges represented a need to cater to a wider sector of consumers.

Modern antiques. Design objects of the recent past were rediscovered in the Eighties. The rhythm of the new, pressing right on the heels of the old, had accelerated the process whereby objects become antiques. The phenomenon of the modern antique (which had worldwide repercussions) dates from March 24, 1984, when the Wolfgang Ketterer gallery in Munich auctioned off pieces from the Sixties (even some from the Seventies) that Fulvio Ferrari, one of the most qualified experts in the "post-antique," had collected over the years. About 200 objects, important because of their linguistic and technological innovations, were selected from among a pool of items manufactured in a small enough number to be of interest to collectors. Pieces by Archizoom, Pesce, Raimondi, Sottsass, Superstudio, and others, were sold at the Ketterer auction to museums and private collectors.

Carlo Mollino was among the designers who profited most by these auctions, thanks to the genius of his work and its rarity (almost all of it was single pieces from his interior design projects).

It is interesting to note how many of these "modernarian" shops (for example, Colombari, Fulvio Ferrari, and Rocca 6 in Turin; Transepoca in Milan; Denis Bosselet, Down Town, and Yves Gastou in Paris; Stefan Vogdt in Munich; and Barry Friedman and Fifty-50 in New York) were also sales points for avant-garde furniture, which held the same sort of appeal for a customer in search of rare items.

Thus, old and "new" antiques were displayed alongside of contemporary pieces by Memphis and Alchimia—as were less famous but no less stimulating objects, which were the fruit of a selective revival of craftsmanship (a departure from the old days, when the designer and producer of the piece were the same person).

FURNITURE

The furniture sector, as has already been seen in the fashion area (and the two sectors were increasingly intertwined), saw the ripening of changes heralded in the previous decade, leading to the disappearance of the mass market. A classical marketing graph would show a pyramid, the tip of which represented the cultural-economic élite and the base the consumers who modeled their lives after those at the peak. Today this figure has been replaced by one showing independent consumers who can no longer be enclosed in a simple geometric shape and form instead a polycentric market. This does not contain the old socieconomic brackets, but rather comprises a series of fluid majorities, the targets of contemporary furniture design.

In this way, the concept of the minority has been scaled down, since its function had not only been recognized but in some way also institutionalized. "The new majority," wrote Andrea Branzi (*Modo*, December 1986) "is thus born many-colored; normality is born as the sum total of many abnormalities." This facilitated the rise of many new products made by companies that stepped into the limelight during these years, adeptly carving out a few slices of the market ignored by more traditional companies.

The first great wave to disturb the still waters of orthodox design at the close of the Seventies was generated by a series of personalities who had begun as exponents of radical design. Founders, in 1973, of Global Tools (an organization that embraced architects of different extraction in order to establish a counter-school of free creativity, though it never got off the ground), they then, when this and other groups formed in the Sixties disbanded, acted as single cultural operators. Among these catalyzing personalities were Alessandro Mendini, in the double role of designer and

From top: "Ring" bed in wood, metal, and tatami mats, designed by Masanori Umeda for Memphis (1981); marble console designed by Ettore Sottsass for Galleria Rocca 6 (1985); "Clesitera," multicolored glass vase produced in Murano by Toso Vetri d'Arte according to Ettore Sottsass' design (1986).

Zabro products.
From top: chairs from the
"Nuovi Animali Domestici"
series, with natural birch
backrests, designed by

Andrea and Nicoletta
Branzi (1985); "Macaone"
table in lacquered wood,
designed by Mendini
(1984).

editor-in-chief of the reviews *Casabella* 1970-76, *Modo* 1977-81, and *Domus* 1980-85; Ettore Sottsass, that charismatic figure whose influence spanned this thirty-year period, affecting many young recruits to Italian design, as it had the "radicals" in their time; and Andrea Branzi, founding member of the Archizoom group, editor-in-chief of *Modo* from 1984 to 1987, essayist and dean of studies at the Domus Academy, the new international school of design.

The focal centers of the New Design were the Alchimia and Memphis groups. Alchimia, founded in Milan in 1976 by Alessandro and Adriana Guerriero, presented its first collection in 1978, followed by the "Bau-Haus uno" collection in 1979 and the "Bau-Haus due" collection in 1980. Alessandro Mendini designed for Alchimia and later became the theorist and coordinator of all the group's activities. His colleagues were Andrea Branzi, Michele De Lucchi, and Ettore Sottsass; the latter broke away in 1980 to establish the Memphis group, calling on architects worldwide to participate. "All the Memphis projects," wrote Barbara Radice, the group's coordinator, "are positive, not critical, proposals, as opposed to those offered by the radical and conceptual poetics…" As the famous Japanese architect Arata Isozaki stated, the immediate success of the Memphis group can be accounted for by the fact that "this initiative appeared at the right time in the field of design, when everybody needed a change, but nobody had yet found the precise way to change the style." Much has been written on Alchimia and Memphis by these two authors, and ample documentation exists at the international level. It is to these groups' credit that they grasped the crisis of the concept of a "standard" as an abstract point of reference, based on the possibility of objectifiable norms. They gave expression to a demand for subjectivity and fantasy with the expansion of the idea of quality to include an object's emotional effect on individuals; they shifted from a high-tech concept to one of "high touch" through the revival of craft techniques and also new technologies and the potential of these to stimulate sensibilities that were neglected in traditional design; they viewed the function of metaphor in the objects they designed as a component on an equal footing with other elements that Rationalism had cloaked in an impregnable aura of science; and they used, after as lengthy prohibition, decoration. This last was a breath of fresh air, and fun, after so many boring products; it opened the way to new links with the fashion world—indeed, decoration became fashion, absorbing its vitality and catering to a discriminating public.

Two of Mendini's works have been selected for description here as representative of his progress during these years toward a "pictorial design." The works contain clear references to Futurism, and the functions and forms of the home are subordinated to the pictorial symbols he designed. The first dates to 1974. It made up part of a series of projects on the fringe of design, where the potential "spiritual" use of the objects proposed was given more emphasis than their "functional" use. It was a coffin-shaped glass table that transcended the inherent function of a table as a surface raised off the floor; attention was diverted from the "over" to the "under"—or better, evoking the funereal, to the "inside." Thus the object's importance per se was eclipsed by the curiosity it aroused in the mind of the viewer. Mendini developed this "conceptual" bent in a number of chairs and tables designed during this period, fully embracing the formal aspects of the objects, so that a chair really looked like a chair, a table looked like a table, a coffin a coffin, but contradicting the function traditionally expected of the object itself and instead suggesting a psychological realization/use.

In "Mobile Infinito," done in collaboration with the Alchimia studio and presented in 1981 by Magazzini Criminali at the Milan School of Architecture, the form itself was destructured and casual. Its components were designed by a number of contributors to avoid their stereotyping - beyond the functional category, which was clearly stated (table, bureau, audiovisual rack, etc.). Each piece was an assemblage of many projects, an open sequence of elements that could be freely juxtaposed thanks to an internal and external lining of magnetic laminate. Decorative elements designed by *transavanguardia* artists Clemente, Chia, Cucchi, De Maria, and Paladino could be applied to these surfaces. The overall effect of eclecticism was accentuated by the fact that each of a piece's components—legs, knobs, lights, knickknacks—was designed by a different person.

Among Ettore Sottsass' works for Memphis, we mention here his colorful 1981 "Carlton" partition unit, which is constructed in a falsely precarious equilibrium, midway between a house of cards and the "human cluster" acrobatic act at the circus. His blown-glass

The chairs and glass-topped table shown on these pages are part of the work Mendini carried out, on the fringes of design, in 1974; the attempt to challenge the functional criterion of the object and replace it with a "spiritual" one later led Mendini to develop a "pictorial design."

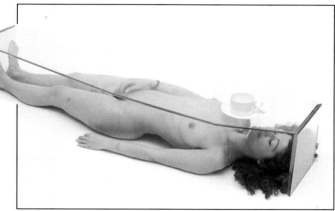

vases of 1986 had multicolored pieces of glass pressed to them, decorated with hanging ornaments.

Andrea Branzi's "Milano" bar unit of 1979, manufactured by Alchimia, was a piece of architectural virtuosity based on the play of perceptual imbalances with large volumes and slender structures that composed themselves, recalling Mondrian's constructive methodology. His "Animali Domestici" (Domestic Pets) series of 1985, manufactured by Zabro, reproposed the "rustic" look in a refined bittersweet key, a blend of the artificial and the natural, a stylistic regeneration, a healthy dip into barbarism for a society that by then had become allergic to delicacies.

While all this took place in Milan outside of the Salone del Mobile circles, the furniture industry offered a series of products that were in general of a high standard, although frequently lacking a comparable innovative charge. Increasingly, innovation was a double-edged sword; on one hand it stimulated formal experimentation, but on the other, it was often restricted to styling—to modest ideas that did not tax to any great extent either the designer or the firm, which was usually ill-disposed toward investing in equipment or molds for products fated for rapid obsolescence. The annual appointment for the release of new models and the forced obsolescence of products called "old" merely because they had been presented at the previous year's exposition (typical of the garment sector) created a number of problems for the furniture industry: it was forced to produce far more than its actual production requirements in order to keep abreast of a volatile and variegated market.

In the field of storage units, the large, specialized companies (Estel, Lema, Malobbia, Misura Emme, Molteni, T 70, and so forth) continued to produce flexible modular systems suitable for all environments, changing some details each year to renew the look, and enriching the range of matching pieces (beds, tables, chairs). Outstanding among the many market offerings were Tito Agnoli's "L 15" system for Lema (1978), which featured a vast range of surface finishes, in lacquers of many colors or in natural wood, and versatility of composition; and Antonio Citterio's "Metropolis" for T 70 (1984), which offered a new "architectural" look with consoles and a "doorway" system that could be set up to store the electronic devices that had increasingly found their way into the domestic scenario. Afra and Tobia Scarpa's "Celario"

(1980) for Cadel (one of the largest Italian companies specializing in wardrobe space) was a system that developed over time, starting out as a mobile wall partition, a room divider with accordian-style panels suspended from a single tack mounted on the ceiling. It later became a wardrobe, or a living-room storage unit. Years of study and testing were needed to perfect its dynamic line, equilibrium, and functionality, but the result was impeccable and offered great flexibility of use.

The salient features of the furniture of the Eighties, however, must be sought in individual products and not in systems. Objects that can, singlehanded, transform an environment most clearly express the concept that developed in this period. Aldo Rossi's "Cabina dell'Elba," a wardrobe/booth done with wooden slats in marine colors, was exemplary. Taking his inspiration from beach-resort bathhouses, Rossi designed this piece in 1980 for Molteni. Another highly original example, presented by Driade at the 1984 Salone del Mobile in the wake of Memphis' success, was Antonia Astori's "Aforismi." These were vertical storage units, often with rolling shutters or glass doors, crowned by cymae, like real, old-fashioned wardrobes and cabinets. These moldings were interchangeable (and therefore manufactured separately from the easily mass-produced rectangular storage units). They were like frivolous hats perched on gray, serious figures, creating an effect of architectonic importance that recalled traditional well-proportioned pieces. Matteo Thun's "Container System" for Bieffeplast (1985) consisted of lacquered metal cabinets featuring double-panel doors, with white sheet metal superimposed on a second black panel; the resulting contrast provided the doors' decoration. In 1987 Rossi revived the old wooden file cabinet with his "Carteggio," again for Molteni.

In an article on the Salone del Mobile published in the December 1984 issue of *Casa Vogue*, Isa Vercelloni noted the existence of two deeply rooted, opposing trends, "the first offering items manufactured in small series, to all appearances one-of-a-kind pieces, almost art copies, furniture that contains a story that must be told, as the personal expression of a given author, selected almost by elective affinities by someone who cherishes that story and knows how to listen to it. The other trend offers increasingly high-technology products—silent, arid, stripped bare—whose designers

Top: "Celario," designed by Afra and Tobia Scarpa for Cadel (1980). It was system of mobile wall partitions and wardrobe space featuring special accordion-style folding panel doors suspended from a track mounted on the ceiling.

Above: "Metropolis", designed by Antonio Citterio for T 70 (1984) and featuring three complementary systems: the Wall

system—compositions of wall storage units assembled from uprights, shelves, and bases on which wood or glass doors, drawers, etc., could be mounted; the Doorway system—single storage units used as freestanding pieces, which could be fitted to house videotape decks, hi-fis, personal computers, etc.; the Console system—various types of cabinets to combine with the Wall system.

were interested in upgrading their products' utility ratings, presenting them as doubly efficient in their functional versatility." Items belonging to the second trend were Pallucco's "Fra Dolcino" expandable bookshelf in aluminium (1984) and Giancarlo Piretti's "Dilungo" table, which could be extended from 31 1/10 to 87 3/4 in. (90 to 225 cm.), or his "Dilemma" ladder/clothes tree, both designed for Castilia and presented in 1984.

Many armchairs and sofas of the Eighties had kinetic devices verging on pure gadgetry, such as movable back- and arm-rests, companion end tables joined to the main framework (Paolo Piva's "Alanda" and "Arca" models for B&B dating to 1980 and 1983, respectively; Toshiyuki Kita's "Wink" armchair for Cassina, 1980; and Vico Magistretti's "Veranda" for the same company, 1983; or the beds that adapted to the tendency for activities to spill over from the living room and into the bedroom (such as Vico Magistretti's "Ermellino" for Flou, 1984, on which the headboard was inclinable; a portion of it could also be turned into an armrest, giving the bed the appearance of a chaise longue).

The close link between fashion and interior design in the Eighties led to the development of a number of articles of furniture that could be "dressed" with interchangeable, washable slipcovers. Examples of this were the pieces designed by Gigi and Pepe Tanzi for Biesse, such as "Grande Numero" (1980), "Margherita" (1982), and "Nudo" (1986); Antonio Citterio and Paolo Nava's "Pasodoble" for Flexform (1980); Vico Magistretti's "Sindbad" for Cassina (1981); and Paolo Nava's "Gli Abiti," with "clothing" by Gianfranco Ferré (1985).

The sofas designed by Paolo Deganello for Driade—"Squash" (1981) and "Back Bottom" (1982)—and his "Torso" (1982), for Cassina, were based on unusual combinations of fabrics. All three of them continued with lucid cogency a style developed by Deganello in 1973 with his "AEO."

Among the most recent items, Antonio Citterio's "Sity" for B&B (1986) met with great success. Its popularity was due not so much to innovative design as to the broad range of possible furnishing solutions offered by the seating plan, with its faultless engineering and the elegant range of fabrics that it came in.

Within this highly varied panorama, the Poltrona Frau company deserves mention for the coherence with which in its seventy-five years of existence it linked its

Top: the "Cabina dell'Elba," a symbolic piece charged with memories and poetry, first designed by Aldo Rossi for Casa Vogue, later presented at Milan's 1980 Salone del Mobile by Molteni and put in production by Longoni in 1983.

Above: "Aforismi," a collection of pieces designed by Antonia Astori for Driade's Aleph division in 1984. The vertical storage units crowned with interchangeable cymae are imposing entities in the rooms they furnish.

corporate image not just with a particular model of furniture but with high-quality products and special treatments for leather. The international success of this company is based therefore on a wealth of manual experience that was skillfully transformed over the years into modern industrial methods. Along with its traditional pieces, which, as fashions changed, never dropped in popularity (indeed, an old piece such as the 1929 "Vanity Fair" armchair seems more modern than many contemporary designs), Poltrona Frau successfully introduced new—even high-tech—pieces over the years, such as Pierluigi Cerri's "Ouverture" of 1982, with steel framework, or Ferdinand Porsche's "Antropovarious" armchair of the following year, with carbon-fiber joints.

During the second half of the Eighties, some accomplishments helped to overcome the impasse in Italian design between the apologists for an imagination rediscovered and the acid defenders of a betrayed modernism. The traditional panorama had changed suddenly. Several new companies had been founded, some of them outside of the mainstream, with the aim of manufacturing not traditional and essential elements of interior decor, but rather a series of small pieces with a special function (clothes trees, end tables, chairs, bookcases, sideboards, carts, flower vases, etc.), normally considered furniture accessories. The linguistic homogeneity of the modern home was shattered and replaced by much freer and more creative combinations of different styles and materials. Pieces were acquired one by one, for their semantic value, and the furniture accessory ceased to be a complement to something else. In substance, interior design shifted from a monocentric vision to a polycentric one, in which the environment was distinguished not so much by the style of its furnishings as by the style of its inhabitant. Harmony was no longer sought among the individual pieces, but derived from their accord with the culture and the lifestyle of the homeowner and his entourage. The passage from furniture style to lifestyle and hence to the multiplicity of lifestyles also marked the passage from furniture accessory to the furniture object *tout court*. A few new companies responded readily to this change, some of them founded by young designers (Pallucco, Zeus, Alias, Baleri, and others) who joined forces to carry out a task that was both design- and management-oriented; or else, new trademarks were launched by companies already well-

Typical of the armchairs and sofas of the Eighties are various moving parts.

Top: the "Alanda" sofa with tilting arm- and backrests, designed by Paolo Piva for B&B in 1980. Above: an example of the osmosis between fashion and furniture is "Gli Abiti," designed in 1985 by Paolo Nava for B&B, "dressed" by Gianfranco Ferré.

Opposite page: two of Cassina's models that owe their striking looks to their innovative use of

upholstery: Vico Magistretti's "Sindbad" (1981), in which a heavy blanket with trimmed edges is placed over a padded framework; and Gaetano Pesce's "Feltri" (1987), an innovative treatment of felt wool fabric stiffened with polyester resin in the lower, load-bearing part, and in the upper part used as is as a form-fitting back- and armrest.

Below: the "Vanity Fair" model of 1920, put back into production by Poltrona Frau.

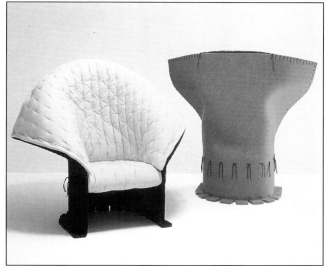

established in the marketplace (Alacta, Bontempi, Castilia, Elam Uno, Molteni & Consonni, et al.), but catering to different consumer strata in a concerted effort to exploit the distribution networks. In this type of production, external production means, materials, and technologies were often employed, thus permitting a flexibility that more rigidly structured companies were not able to match.

One material highly favored by these companies was metal, lacquered black or silver—decidedly "minimal" colors after the glut of pastels seen in the late Seventies and early Eighties. Many chairs were made in this material, as were tables, cupboards, carts, and clothes trees. Of the many products offered by these new companies, we can start with those by a company that is not new to us, Zanotta; over the years this company presented alongside its traditional sofas and armchairs some of the most attractive furniture accessories: Achille Castiglioni's series of dumbwaiters, starting with the "Servomuto" service table of 1974 (and expanding the line with a standing ashtray, an umbrella stand, a towel rack, a clothes tree, and so forth), his folding "Cumano" tea table (1979), and "Albero" plant stand (1983); Enzo Mari's "Tonietta" chair (1985), with aluminium framework and leather-upholstered seat and backrest; and Tusquets and Coltet's television and hi-fi rack (1987). Alias got its start in 1979 as manufacturer of basic, cut-and-dried pieces quite unlike the postmodern articles that were then appearing on the market: Giandomenico Belotti's "Spaghetti" series (1979–81) with a tubular metal framework covered in PVC cordage; Marco Botta's "Prima" and "Seconda" chairs (1982–87), whose steel framework supported a perforated sheet-metal seat and polyurethane cylindrical backrest; Botta's "Quinta" and "Latonda" in which he pursued his research into perforated sheet metal, here suspended from a tubular steel framework. Alberto Meda's "Light-Light" chair (1987), the first to be made of carbon fiber, was also manufactured by Alias.

Enrico Baleri, one-time art director of Alias, founded Baleri Italia in 1984 for the manufacture of articles he'd designed as well as those of others, including Hans Hollein, Alessandro Mendini, Guillaume Saalburg, Hannes Wettstein, Bruno Rota, and Philippe Starck, who got his start in Italy and later went on to become the new French star of international design.

Bontempi presented a collection designed by

Giuseppe Raimondi at the 1986 Salone di Milano, demonstrating an encouragement of innovation and the development of an "attractive functionality" rooted in Italian rationalism. Its attention to constructive details brought to the furniture accessory the precious benefits of technological and material research. Included in this collection was the "Delfina" chair, a 1987 Compasso d'Oro winner, whose molded polyurethane seat provided both softness and a load-bearing structure; the backrest, a series of curved steel rods, offered both elasticity and comfort. The "City" bookcase was a composition of molded sheet-metal uprights of various heights that doubled as casings for lighting fixtures. The sheet metal was perforated to allow the insertion of a number of optionals—shelves, cabinets, record holders, clothing racks (so that it was suitable for commercial settings as well)—and this also permitted the light to filter through, illuminating the objects on display and the immediate area. The product's appeal was enhanced by the upright's specific volume, substance, and possible variations in height, inviting the owner to create a domestic stage set inspired by the metropolitan landscape.

Castilia debuted at the 1984 Salone del Mobile as a trademark of the domestic division of Castelli, one of the largest European manufaturers of office furniture. Its "Dilungo" table, designed by Giancarlo Piretti (creator of the "Plia" chair), could be extended to three times its original length, using an invisible mechanism; the "Dilemma" ladder by the same designer could be transformed beyond all recognition, into a clothes tree; Mario Bellini's *Diletto* bed had kinetic devices so that it could be positioned for normal repose or a semi-reclining posture, and the footboard offered precious additional surface area to use for sitting, packing one's suitcases, or holding the television. In 1987 Castilia added to its product line a strange chair by Nando Cuniberti, the "Chrysalys," which could easily be changed from a comfortable armchair into a table and back again.

As people's home activities that had once been confined to the living room started to filter into other areas of the home, the bedroom became a zone for relaxation, conversation, socializing, reading and even work, and in the Eighties this stimulated a new look in beds and in bedroom furniture in general. Every traditional furniture manufacturer introduced new bed designs, and a number of new, specialized companies

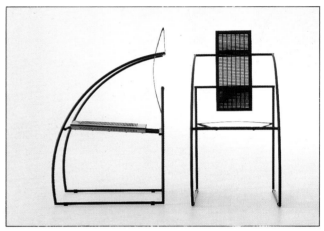

Top: two furniture accessories designed by Achille Castiglioni for Zanotta: the small folding "Cumano" table of 1979, and the "Servomuto" of 1974.

Above: the "Quinta", a chair in tubular steel and perforated sheet metal designed by Mario Botta

for Alias (1985).

Below: the folding "Francesca Spanish" chair in tubolar steel and rigid polyurethane, and the "President M" table in steel and aluminum with glass top, designed by Philippe Starck and produced by Baleri in 1984.

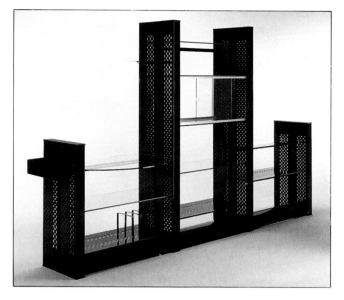

From top: the "City" bookcase in molded sheet metal, designed by Giuseppe Raimondi for Bontempi (1986); the extensive "Dilungo" table and "Dilemma" clothes tree/ladder, designed by Giancarlo Piretti for Castilia (1984).

were founded: Flos, Frauflex, and Axil offered the textile look; Interflex, Bontempi, and Bonaldo made use of exposed metal frames; and Adile, Campeggi, Meta, and Mimo focused on sofa beds.

Interflex paid particular attention to the structure of the bed, starting with the springs. Examples are Vittorio Prato's "Chassis" (1982) and "Flash" (1987), and Achille Castiglioni and Giancarlo Pozzi's "Itititi" (1986). The latter, one of the most interesting designs of the decade, revolutionized the traditional approach of the perimeter frame: Castiglioni and Pozzi proposed an original system of fiberglass rods laid out longitudinally and joined to two cross pieces. These rods were separate and easily unmounted so that beds of any length and width could be constructed. The design of the bed—from the leg joints to the head- and foot-boards—was a display of elegant coherence.

Paolo Piva's "Adia" bed for B&B (1987) was a response to the new polyfunctional interpretation of the bedroom: it was a soft platform with no evident head-foot axis. The headboard was made up of movable cushions that revolved around the bed's perimeter, also equipped with a number of tables.

During these years a broad range of proposals for the kitchen emerged, all of high quality. These were marketing-oriented products with stylistic features that permitted personalization through numerous optional parts. A twofold supply developed to meet various demands at this time. For example, in 1984 ArcLinea (a large manufacturer of medium-high-price kitchens) launched its Aiko division at a young public (culturally sophisticated twenty- to twenty-five year-olds). Aiko offered eight models at accessible prices; its "Brooklyn" kitchen, by Lucci and Orlandini, was a best-seller that featured in lieu of cabinetry, shelves anchored to the work surface. An opposite tack, aimed at people with large kitchen areas at their disposal, was the Abaco trademark, a spin-off of Snaidero. The Abaco models Giovanni Offredi and Angelo Mangiarotti designed for an elegant and demanding clientele used lacquered surfaces, natural stone, and electrical appliances hidden from view, all in compliance with rigorously high standards of efficiency. Giovanni Offredi's 1986 "Kalya" model played up the contrast between the severe orthogonal layout of the uprights and bases and the pronounced curves of the work surfaces; a contrast further highlighted by the designer's use of colors and materials. The doors and panels were white polyester or metalic pale or dark gray lacquer, and the work surface was multilayered wood covered with post-formed laminate, available in different colors.

Other kitchen models produced in these years were Citterio and Nava's "Factory," presented by Boffi at the 1980 Eurocucina exposition, where everything, including the lower storage cabinets, was raised off the floor to permit thorough cleaning. The system included wall-shelves that could be closed off by fabric-lined doors or wooden shutters; these opened upwards on special friction hinges that made it possible to leave everything on the shelves in view. The high-tech look of the chromed-steel gridiron shelves in the interior contrasted with the domestic warmth of the copper hearth in the cooking area.

Tito Agnoli's "Libro," presented by Disegno Due in 1984, was so named for its folding, sliding doors mounted on aluminium tracks, which opened up book-fashion. The Kairos Studio's "Futura" and Paolo Piva's "Quinta" were presented by Dada in 1986. The former was distinguished by its cabinet doors, which opened (again, book-fashion) upwards by means of special hinges. The latter had a beechwood framework with a series of vertical separators and sliding doors. R.B. Rossana presented its "214," designed by Michele De Lucchi, at the Eurocucina show. Depending on the play between varying depths (from 23 2/5 to 30 2/5 to 35 1/10 in. [60 to 78 to 90 cm.]), two registers of storage cabinets are available: one for everyday use, with everything at arm's reach, and one for utensils, accessories, and provisions used less often.

Lighting fixtures. The many lamps of the Eighties show a growing link between the lighting fixture and the actual energy source: the release of new types of light-bulbs on the market often prompted the creation of new fixtures. The Seventies had seen the incandescent bulb produced in new shapes and sizes (the globe), or partially mirrored; the Eighties was the decade of halogen, which in addition to permitting smaller bulbs offered an extraordinary quality of light, greater efficiency, and excellent chromatic yield. The new, smaller fluorescent bulb in a broad range of colors also found many applications. In its lengthier form, the fluorescent tube was used in combination with other types of lighting in many office and industrial designs, and the smaller version, with E 27 attachment and incorporated starter, penetrated the home front and began to replace incandescent lighting.

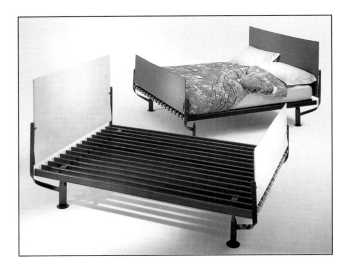

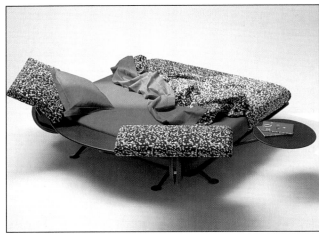

From top: the "Itititi" bed, designed by Achille Castiglioni and Giancarlo Pozzi in 1986 for Interflex, which revolutionized the framework with new materials used in a logical and innovative way; the "Adia," designed by Paolo Piva for B&B in 1987, is a platform-bed fitted with a series of accessories and mobile cushions along its perimeter; the "Brooklyn" kitchen by Lucci and Orlandini for Aiko, whose cabinets have been replaced by shelves anchored to the work surface.

Fontana Luce's displays at the 1980 Euroluce exposition aroused interest in a new look: delicately tinted blown glass. Gae Aulenti and Piero Castiglioni's "Parola" table and floor lamps and Umberto Riva's "Metafora" launched a multitude of glass lamps and design objects that gained in popularity over the years because of the look's originality. Some of the most important pieces were Franco Raggi and Daniela Pupa's hanging "Oz" lamp (1980), Gregotti Associati's "Segno Uno" floor lamp (1981), and Daniela Pupa's "Olampia" hanging lamp (1984). Livio and Piero Castiglioni's "Scintilla" lighting system (1983), based on the suspension of bare halogen light bulbs from the wall or laid out along cables stretched from wall to wall, was a best-seller.

The following designs all date to 1981: Ettore Sottsass' "Callimaco" floor lamp for Artemide; King, Miranda, Arnaldi's "Crisol" hanging lamp with pressed-glass diffusor suspended from two fine low-tension cables for Arteluce; Achille Castiglioni's "Cibigiana," an unusual and amusing object for illuminating bedtime reading, with a small, swiveled mirror used in orienting the concentrated beam of light, for Flos.

Porsche Design's highly flexible "Kandido" lamp (in versions for table, wall, or ceiling), for Luci, dates to 1982. It was made up of an adjustable system of three telescopic radio antennae, that also conducted low-voltage current, and a small 50-watt halogen bulb.

Dating to 1984 are Umberto Riva's "Veronese" table lamp for Barovier & Toso, a blown glass amphora containing e suspended, transparent glass butterfly that created a prismatic effect with the light that filtered out from the base; Carlo Forcolini's "Icaro" wall lamp for Artemide, featuring a tube-shaped halogen bulb inserted into a thick piece of glass, and two aluminium side "wings" that served as shades; Rodolfo Bonetto's "Ala" table lamp for Guzzini, with jointed arm: Asahara Sigheaki's "Palomar" floor lamp for Stilnovo, whose orientable diffuser resembled a beacon; Vico Magistretti's "Kalaari" for O-Luce and Michele De Lucchi's "Cyclos" for Artemide, two of the few hanging lamps produced in these years; and Mario Barbaglia and Marco Colombo's "Dove" for Paf, in polymeric plastic lamina covering the electrical parts and mounted on gimbals over a base that contained a transformer. It presented a new look that had broad repercussions and was a great commercial success.

Dating to 1985 are Mario Botta's "Shogun" lamp

Above: the "Cibigiana" reading lamp by Achille Castiglioni for Flos (1981).

Right: "Parola," designed by Gae Aulenti and Piero Castiglioni for Fontana Arte (1980).

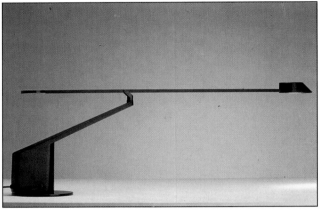

Top, from left: "Icaro," designed by Carlo Forcolini for Artemide (1984); "Aladino," designed by Giuseppe Raimondi for Valenti (1986), featuring, for the first time, glass as a conductor of electrical current, due to a silver decoration applied to the surface.

Above: "Ala," designed by Rodolfo Bonetto for Guzzini (1984).

for Artemide, a lamp-personality based on the play of two movable helmets of perforated sheet metal casting lacy patterns of shadow and light; Giuseppe Raimondi's "Taitu" lamp for Valenti, which stretched from floor to ceiling and was made up of two low-tension cables with three swiveled light sockets for dichroic halogen bulbs that could be fixed at any height; De Pas-D'Urbino-Lomazzi's "Valentina" table lamp for Valenti, with anodized aluminium rods and plastic joints that lent the maximum possible flexibility to the movement of the reflectors; Afra and Tobia Scarpa's "Butterfly" wall and floor lamps, producing a filtered, indirect light by means of a frosted glass diffusor and swivel-mounted, flame-resistant, pleated fabric shades.

Dating to 1986 are Michele De Lucchi and Giancarlo Fassina's "Tolomeo" reading lamp for Artemide, with a jointed arm in polished aluminium, and visible mechanisms: Giuseppe Raimondi's "Aladino" table lamp for Valenti, which featured, for the first time, glass used not just as a filter but as a conductor of electricity, due to a silver decoration applied to the surface. The light source seemed to be suspended, exalted by the transparency of the glass and the lack of visible metal elements.

Alberto Meda and Paolo Rizzato's "Lola" floor lamp, for Luceplan, dates to 1987. Here high technology was used to great effect: the lamp had a telescopic, carbon-fiber upright supported by a jointed tripod in flexible polyurethane, a forked head in thermoplastic polyester holding the light socket and photo-engraved metal reflector, and a 300-watt halogen bulb that could be set to four different levels of intensity with a dimmer switch. In the same year Valenti presented Giuseppe Raimondi's "Miriade" lighting system. This consisted of a pair of low-tension cables that could be extended from wall to wall and a series of dichroic light with gyroscopic swivel mechanisms. These light sockets could be fixed directly on the cable or suspended in space from rigid or telescopic supports that enhanced the environment with a sort of luminous, aerial dropped ceiling in which each light source could be directed as desired.

THE TRIENNALES

The new Triennale was presented in 1979 as a museum in progress, a permanent and systematic cultural display of design and production.

The XVI Triennale, inaugurated on December 15, 1979, was subdivided into three exhibition cycles that concluded in 1982.

The 1983 XVII Triennale presented an exhibition entitled "Le Case della Triennale, Otto Progetti di Ambienti Domestici Contemporanei" (Homes of the Triennale, Eight Projects for Contemporary Domestic Settings); the installation was designed by Franco Raggi and Francesco Trabucco. In his introduction, Raggi wrote: "In a society that registers a dramatic gap between the urban/collective and the domestic/private, the home increasingly figures as the last space in which to let one's imagination go. This exhibition should therefore be interpreted as a statement of opposition to the all-inclusive design package, against design offering easy solutions. Through a series of old and new themes for settings, it investigates the evocative force of the decorative arts."

As Francesco Trabucco, has elsewhere commented, "The home—storehouse of the memory, museum of ourselves, where objects' meaning often carries more weight than does their utility, the last frontier of personal design—continues to be a terrain of personal renewal, because the design of domestic objects does not attribute to functionality the capacity to express the poetic that instead arises more clearly, intelligibly, and evocatively from the relationships between objects and the space that holds them: the light, the color, the sounds of a home."

Four of the themes that Raggi mentioned dealt with "historical" issues already examined in past Triennales, especially that of 1933: "The Newlyweds' Home," "The Vacation Home," "The Artist's Home," and "The Luxury Home." To cover modern lifestyles, four other themes were added: "The Working Home," "The Restful Home," "The Shared Home," and "The Oneiric Home." Eight different designers, representing a third generation of Italian designers, made use of series products as well as appositely designed new pieces in their projects. The results were displayed in separate square areas, each of which represented a different domestic theme. What emerged from this exhibition—in which the various designers had each given more weight to poetic aspects, to allusive, theatrical paradoxes than to making proposals of ideal settings —was the idea that "symbolic value was a greater factor than practicality in determining interior decoration."

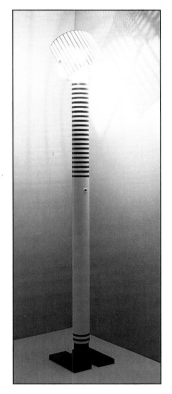

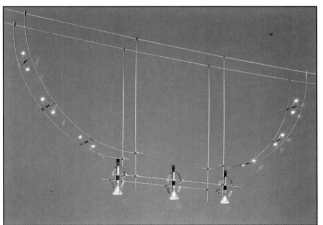

Top: "Shogun," designed by Mario Botta for Artemide (1985); "Lola," designed by Alberto Meda and Paolo Rizzato for Luceplan (1987).

Above: "Miriade," designed by Giuseppe Raimondi for Valenti (1987).

XVII Triennale (1983): "Homes of the Triennale."

Top: "The Vacation Home," by Michele De Lucchi.

Above: "The Artist's Home," by Lucci and Orlandini.

Opposite page, from top: "The Working Home," by Pietro Derossi; "The Shared Home," by Paolo Deganello and Alberto Magnaghi; "The Oneiric Home," by Denis Santachiara.

"The Newlyweds' Home" was designed by Alessandro Guerriero with Alchimia. Its foyer, with mosaicked door, opened onto a lobed-plan setting, cornerless and completely lined in lavender-colored quilted fabric, including the soft floor, which also served as a resting place. A decorative lighting system made up of pink modular cones was attached to the walls and ceiling; tiny lights flashed on and off in this closed universe without doors and windows. The interior was bare, containing only a sculpture by Mendini and a fruit bowl by Oscar Tusquets.

"The Vacation Home," designed by Michele De Lucchi, was a sort of modern version of a prospector's cabin, made to be experienced and used more outside than in. The great cylindrical beams that were laid out horizontally to form the walls were hollow and were set up inside to house the various household appliances.

"The Artist's Home," designed by Roberto Lucci, Paolo Orlandini, and Federica Zanuso, was conceived for a designer and appeared as a transparent space made of double-weight nylon netting over extruded light alloy panels. Inside, a collection of prototypes gathered by the architects in the course of the design process were displayed.

"The Luxury Home," designed by Gian Franco Gasparini with Studio Arcanto, was a vague setting in a functional key. A cubical space at the center was delineated by four plates of mirrored glass that, as the intensity of the light changed, either revealed or veiled a totem-like furnishing placed at its center; this was a receptacle for remembered objects.

The "Working Home," designed by Pietro Derossi with Renato Brazzani, Giorgio Ceretti, Francesco Di Suni, Franco Lattes, and Giulio Paolini, was an imaginary setting within an abandoned factory. A gigantic poster, covering an entire wall, may have represented an extreme of production decentralization (work in the home, black-market work) or an extreme of metropolitan nomadism in search of an existential refuge. In this house there existed no distinction between workplace and home: only two elements furnished it, an all-purpose table in polyethylene and an industrial shelving system holding various work tools. Descending from on high was an angel by Giulio Paolini.

"The Restful Home," designed by Franco Mirenzi, was structured on a perfectly square floor plan divided into four areas around a convertible wall unit designed by Marenzi for Citterio. These interlocking spaces represented mental and psychophysical repose, physical hygiene (physical education), and alimentation.

"The Shared Home," designed by Paolo Deganello and Albert Magnaghi, was laid out on three floors: spaces with individual identities for solitary use occupied the second floor, where the rooms had personalized terraced openings, each with a differently designed window casing; below these, on the ground floor, were the shared spaces, completely open to the urban panorama; the third floor, which was left unplanned, was an undefined place for experiential encounters and urban information exchange, among different communities as well as individuals.

The "Oneiric Home," designed by Denis Santachiara, was a dark interior based on a square floor plan. A hall illuminated with torch-sconces, designed by Santachiara for Vistosi, diagonally traversed the floor plan and provided access to the zones for day and night use. Different technologies were employed in the furnishings of the two rooms, and new typologies of objects were invented (a luminous bedspread, a radio-bench, a sofa that produced small rotatory movements), which Santachiara defined as "neocommodities" and which later were the focus of an exhibition that he organized in 1985 for the Triennale.

In February 1985, at the same time as the Triennale, an exhibition organized by Carlo Guenzi entitled "Le Affinità Elettive" (The Elective Affinities) was inaugurated. Twenty-one designers around the world had been called on to express their visions of the poetics of interior design. The furniture was realized through the Ente Comunale del Mobile in the township of Lissone, one of the most important Italian furniture production and sales centers, which sponsored the exhibition. Two projects were requested of each designer. The first, a room/stall space, was a setting in which the designer was to document the cultural points of reference, the "elective affinities" that gave rise to the matrix or the stimuli of his creative processes. The second project was the realization of an object that would testify to the conditions, the work, the needs, and the hopes of contemporary man.

In Mario Botta's room/stall, he attested to two points of reference for his design approach—Romanesque art and folk art—with a fragment of the capital of a Romanesque column and a granite votive fountain. His second project, the "Guscio" bookcase unit, was designed to accomodate two people seated

facing one another. Done in spaced beechwood slats, "Guscio" created a stage curtain, a womb-space for "looking at and talking to one another, writing, reading, thinking, idling."

An exhibition entitled "Il Progetto Domestico—La Casa dell'Uomo: Archetipi and Propotipi" (Domestic Design—Man's Home: Archetypes and Prototypes) was inaugurated at the Triennale in January 1986. Conceived by Mario Bellini with contributions by George Teyssot in the historical section, it was above all a great exhibition on Western man's home designs, from the seventeenth century to today. Supported by a vast collection of materials, including paintings, models, furniture, inventions, books, and photographs from museums and collections all over the world, the design section presented twenty-five installations by as many internationally known architects, designers, and artists. The exhibition's basic thesis was that the designer or inhabitant wishing to think of how a home should be planned today is faced with two problems: the many existing models and the absence of an absolute model. In an attempt to achieve clarity, the participants were asked to evoke, with their work, given dwelling archetypes, avoiding the design of prototypes and instead proposing metaphors of possible methods.

Achille Castiglioni was assigned the theme of a 78³/₄-cubic-yard (72 sq. m.) dwelling space for six people, a reinterpretation, in a modern key, of a project by the late-nineteenth-century English architect D.G. Hoey, entitled "Improved Dwellings for the Poorer Classes." This project consisted of a sort of ship's cabin 18¹/₂ sq. yd. × 45⁹/₁₀ yd. (17 sq. m. × 4.2 m.) high, a living space for six people. Castiglioni conceived of a bright cage which in all of its intentional abstraction permitted the introduction of one concrete product, an all-purpose table designed for one or more individual pursuits and free groupings, independent of the restrictions of space.

Paolo Deganello's theme was "Special, All-Purpose Furniture." This involved the examination of a trend that had begun in the nineteenth century with convertible furniture (the bed-closet, kitchen-closet, armchair-desk), or the Modernist tradition (the built-in closet, stepladder-chair, library-bar). For this purpose, he designed a sofa-bed and a multipurpose element, a glazed base made of a sort of quartz terrazzo cement, which artificially recreated the natural contours of hills.

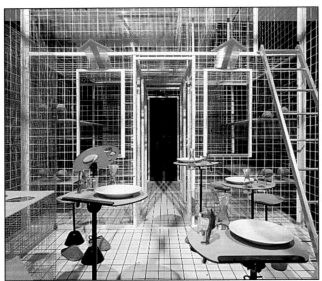

XVII Triennale (1985): "The Elective Affinities."

Top: Mario Botta's "Guscio," a bookcase unit that accomodates two

seated people.

Above: a 78 3/4-square-yard (72 sq. m.) space for six people, designed by Achille Castiglioni.

Thus, by driving various types of uprights into a composition of these base elements (each element differently shaped), he obtained tables, lighting fixtures, bookcases, and sofa-beds.

Richard Sapper tackled the "Dens and Rumpus Room" theme. He designed a large work table with drawers, over which he suspended a metal structure for tool storage that could double as a sideboard. The room's lighting system was later produced in series by Artemide.

Denis Santachiara's theme was of extreme actuality: "The Return to Domestic Work: The Home as the Terminal," that is, the overlapping of the workplace and the dwelling as made possible by telematics. Santachiara's interpretation included "Ines," a talking, all-round-use robot.

The American Pop artist George Segal—famous for his life-sized plastic figures that capture with disturbing realism the gestures of our daily lives—contributed four of his works to a space designed by Mario Bellini: *The Shower Stall*, plaster and metal, 1968; *Blue Girl on the Threshold of a Blue Door*, painted plaster and wood, 1977; *The Restaurant Window*, plaster on wood, 1971; and *Two Girls on Bed*, plaster, 1969.

"Beyond the Bed: The Places and Machinery of Sleep" was the theme assigned to Ettore Sottsass. He envisioned a well-furnished room containing a canopied fourposter bed, the headboard of which was in reality a bookcase. The room was filled with technological objects—racks of amplifiers, columns of televisions, mobile storage units for records, videocassettes, and so forth—which amid the special atmosphere became suffused with irony.

THE COMPASSO D'ORO AWARDS

Seven hundred products and sixty studies were presented at the twelfth edition of the Compasso d'Oro competition, in 1981. The introduction of a "studies" category responded to the need to stimulate further exploration of developments in the field of technology and production, as well as in that of expressive idioms. This broadening of the concept of design was also reflected in the awards conferred; these were no longer restricted to single products, but extended to companies that were distinguished by their overall image and to a few non-designer personalities operating within the design sector. Award-winners included Giorgio Giugiaro for his "Panda" automobile; Francesco Soro for his "Siglo 20" sofa, manufactured by ICG;

XVII Triennale (1986): "Domestic Design."

Top: "Special, All-Purpose Furniture," by Paolo Deganello.

Above: "Beyond the Bed: The Places and Machinery of Sleep," Ettore Sottsass.

Sandro Colbertado and Paolo Rizzato for their "D 7" lamp, manufactured by Luceplan; Angelo Cortese for a "Furniture System for the Bedroom," manufactured by Tosimobili; and Riccardo Dalisi for his study of the production of a Neapolitan coffeemaker, done for Alessi.

The Compasso d'Oro award for outstanding research went to three companies: Driade, Alchimia (interior design) and Zanussi (electrical appliances), while awards for contributions to culture and theory went to Guido Jannon, the creator of the image of Abet Print plastic laminates; Renzo Piano, internationally known architect, designer of the Beaubourg; and Carla Adamoli who was awarded a special Compasso d'Oro in recognition of her years of dedicated activity at ADI and her contributions to the diffusion of design.

In 1984, the jury, which included Cini Boeri and Bruno Zevi, expressed its firm stance against "the elements of neodecorative, irrational and narcissistic design and the contemplations of a more or less hedonistic private life" that were gaining force, carried by the swell of postmodernism; in the same breath it criticized the consistent insensitivity of the public authorities to quality in design. It honored, among others, Giorgio Giugiaro for his activities in various design sectors in recent years; Achille Castiglioni for his "Dry" flatware, manufactured by Alessi; and Studio Kairos for its "Sisamo" wardrobe, featuring a new type of door mechanism, manufactured by B&B.

In 1987, both to celebrate its twentieth anniversary of administration by ADI and to participate in the emergent phenomena of international design, the Compasso d'Oro invited an international jury to preside over its 16th edition. This jury included the famous French designer Philippe Starck and the curator of the design division of New York's Museum of Modern Art, Cara McCarty, as well as ADI's president Angelo Cortesi, and Rodolfo Bonetto, a prominent figure in Italian design. After examining 673 products and studies, the jury assigned twenty-one Compasso d'Oro awards, noting that "Italian design has survived a dangerous phase of hedonism, reestablishing the close relationship between its work and technological and scientific progress. Consequently, more consideration is being given to the evolution of man's behavior at home, in the city, in sports and at the workplace, rendering obsolete the simple solutions of production rationality and quality as ends in themselves and re-

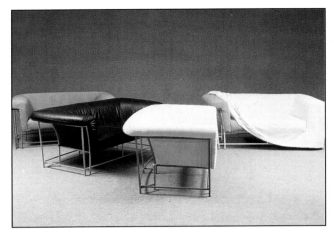

The Compasso d'Oro award (1981).
Above: "Siglo 20," a sofa with tubular steel framework and self-supporting upholstery, designed by Francesco Soro for ICF (1980).

The Compasso d'Oro award (1987).
Right: "Delfina" chair, framework in painted tubular metal, seat in polyurethane, backrest of curved steel rods conceived for flexibility and comfort, designed by Giuseppe Raimondi for Bontempi (1986).

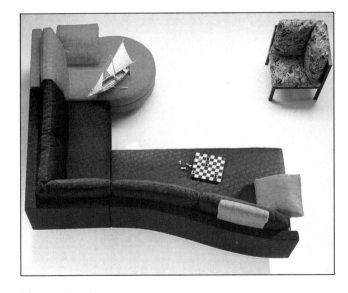

Above: "Sity" seating system, designed by Antonio Citterio for B&B (1986).

placing them with a greater and more up-to-date consideration of use relationships."

Other awards were given: to Abete Laminati for "Diafos," a new plastic laminate that for the first time paired the laminate's technological properties with a transparent effect; to Antonio Citterio for his "Sity" seating system, manufactured by B&B; to Giuseppe Raimondi for his "Delfina" chair, manufactured by Bontempi; to Andrea Branzi for his activities as designer and critic; and to Cosmit, the organizing committee of Milan's Salone del Mobile, for its contributions to the diffusion of design.

ART SHOWS

At the close of the Seventies, the art market seemed to be overwhelmed, and indeed saturated, by a wave of conceptual operations that were difficult to market. As a result, the market changed course, parallel with a revival of color and figurative decoration that soon proved to be a real reversal of trends. It is necessary to define the term "postmodern" before discussing its particular iconography. In the field of art, the postmodern appeared almost as a vendetta of the past (the modern), whose validity it acknowledged and commemorated, after the avant-garde had destroyed the past and dismissed tradition. Conceptual art was the last stage of modern art's innovative process.

In architecture in the early Eighties this term was widely abused and had become a catch-all category for a series of fundamentally different operations, so much so that the French philosopher and author of *The Postmodern Condition*, Jean-François Lyotard himself, felt compelled to take issue with it.

The objections that arose regarding postmodernism can be traced not only to the term's ambiguity but also to the confusion that often surrounded the concept of modernity that postmodernism rejected or claimed to replace. According to Umberto Eco, postmodernism is not a trend that can be pinned down in time: "Every era has its own postmodernism, just as every era has its own mannerism." For Tomás Maldonado, a harsh critic of the postmodern ideology—which he denounced as "a philosophy made of papier mâché [which] seems to correspond to an architecture made of papier mâché—postmodernism, just like postindustrialism, essentially finds expression in two contrast-

The Compasso d'Oro award (1987).

Abet's new "Diafos" plastic laminate, which paired the technical properties of laminates with a new transparent effect.

ing forms: the premodern, that is, the nostalgic exaltation of traditional values; or as the supermodern, that is, the boundless faith in the idea that it is possible to change society through a technological (and above all, technocratic) revolution without damaging (indeed, renewing) the present late-capitalistic social order. The first clearly shows its desire to reject *en bloc* modernization; the second, its desire to resurrect it but this time according to a neoconservative ideology" (*Il Futuro della Modernità*).

After being broadly diffused within the world of art, the term "postmodern" was applied to architecture from 1976 on, when a few American reviews used it to describe a type of architecture that had broken with the orthodox dictates of modernism and the moralistic dictates of functionalism and rationalism to embrace a number of metaphoric expressions, going as far as to revive kitsch. The term was definitively adopted in 1978 following the publication of the British architectural historian Charles Jencks' controversial book *The Language of Post-Modern Architecture*. The same author participated along with Paolo Portoghesi at the 1980 Venice Biennale, which officially consecrated the term in architecture, design, graphic arts, and fashion with the construction of the "Strada Novissima" (The Latest Street) in the "La Presenza del Passato" (The Presence of the Past) section.

The "Strada Novissima" was a street made up of a row of façades with many arches and columns, built on the design of twenty world-famous architects who worked in the postmodern idiom, from Leon Krier to Michael Graves, Arata Isozaki, Robert Venturi, Franco Purini, and others. In it, the "lost language of architecture" was resurrected after so many years of identification with politics, urban planning, design, and so forth. "What I am interested in proving," stated Portoghesi in an interview in Andrea Branzi's book *Moderno Postmoderno Millenario*, "is that the history of architecture is all on a single level, and that the great repertory of historical forms, with all that it has to teach and with all of its meanings, is at our complete disposal, regardless of hierarchies. I believe that the hierarchies that were established were truly only the fruit of inhibitions and lack of clarity about ourselves. I am in favor of a free architecture, one which consists of a game that involves the observer, or at least offers itself for involvement."

The Architecture section of the same Biennale pre-

Venice Biennale, (1980): "The Latest Street."

View of the total effect and detail of the façade designed by Hans Hollein, who, starting with two stone columns that defined the space at his disposal, imagined

possible variants of them, such as a tree trunk, a building (whose base is a model of Adolf Loos' entry in the "Chicago Tribune building" competition), a broken aerial column that becomes an entryway, and a vertical hedge.

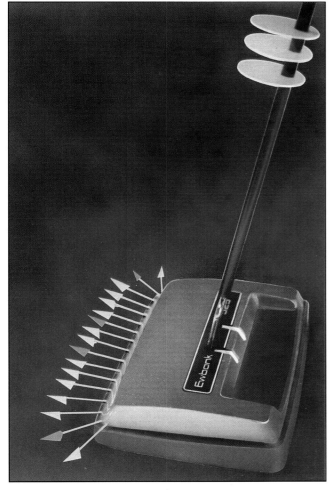

sented at the Arsenale an exhibition entitled "L'Og-getto Banale" (The Ordinary Object), organized by Alessandro Mendini, Paola Navone, Daniele Pupa, and Franco Raggi. The objects selected for display were small, commonplace, and available in the large department stores of many countries (an iron, an electric space heater, a woman's shoe, a carpet sweeper—anything, as long as it was "aesthetically drained, or in any case, utterly devoid of formal qualities that could be attributed to good design." Small cosmetic operations were carried out on these, applying small arrows or disks in fluorescent colors to inject them with energy—leaving, however, the basic image as unchanged as possible. The objects were displayed along the sides of the walkway, on two counters covered in an imitation veined-white-marble plastic laminate designed by the contributors to the exhibition. The exhibition space was dominated by a large oil painting by Arduino Cantà-fora. Passing through the exhibition one entered an "Interno Banale" (Ordinary Interior), a room decorated in a Fifties style, with obviously banal pieces, vases with plastic flowers, and a reproduction of a Mondrian work on the wall. The purpose of all this was not merely to extend to architecture and design the revival of mass culture and its aesthetics that had taken place fifteen years earlier with Pop art, but rather to express the functional possibilities of objects removed from their ordinary context, reproposing them as the starting formal point of a "strong" operation on a "weak" substrate. In the Visual Arts section, two exhibitions were presented side by side: "Art of the Seventies" and "Open 80." The latter was organized by Achille Bonito Oliva and Harald Szeemann and focused on new artists of this decade whose work represented the recovery of figurative values.

In Italy, these artists were channeled into three main groups, singled out, and presented to the public by as many critics. Achille Bonito Oliva identified the "Trans-avanguardia" artists (including Clemente, Cucchi, Chia, De Maria, and Paladino), who appeared on the national and international scene at the end of the Seventies. In 1980 they presented a group exhibition at the Sperone gallery in New York. Their main innovation consisted of a new attitude toward the artistic patrimony of the past; this was one avant-garde that was bent on reviving the past rather than transcending it. The key to understanding this revival is in realizing that in our era everything becomes history before its time;

Top: the "Theater of the World," Aldo Rossi's evocative floating construction for shows, debates, and concerts to be offered by the Biennale. Towed by the shipbuilder as far as the Customs point, the theater's silhouette was added to that of the city's other buildings, creating a cityscape in continual transformation.

Above: a carpet sweeper presented at the exhibition "The Ordinary Object," conceived by Alessandro Mendini, Paola Navone, Daniela Puppa and Franco Raggi.

this accelerated form of communication also fans the combustion of the new to a level that is not always realistic and that may leave a residue that has meaning. "The art of the past proves more and more to be a mine of materials that the artist can render contemporary, or renew, giving them new ambiguity and density, by setting them in relation to modernity" (Omar Calabrese, *L'Età Neobarocca*).

Francesco Clemente, for example, adopts the mythology of the past by adopting visual references that ran through the Viennese Secession, Expressionism, and the "Oriental" perception of space. Enzo Cucchi constructs landscapes with a precarious light where "color, sign, fantastic architectures, trees, boats, and skulls are the source of an incessant flow that interrupts the head-on impact of the work." The visual result catches the viewer in a breakdown of his sensibilities that erases all rules of rational interpretation of the work. Renato Barilli was the official critic of the "Nuovi Mondi" group, which provided a link between the Eighties and the previous decade, although without lapsing into excessive quotation. Some of its exponents, such as Salvo and Ontani, had already been active in previous years; a sculptor of the new generation, Luigi Mainolfi, lucidly told the story of the earth and of man, using raw materials such as terra-cotta, tufa, and bronze to create an image in which the theme of the archaeological find became a fantastic vision. Other artists within this group are Faggiano, Spoldi and Jori—whose works display a tactile charm although the artists' training was in photography; and Salvatori, Levini, and Pagano, who seem to favor a symbolist preciousness.

The artists introduced by Maurizio Calvesi at the 1984 Venice Biennale were defined as the "Anacronisti" or "painters of memory." This pictorial school marches under the banner of anachronism; of its members, Maurizio Calvesi has written, "Anachronistically (in conflict with their own time) they reject the compromise between art and consumption, registering in art a value that stands in contrast with the non-values of consumption. With this aim, they repropose painting in all of its slow, sedimented processes, whereas the avant-garde had cut short the rhythms of painting, arriving at the immediacy of the gesture." Some of them (Mariani, Ongaro, Piruca, Galliani, Di Stasio) verge on mannerism, a "mental masquerade," while painting in the manner of a painter of the past.

Top: Figlio del Figlio *(Son of the Son) by Sandro Chia (1982).*

Above: "Porta" (Door) by Mimmo Paladino, done on the occasion of the "Le Stanze" exhibition at the Castello Colonna di Genazzano (1980).

With Arduino Cantàfora and Luigi Serafini, Massimo Scalari is one of the most famous of the architect-painters who introduce fantastical architectural elements into their painted works.

Top: "Seaport City Gate,"

axonometric façade inspired by one of the artist's 1979 paintings, presented at the 1980 Biennale.

Above: Narciso by Luigi Stoisa oil on tar exhibited in 1988 at the Tucci Russo gallery in Turin.

Perspective—or better, the classical version of perspective invented in the first half of the fifteenth century, endowed with a single vantage point and a single vanishing point—was the subject of an investigation in the "Spazio" section of the 1986 Venice Biennale dedicated to the relationship between "Art and Science." Although the market's interest in the recent past had reached its saturation point, and there was an evident "disparity between the postmodern in architecture and in the visual arts and the progressive winding down of the phenomenon" (Vittorio Fagone), in the late Eighties new perspectives opened up in Italy as well, with a highly composite range of experiences, from a return to abstract art to a recovery of those artistic situations that in the Sixties, until 1968, had offered a fertile terrain to the Italian avant-garde. Constructivist and minimalist models were dusted off, even though in their new incarnations they were no longer marked by the cold rigor of their historical precedents. As had occurred with *arte povera*, it was the materials that defined the works of such young artists as Luigi Stoisa or Nicola Ponzio.

Deserving of mention without placing it in the context of a group or precise trend is the work of a few architects who brought to the medium of paint important features of their rightful discipline. Arduino Cantàfora offered "painted architecture" that recalls the architectural compounds of the Thirties. Massimo Scolari dealt with lost ancient mythologies, from Noah's Ark to the Tower of Babel. Lastly, Luigi Serafini was a sophisticated and ironic portrayer of fantastic architecture, such as that in his book *Codex Serafinius*, an eighteenth-century-style memoir of imaginary travels. He also designed objects—tables, chairs, and ceramics that emanate the fragrance of his oneiric eclecticism.

Along with these painter-architects are other architects or designers in many countries who created objects or mini structures that trespassed upon the world of art. The visual arts have recovered the powerful neoconstructivist dimension of the art object, with many points in common with the free design injected with fantastic figuration that characterized the avant-garde. "Documenta 8,"—whose members included Lapo Binazzi, Andrea Branzi, Paolo Deganello, Alessandro Mendini, Denis Santachiara, and Ettore Sottsass—demonstrated the consistency and quality of the Italian contributions to this worldwide trend.

INTERIORS

ALBERTO SALVIATI AND AMBROGIO TRESOLDI

nyone who has driven on the Milan-Venice highway near Bergamo has no doubt noticed one of the few Italian examples of graphic design on a large scale. It is the colorful façade, in stripes of diminishing width in shades ranging from carmine red to white, designed by Salvati and Tresoldi for a furniture exposition center. This project represents a brilliant solution to the problem of how to use the flat façade of an industrial warehouse (many examples of this can be found in the work of Japanese architects Minoru Takejama and Ryoichi Shigeta in Tokyo, in that of Cesar Pelli in Los Angeles, and in Jean-Philippe Lenclos' transformations of existing structures in France), but it is Salvati and Tresoldi's use of colors in interiors that truly distinguishes their projects.

The building presented here, rising above the slopes of Lake Maggiore, is of stone and wood. It contains two dwellings: a smaller one for the parents, who live there for periods throughout the year; and a larger one (shown here) made up of a large living-dining room, a kitchen, three bedrooms, and two bathrooms, for a four-person family and guests.

All the rooms are laid out with extreme simplicity on a single level that follows the contours of the terrain. There is a long porch with a wooden truss-work overhang supported by concrete columns. The bright colors of the exterior—yellow, light blue, white, red, and pink—are picked up inside, where different materials are joined in a difficult union of the rustic and the elegant: ceilings in larchwood, floor in rough-cut gneiss flagstones, chimney in granite fieldstone, sofas in pink cotton fabrics, wall decorations of various types. Wide sliding panels in lacquered wood separate the rooms in a dynamic way, creating a spatial continuity highlighted by the painted geometric motifs on them, in rose tones, by Giuliano Barbanti. A central stone fireplace separates the living room from the master bedroom, which can be made an integral part of the former by opening the panels.

The second interior is the architects' studio, an office space created in a renovated industrial warehouse with a shed roof. The ceilings were high enough to create two floors, linked by a wooden staircase. The upper floor houses the office files and two meeting rooms. White lacquered wood panelings, fixed or sliding, separate the rooms on the ground floor overlooking the courtyard garden. A series of round concrete pilasters painted in various tones of high-gloss gray enamel support the blue-beamed structure of the loft space. A staircase and the pink-enameled wood parapet of the loft wrap around the pilasters. The floor and ceiling panels are of larchwood planks.

Preceding pages: view of the living room with door opening on to the dining room, interior design by Ettore Sottsass with Aldo Cibic. Foreground: "Lido" sofa by Michele De Lucchi for Memphis (1982).

Left: the villa decorated by Alberto Salvati and Ambrogio Tresoldi with view of the granite fireplace. Background: mobile wall panels painted by Giuliano Barbanti.

Top: the night zone, with a central fireplace separating the living room from the master bedroom.
Above: the villa's porch has painted blue trusswork supported by concrete columns,
and broad, full-height openings take the living room into the outdoors (photo Laura Salvati).
Right: the view of the night zone through the living room. The floor is rough-cut
gneiss flagstones, and the ceiling is larchwood.

250

Top: Salviati and Tresoldi's studio seen from the loft structure. The bureaus, table, and other work surfaces were designed by the architects for Teknomeli. Foreground: a sculpture by Lucio Del Pezzo. Above: the meeting room. The chairs around the table were designed by Salviati and Tresoldi for Pozzi.
Right: the stairwell and parapets are pink-lacquered wood; the ceiling of larchwood panels matches the parquet floors.

ROSANNA MONZINI

Milan-born Rosanna Monzini received her degree in architecture in 1955 from the city's university. She immediately plunged into intense professional activity in the construction, interior decoration, and interior design sectors, and from 1968 to 1981 acted as interior design and show installation consultant to the Milan La Rinascente department store.

Her varied portfolio includes villas in Sardinia and on Lake Maggiore, the complete remodeling in terms of spatial layout and end-use of a number of villas and buildings in Bergamo and Novara, and several domestic interiors. She has also designed and carried out commercial interior-design projects—showrooms, boutiques, and stores—for Enrico Coveri in Italy and abroad.

One feature runs throughout Monzini's work, and that is her way of exalting the expressive potential of the spaces she shapes, often making brave and open-minded choices as she tries to achieve harmonious results that respect the settings, dimensions, and styles sought for or given. The apartment shown here is in the garret of a building in Venice with strong structural givens. In collaboration with the engineer Walter Gobbetto, Monzini designed a new iron truss structure straddling the external walls and capable of supporting the new floors and walls.

These trusses, painted in red lead color, were left in sight, and through them one can glimpse the old roofing in wood and terra-cotta tiles, which when restored set up a dialogue with the new construction technology of the room dividers. The peaks of the trusses correspond to the hallway, along the course of which, to the sides, are the kitchen and three bedrooms with bathrooms. At one end of the sequence, the hall opens into the living-dining area, and on the opposite end is the studio.

The living-dining area is made luminous by bay windows and a doorway to a terrace overlooking the courtyard. It is furnished with antiques (a 1935 hope chest in briarwood, two French chairs in the Charles X style, an eighteenth-century table, and a briarwood piece by Giò Ponti), as well as modern pieces (Caccia Dominioni's table for Azucena, Charles Eames' chairs for Miller). Monzini designed the sofas with iron bases painted in the same color as the trusses; she also designed all the storage units that line the walls of the rooms, optimizing the use of the lower spaces.

The studio has a long birchwood tabletop all along the windowed wall that serves as a desk and bookshelf. The floor is in a special composite marble, made according to a traditional Venetian process, as are the walls, which are rough-plastered and treated to produce an orange-peel effect.

Left: the garret hallway with iron trusswork. In the background is the studio, with bookshelves and a long tabletop/desk with two chairs, designed by Giò Ponti for Cassina in 1957.

Following pages: a view of a corner of the living room with armchairs designed by Monzini.
The briarwood console in the foreground is by Giò Ponti: a lamp with a glass vase base dating to the Fifties, by Barovier & Toso, rests on the small eighteenth-century table. The carpet reproduces a design done in 1918 by Balla.

Above: another view of the living room, based on a number of stepped areas, and overlooking a courtyard terrace. In the foreground, to the left on the briarwood console, are an old Murano vase and a bowl by Clarice Cliff; to the right is an eighteenth-century table and Louis Philippe armchair.
Right: a children's room with an iron staircase leading to the rooftop and a metal grating flyway leading to the garret.

Top: bedroom with two nineteenth-century walnut twin beds, reflected in a large round mirror with a silkscreened grid-pattern.
Above: the area of the studio with a fireplace; in the foreground, a chaise longue designed by Bruno Mathsson (1935) and a chair by Giò Ponti.

PIERO PINTO

iero Pinto was born in Alexandria, Egypt, of Italian parents. He grew up in a sophisticated and cosmopolitan environment that greatly influenced his future career. At eighteen, he went to study in Italy at Bologna's Accademia di Belle Arti under professors such as Giorgio Morandi and Virgilio Guidi. In 1952 he moved to Milan to continue his studies in set design at the Accademia di Brera. He started his career as an antiques dealer and buying consultant to an élite clientele and soon achieved world reknown.

He has done a number of projects for very prestigious private homes in Italy and abroad, for stores (Galtrucco, Rocca, Rossetti, Krizia, Biagiotti, and so forth), and for larger establishments including the Hotel Royal in Courmayeur, the Casino Internazionale in Nairobi, the El Toulà restaurants in New York and Peking, and the American Embassy in Rome. The first interior shown is his home in Venice, a nineteenth-century oratory in the Italo-Byzantine style with an annexed deconsecrated chapel adorned with thirteenth-century elements. Once an extensive restoration of the external façades and internal walls had been carried out—bringing to light splendid marble facings—Pinto came up with an innovative solution for the living room: this was an iron loft structure that left the original architecture intact and in sight. The floor of the loft—which runs along the entire perimeter of the chapel—is done with industrial grating. Thus the light of the high windows can filter down to the floor below. Finally Pinto selected, with loving care, antique furnishings of various periods.

The second dwelling is the home of Mariuccia Mandelli, famous creator of Krizia fashions. The job required the renovation of a neoclassical building in Milan to include, in addition to the living area, offices and a polyvalent space for fashion shows, theater, and music.

In this environment Pinto freely juxtaposed various elements, leaving each its historic and material uniqueness. The pieces are inserted in a warm, golden space made homogeneous by the same color of enamel for the walls and ceilings, applied in glazed layers by expert craftsmen.

Curiosity and the joy of discovery start at the full-length mirror placed at an angle in the entrance hall to surprise visitors with a view of the living room. A seventeenth-century Chinese screen occupies one of the living-room walls; opposite stands a Fontana "slash" of 1953. There is a nineteenth-century Russian armchair in briarwood, as well as a two-tone leather armchair of 1982—Ettore Sottsass, "Westside" for Knoll; the Art Nouveau decoration of the Tiffany lamps is picked up in the floral designs of the stairway-sculpture leading to the dining room, designed by Claude Lalanne.

The upper floor holds the kitchen and dining room, which opens onto a terrace alive with flowers and plants, echoed inside by the printed fabric lining the walls. The same leaf motif is repeated in paint on the mirrored facings that camouflage the pilasters. On the stair parapet, two disquieting figures animate this artificial jungle: a pair of papier mâché panthers standing guard.

Left: the large renovated oratory space, transformed into the day area. The staircase and flyway are done in industrial grating that created two interrelated levels.

Top and opposite page: two views of the flyway that follows the contours of the walls.
Above: a view of the Venetian campo *showing the nineteenth-century oratory that Pinto transformed into a weekend home.*

Detail showing the living room of the second interior by Piero Pinto.

Above: a view of the living room toward the entrance hall. An old Chesterfield stands below the work by Fontana, and in front of it is an armchair designed by Sottsass for Knoll (1982). The serpent floor lamp with Daum glass shade was designed by Edgar Brandt; on the table are Gallè vases and animal figures of tin and iron.
Right: the dining area, slightly raised, with walls lined in a Krizia fabric decorated with leaf motifs. The same decoration is repeated in the mirrors that camouflage the pilasters. Two papier mâché panthers stand guard on the staircase parapet.

GAE AULENTI

This interior by Gae Aulenti shows her remodeling of an apartment located on the top floors of a prestigious turn-of-the-century Milanese building. Its original floor plan was traditional, with a long hallway that gave onto the various rooms. Aulenti transformed the look of the house, giving it a different layout carved from the available space and strongly characterized on a perceptive level, using all the tools of her trade to create a scenic space that changes depending on the viewer's vantage point.

The long corridor was transformed into an entrance hall that shares the living room space, glimpsed through a series of square pilasters. It creates an effect of pure abstraction (accentuated by the homogeneous treatment of the walls and ceiling), a perspective vanishing point cadenced by substance and void, light and shade. These pilasters with their smooth surfaces (with no plinth or other element that could disturb their conceptuality) rise up from an equally abstract surface, the wall-to-wall-carpeted floor in a single color. This play of successive permeability, sequences echoed by others, is continued in the living room. This area is made up of two contiguous rooms separated by a second row of pilasters at right angles to the

first—an illusory stage curtain. The far wall holds a fireplace the mantelpiece of which is painted with a trompe-l'œil decoration, a continuation of this play of perspective.

This ability to captivate the gaze of the visitor shows not only Aulenti's talent as an architect but her skill as a set-designer accustomed to employing the tools of perspective in her theatrical work and knowing how to use the appropriate amount to communicate the desired effect.

The courtliness and serenity transmitted by this construction are those handed down to us by the fifteenth century, with a single vantage point and a single vanishing point. The resulting space is crystalline, immobile, hierarchically coordinated in every respect, dominated by the golden rule of harmony. It reflects a Ptolemaic vision of the world, a vision that is dense with certainties, that perceives man as the center of the universe and in a harmonious relationship with it.

In such a strongly characterized setting, Aulenti introduced with studied nonchalance a few furnishing elements of her own design: the "Orsa Maggiore" sofas (Elam), and lamps ranging from the "Pipistrello" and "Ruspa" (Martinelli Luce) to the "Patroclo" (Artemide) and "Parola" (Fontana Arte).

Left: the vanishing perspective of the entrance-hall colonnade, which replaced the corridor that originally provided access to the rooms. On the back wall is a family heirloom—a portrait done in the early twentieth century.

Left and top: the two contiguous spaces of the living room, enhanced by the shifting perspectives. In the foreground, a long table by cabinetmaker Pierluigi Chianda, and Aulenti's "Ruspa" lamp for Martinelli Luce (1968). The fireplace mantelpiece has a painted trompe l'œil *decoration that fits in well with the visual play that dominates this environment. Above: the bath is conceived as a series of separate but interpenetrating areas. In the foreground, Aulenti's "Parola" lamp for Fontana Arte (1980).*

ETTORE SOTTSASS

For thirty years Ettore Sottsass has been to many young architects, and others, not a master to be revered but a fellow traveler with a wide range of experience.

His youthful personality (he is now over seventy, and as exuberant as ever) has come down to us through his theories, his writings, his accounts of his travels, and the ceramic pieces, jewelry, and furniture in which he skilfully reinterprets features of the Indian, Japanese, and American cultures. He has designed typewriters and computer terminals for Olivetti, office furniture, housewares and flatware for Alessi, and fashion stores both in Italy and abroad for Fiorucci and Esprit.

It has been written that Sottsass penetrates the world of recurrent ideas with a candor and a wisdom that unmask the banal and humdrum aspects of religion, politics, rationalism, functionalism and technology. His is a metaphorical design, in which the object itself holds little importance. Rather, the style of the objects and his use of color create his bold messages.

One of his few interior design projects for a private home was the one he did in 1960 for a Chinese family in Milan. The Tchou home represented "a design conceived to be as fluid as possible, where the symbols and cultural references could circulate freely in the spaces, and could overlap, contaminate one another, encounter one another, having arrived from distant and disparate places." Here for the first time appeared a "tower"

piece—a constant in Sottsass' work from then on—one that extends from floor to ceiling, with shelves, drop leaves, gratings, columns, and special doors made to communicate something even when they are closed, contributing to make the look different on each of the four sides.

"The doors in a home, like those in films, communicate emotions, suspicions, surprises," wrote Sottsass at the time.

We find the continuation of all this in the interior shown here, done twenty-five years later for the famous silversmith Cleto Munari in an old *palazzo* in Venice. Here, too, a large, all-purpose piece is placed in the entrance foyer; it is a good totem, standing between the day and night areas of the home. Made of pearwood, the structure has four uprights supporting as many large disk-shaped lighting fixtures in glass; one side has a low cylindrical table with marble top, illuminated by an extensible halogen lamp; the side toward the wall has an arched mirror that echoes the shape of the entrance door; the side facing the living room is a bookcase-desk with a space that can serve as a bar, behind which are a record holder and hi-fi.

Other strong presences in the living room were the long neo-Biedermeier sofa designed by Sottsass for this house, and Michele De Lucchi's sofa for Memphis; but the true protagonists of the interior are the doors, each of which implies through its own particular design, as in Baroque structures, the nature of the room that lies beyond.

Left: Ettore Sottsass' "Agra" sofa in veined white marble, with armrests in black marble, for Memphis (1982).

Following pages: the living room in Cleto Munari's house, designed by Sottsass and Aldo Cibic. To the right: the all-purpose piece separating the day and night zones.

Another view of the living room, with, in the foreground, Michele De Lucchi's "Lido" loveseat for Memphis. Right: the dining room, with an eighteenth-century frescoed ceiling and Aldo Rossi and Luca Meda's "Teatro" chairs for Molteni (1982; photo by Aldo Ballo).

TONI CORDERO

oni Cordero was born in 1937 in Lanzo Torinese. After a lengthy collaboration with architect Sergio Hutter and engineer Franco Ossola (with whom in 1986 he won the competition for the new stadium in Turin), in 1981 he established his own studio for interior decoration, design, and construction. He has designed the Japanese stylist Kenzo's stores all over the world and has done projects for the renovation and remodeling of offices in prestigious Milanese buildings.

The projects shown here—very different from one another (the first was covered in *Gran Bazaar's* May 1982 issue, the second in *Casa Vogue's* November 1985 issue)—clearly mark two phases of his development. The first arose from an examination of the problem of how to relate to the history of architecture and to the masters he so admired—from Scarpa to Chareau, Le Corbusier, and Rietveld—as well as to the history of furniture, of the antique or modern decorative object. This pursuit, evident in Cordero's projects of the early Eighties (the Tivoli home in Milan, 1980; the one shown here, in Rome, 1981; and a London home, 1983) blossomed into a learned style, rich in cross-references, of great appeal for its abstraction that is devoid of carnality. They were uncorrupted and incorruptible homes. They showed an exaltation of the structures, a sophisticated treatment of surfaces, a graphic use of metal, attention to constructive detail, and the presence of the staircase as an event in space, around which a story was constructed. (Vanni Pasca dedicated an article to Cordero's staircases, published in the June 1984 issue of *Casa Vogue*.).

Having accomplished these projects, Cordero did an abrupt about-face. His doubts about relating to the history of architecture overcome, he engaged in a much more rewarding but also more demanding type of intercourse: that of the designer and his client (the client and his family, their past, and the successive layers of their meaning that made up and continue to make up his life project) in relation to which Cordero has assigned himself the role of creator of a work that is open to other adaptations, an interior that speaks of many specific details, no longer of utopian subjectivity. It is a system that allows for subsystems to be added at a later date. That is the case with this farmhouse on the hills near Turin, which dates back to the seventeenth century. Here Cordero worked to design not only a house but the serenity, the joy, and the playfulness that a house can offer. He respected the existing architectural and technical conditions, highlighting new interventions but somehow adapting them to their precedents (the reinforced concrete wall of the stairway is softened by decorations; the iron window and door frames exalt rather than deny the original arched openings.). He mixed furnishings of different periods and resorted to "poor" decorative techniques such as using carved-rubber rollerstamps. He brought a piece of sky into the house (Tobas' *Ciel Portatif* hung from the living room rafters), and evocative safari trophies (a bloodless safari, Claudio Parmiggiani's vacuum-molded plastic "Zoo.").

Left: the home's entrance and passage to the tower. In the background: the staircase leading to the studio. Floor and parapet of pietra serena, walls finished in plaster made of pulverized pozzuolana. The Roman bust dates to the second century a.d. and is mounted on a structural element of the stair.

The dining room, with a ceiling lamp designed by Cordero after a piece by Adolf Loos for the Scheu house. Top right: the stone staircase leading to the tower. Below: the bath with accessories carried out according to design.

Top: a view of the fireplace, roller-decorated with a number of overlapping patterns.
Above: the inner door that links the entrances of the two apartments built on different levels.
Right: a view of the upper-level living room, featuring a striped cement partition that also serves as supporting structure for the rebuilt floor.

SELECTED BIBLIOGRAPHY

Archizoom, "Le Stanze Vuote e i Gazebi," *Domus*, n° 462 (1958).
Nuovi Disegni per il Mobile Italiano. Exhibition catalogue, Osservatore delle Arti Industriali, Milan: 1960.
Dorfles, G. *Ultime Tendenze dell'Arte Oggi.* Milan: Feltrinelli, 1961.
– *Simbolo, Comunicazione, Consumo.* Turin: 1962.
Eco, U. *Opera Aperta.* Milan: Bompiani, 1962.
Formaggio, D. *L'Idea di Artisticità.* Milan: 1962.
Dorfles, G. *Il Disegno Industriale e la sua Estetica.* Bologna; Cappelli, 1963.
"Sei domande a Otto Designers," *Edilizia Moderna*, n° 85 (1964).
Menna, F. "Design, Comunicazione Estetica e Mass Media," *Edilizia Moderna*, n° 85 (1964).
Argan, G.C. *Progetto e Destino*, Milan: 1965.
Dorfles, G. *Nuovi Riti e Nuovi Miti.* Turin: 1965.
La Casa Abitata: Biennale degli Interni di Oggi. Exhibition catalogue, Arti Grafiche Meroni, Florence: 1965.
Munari, B. *Arte Come Mestiere.* Bari: Laterza, 1966.
Santini, P.C. "I Castiglioni Designers," *Ottagono*, n° 3 (1966).
– *Il Kitsch, Antologia del Cattivo Gusto.* Milan: 1968.
– *Artificio e Natura.* Turin: 1968.
Maldonado, T. *La Speranza Progettuale.* Turin: Einaudi, 1969.
Sottsass, F. "Memorie in Panna Montata" (series) *Domus*, (1969).
"Compasso d'Oro: Quindici Anni di Design Italiano," *Ottagono*, n° 17 (1970).
Bellini, M., and Romano, M. "I Sedili," *Ottagono*, n° 19 (1970).
Bonito Oliva, A. "Assalto all'Oggetto," *Domus*, n° 483 (1970).
Celant, G. *Conceptual Arte Povera Land Art.* Exhibition catalogue, Galleria Civica d'Arte Moderna, Turin: 1970.
Dorfles, G. *Le Oscillazioni del Gusto.* Turin: 1970.
Frateili, E. "Fortuna e Crisi del Design" *Zodiac*, n° 20 (1970).
Mari, E. *Funzione della Creatività Estetica.* Milan: 1970.
Migliorini, E. *Conceptual Art.* Florence: 1970.
Calvesi, M. *Le Due Avanguardie.* Bari: Laterza, 1971.
Della Volpe, G. *Critica del Gusto.* Milan: 1971.
Dorfles, G. *Marco Zanuso Designer.* Rome: Editalia, 1971.
Munari, B. *Artista e Designer.* Bari: 1971.
Rosselli, A. "I Problemi dell'Azienda del Mobile in Italia," *Rassegna*, n° 9 (1971).
Baudrillard, J. *Il Sistema degli Oggetti.* Milan: Bompiani, 1972.
Eco, U "Dal Cucchiaio alla Città," *L'Espresso*, n° 23 (1972).
Fossati, P. *Il Design in Italia.* Turin: Einaudi, 1972.
Muller, G. *La Nuova Avanguardia–Introduzione all'Arte degli Anni '60.* Venice: 1972.
Italy: The New Domestic Landscape. Exhibition catalogue, Museum of Modern Art, New York: 1972.
Alison, F. *Le Sedie di Charles Rennie Mackintosh.* Milan: G. Milani, 1973.
Archizoom, "La Distruzione degli Oggetti," *In*, nos.2–3 (1973).
Rubino, L. *Quando le Sedie Avevano le Gambe.* Verona: Bertani, 1973.
Santini, P.C. "Ottagono Numero Trenta (Monografie dell'Arflex, Artemide, Bernini, Boffi, Cassina, Flos, De Padova e Tecno)," *Ottagono*, n° 20 (1973).
Atti del Convegno Industrial Design Promosso dal Centro Studi e Ricerche Busnelli. Misinto: 1973.
Baudrillard, J. *Per una Critica della Economia Politica del Segno.* Milan: 1974.
Maldonado, T. *Avanguardia e Razionalità.* Turin: Einaudi, 1974.
Rosselli, A. *Lo Spazio Aperto: Ricerca e Progettazione tra Design e Architettura.* Milan: Pizzi, 1974.
Vergine, L. *Il Corpo Come Linguaggio.* Milan: 1974.
La Sedia in Materiale Plastico: Mostra Internazionale: Atti del Convegno. Milan: Centrokappa, 1975.
Balbo, L. *Stato di Famiglia, Bisogni Privato Collettivo.* Milan: Etas, 1976.
Favari, R., and Favario P., "Il Salotto Cattivo: Splendori e Miserie dell'Arredamento Borghese," *Almanacco Bompiani.* Milan: Bompiani, 1976.
Orlandoni, B., and Vallino G., *Dalla Città al Cucchiaio: Saggi sulle Nuove Avanguardie nell'Architettura e nel Design.* Turin: Studio Forma, 1977.
Santini, P.C., *Facendo Mobili Con...* Florence Poltronovo, 1977.
Albini, F., *Architettura e Design 1930-1970.* Florence; Centro Di, 1979.
Aulenti, G., *Architettura È Donna.* Milan 1979.
Dorfles, G., *Moda e Modi.* Milan 1979.
Mendini, A., "Oggetti Semplici per Funzioni Complesse e Poi Anche Architettura" *Modo* n° 20 (1979).
Paesaggio Casalingo: La Produzione Alessi nell'Industria dei Casalinghi 1920-1980. Milan 1970.
Shapira Nathan, H. *Design Process Olivetti 1908-1978* Milan: Olivetti, 1979.
Battisti, E., ed. *Gae Aulenti.* Milan: Electa, 1979.
Caroli, F., *Nuova Immagine: New Image.* Milan: Mazzotta, 1980.
Castronovo, V. *L'Industria Italiana dell'Ottocento a Oggi.* 1980.
Grassi, A., and Pansera A., *Atlante del Design Italiano 1940-1980.* Milan: Fabbri, 1980.

Marcolli, A. "Panda", *Ottagono*, n° 58 (1980).
Pedio, R. *Enzo Mari Designer.* Bari: 1980.
Van Onck, A. "Progettare il Bianco" (Elettrodomestici Zanussi), *Domus*, n° 606 (1980).
Vercelloni, I. *1970-1980, Dal Design al Post Design.* Milan: Condé Nast, 1980.
Design Giugiaro: La Forma dell'Automobile. Milan: 1980.
Pop Art: Evoluzione di una Generazione. Milan: 1980.
Baroni, D. *L'Oggetto Lampada.* Milan: Electa, 1981.
Raggi, F. "Biennale e Banale" *Modo*, n° 36 (1981).
Del Buono, O., and Tornabuoni L. *Album di Famiglia della TV.* Milan: 1981.
Gavinelli, C. and Pierlorenzi, G. *Design: Né Arte Né Industria.* Rome: 1982.
Gregotti, V., Zozi, R., Bocca, G., Dorfles, G., Baroni, D., and Vidari, P. *Un'Industria per il Design.* Milan: Immagine Lybra 1982.
Alferj, P. and Cernia F. *Gli anni di Plastica.* Milan: Electa, 1982.
Boatto, A., *Pop Art.* Bari: Laterza, 1983.
Raggi, F. and Trabucco, F. *Le Case della Triennale*, Milan: Electa, 1983.
Branzi, A., *La Casa Calda: Esperienze del Nuovo Design Italiano.* Milan: Idea Books, 1984.
Casciani, S. *Mobile Come Architettura: Il Disegno della Produzione Zanotta.* Milano: 1984.
Celant, G., *Michelangelo Pistoletto.* Milan: Electa, 1984.
Morello, A., and Ferrieri, A.C. *Plastiche e Design, dal Progetto al Prodotto.* Milano: Arcadia 1984.
Radice, B., *Memphis: Ricerche, Esperienze, Risultati, Fallimenti e Successi del Nuova Design*, Milan: Electa, 1984.
Centrokappa, *Il Design Italiano degli Anni '50.* Milan: 1985.
De Fusco, R. *Storia dell'Arredamento.* Turin, Utet, 1985.
Storia del Design. Bari: Laterza, 1985.
Dorfles, F. *Ultime tendenze nell'Arte d'Oggi dall'Informale al Postmoderno.* Milan: 1985.
Gramigna, G. *1950 Repertorio 1980: Immagini e Contributi per una Storia dell'Arredo Italiano.* Milano: 1985.
Salvati and Tresoldi, *Lo Spazio delle Interazioni.* Milan: 1985.
Scarpa, A., and Scarpa, T. *Architetti e Designers.* Milan: 1985..
Sottsass, E. *Mobili e Qualche Arredamento.* Milan: 1985.
Vercelloni I., *L'Arte di Abitare Secondo "Casa Vogue"* Milan: Longanesi, 1985.
Compasso d'Oro 1954-1984. Milan: Electa, 1985.
Il Mercato del Mobile in Italia. Cosmit: Relazione Cirm, 1985.
Ferrari, G. *Gabetti e Isola Mobili 1950-1970.* Turin: U. Allemandi 1986.
Gregotti, V. *Il Disegno del Prodotto Industriale Italia 1860-1980.* Milan: Electa, 1986.
Manzini, E. *La Materia dell'Invenzione, Materiali e Progetto.* Milan: 1986.
Meneguzzo, M., and Quirico, T. *Bruno Munari.* Milan: Electa, 1986.
Sambonet, G. *Alchimia: Archivi di Arti Decorative.* Turin: U. Allemandi, 1986.
Italia Moderna 1860-1980: Il Paese Immaginato. Milan: BNL, 1986.
Il Progetto Domestico - La Casa Dell'Uomo: Archetipi e Prototipi. Exhibition catalogue, Milan: 1986.
Barilli, R. *Il Ciclo del Postmoderno - La Ricerca Artistica negli Anni '80.* Milan: 1987.
Bonito Oliva, A. *Antipatia - L'Arte Contemporanea.* Milan: 1987.
Calabrese, O. *L'Età Neobarocca.* Bari: Laterza, 1987.
Sylos Labini, P. *Le Classi Sociali negli Anni '80.* Bari: 1987.
Maldonado, T. *Il Futuro della Modernità.* Milan: Feltrinelli, 1987.
Scarzella, P. *Steel & Style: From Project to Product.* Milan: Arcadia, 1987.
Vercelloni, V. *L'Avventura del Design: Gavina.* Milan: Jaca Book, 1987.
La Pietra, U. *Argomenti per un Dizionario del Design Italiano.* Milan: Franco Angeli, 1988.
Pettinati, S. *Tivù, Cronaca della Televisione.* Turin: Sei, 1988.
Moderno Postmoderno. Soggetto, Tempo, Sapere nella Società Attuale. Milan: 1988

Reviews and Periodicals

Domus, Mazzocchi Bordone, Milan: 1928.
Casabella. Milan: 1929.
Interni / La Rivista dell'Arredamento. Milan: Elemond, 1954.
Il Mobile: Quindicinale dell'Industria, dell'Artigianato e del Commercio dei Mobili. Milan: 1957.
Abitare. Milan: Minetto, 1962.
Ottagono: Rivista Trimestrale di Architettura, Arredamento e Industrial Design. Milan: 1966.
Casa Vogue. Milan: Condé Nast, 1968.
Arredorama, il Mobile Italiano nel Mondo. Milan: 1969.
In - Argomenti e Immagini di Design. 1971-74.
Modo: Mensile d'Informazione sul Design. Milan: 1977.
Gran Bazaar. Milan: 1978.
Gap casa. Milan: 1980.
L'Arca. Milan: 1986.

INDEX

Numbers in italic type indicate pages on which illustrations appear.

286

287

DATE DUE

GAYLORD   PRINTED IN U.S.A.